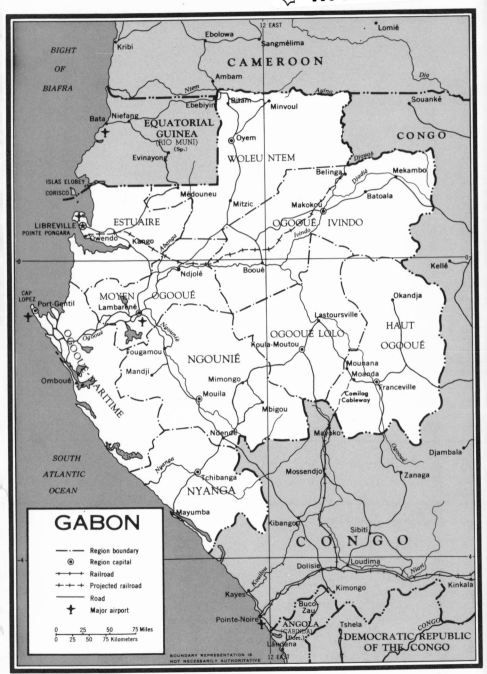

W9-ADC-467

GABON

- —·— Region boundary
- ⊙ Region capital
- ┿┿┿ Railroad
- ┿┿┿ Projected railroad
- ⎯ Road
- ✈ Major airport

0 — 25 — 50 — 75 Miles
0 — 25 — 50 — 75 Kilometers

BOUNDARY REPRESENTATION IS
NOT NECESSARILY AUTHORITATIVE

AFRICAN BETRAYAL

AFRICAN BETRAYAL

By Charles F. Darlington
and
Alice B. Darlington

DAVID McKAY COMPANY, INC.

New York

AFRICAN BETRAYAL

Library of Congress Catalog Card Number: 67-24783

MANUFACTURED IN THE UNITED STATES OF AMERICA

VAN REES PRESS • NEW YORK

This book is dedicated to
Our children and grandchildren

Charles III and Janet
Mark and Matthew

———

Letitia and Fernando Esponda
Leticia Esponda

———

Christopher

Contents

Preface   ix

Part One by Ambassador Darlington

I   The Government of Gabon   3
II   Gabon: Rain Forest Equatorial Africa   19
III The Setting in Which the United States
     Opened Its Embassy   35
IV   An American Ambassador in a New Country   49
V   American Interests and Roots in Gabon   61
VI   AID   74
VII The Peace Corps   101
VIII The Deteriorating Situation   111
IX   The Coup d'État, February 18-20, 1964   126
X   The Seamy Side of Grandeur   142
XI   A Long Way from Lafayette   156
XII Epilogue   172

Part Two by Mrs. Darlington

XIII   Opening a New Embassy and a New Life   185

XIV   Our Household Staff   213

XV   Some Neighbors at the Residence   223

XVI   Women in Gabon   235

XVII   The Woleu N'Tem and Río Muni   252

XVIII   Independence Ceremonies of the Kingdom
        of Burundi   276

XIX   Albert Schweitzer   285

XX   Our Last Trip in Gabon   301

XXI   Violence: The Congolese Riots,
        September 18-20, 1962   326

XXII   More Violence: The Coup d'État
        and Its Aftermath   334

        Index   349

Illustrations between pages 148 and 149

Preface

THIS is a very personal book. It does not purport to be history, or economics, or a travelogue, although it is some of each of these. We have intended it as the story of our years in Gabon, recording, as faithfully as possible, what we encountered, learned and felt, and what we attempted to do.

The United States has more than 120 ambassadors serving throughout the world, 36 of whom are accredited in African countries. If each were to write a book after completing a tour of duty, it would be insufferable. Why, then, do we presume to do so?

Few American ambassadors have in fact made public their experiences. For the many still in active service this would not be appropriate, and of those who have been able to summon the energy after retirement most have written general books about the Foreign Service and their careers. This is a book about a single country little known to Americans, but one of the most important in that vast expanse of Black Africa that not long ago belonged to France.

The great majority of Americans who visit Black Africa go to the English-speaking countries. They will stop in Nigeria, or they will find their way to Kenya and Tanganyika to see the big game. Not many are interested in that other world of French-speaking Africa, and they mostly will choose the better-known countries in the West, Senegal or the Ivory Coast. Few venture further, into the lands that formed French Equatorial Africa: the Brazzaville Congo, Gabon, the Central African Republic and Chad, or neighboring Cameroon.

I have been amazed at how many people, when I would tell them where I was stationed, would give me a stock four-word reply, "Never heard of it." When I would then add that Gabon is the country where Dr. Schweitzer lived, they would light up with an "Oh, yes," but they would still not be able to say within a thousand miles in what part of Africa it is to be found. And what Gabon and its people are like, few of my countrymen have even the haziest idea. Marguerite Mba, the first Gabonese woman to visit the United States, met here an American woman who looked at her with surprise and said, "Oh, you wear clothes."

So, one purpose of our book is to tell about Gabon and the Gabonese. But Gabon is not an island; it is very conscious and proud that it is African, it feels particular kinship with all Black Africa, it is a part culturally and economically of French-speaking Black Africa, and it has much in common and special ties with its Equatorial neighbors. The story of Gabon, therefore, throws light elsewhere in Africa. The *coup d'état* in Gabon was one of more than a dozen that have taken place in Africa, but it was the only one to have been reversed by a foreign power.

A second purpose that we have is to give a picture of what an American ambassador in a small post does. Again I have been amazed at how little many people know of what an ambassador's job consists. "What is it that you do, anyhow?" How often have I been asked that question! I suppose that the question really meant, "How could you possibly find enough to keep yourself occupied in so small a country with which we have so few problems?" This, of course, reflects misunderstanding. The United States has important interests in Africa and many in Gabon. Our job was intensely demanding, with pressure all the time and never an idle moment. It was particularly interesting because we were starting something— we were the first American ambassador and wife resident in Gabon—and it was exciting because of the tense political developments through which we lived.

Our story is critical of some of the policies followed by President de Gaulle's Government toward Gabon, but we must make it clear that our judgment in these matters has nothing to do with our sentiments toward France. We have always been, and we are, devoted to France and admirers of the charming and gallant French people. Nor are our conclusions a personal reflection of present differences between the United States and President de Gaulle, into which we had hoped, and tried, to avoid being drawn. Our concern is for the welfare of the Gabonese people and for the interests of the United States in Gabon and in Africa. If some of the stories that we tell about our Gabonese friends appear a bit personal we assure them that we mean no offense and that nothing in our book should be taken as detracting from the great affection and respect we have for them.

We enjoyed our years in Gabon immensely. We had a sense that we were doing something really worthwhile. We hope that our book will give an understanding of the Gabonese and a picture of what life is like in Equatorial Africa. And we will be happy if our readers can share a part of the feeling that we have for this friendly little country and its sympathetic people.

CHARLES F. DARLINGTON
ALICE B. DARLINGTON

Mount Kisco, New York
May, 1967

PART ONE

by AMBASSADOR DARLINGTON

I

The Government of Gabon

I WAS sitting on a packing case looking through the open French doors of the official Residence that was to be our home for the next three years. Across the broad terrace I could see the white buildings of Libreville among dark trees, and in the background the blue waters of the Estuary and the Atlantic sparkled in the morning sun. A pair of medicine birds chased each other up into the great mango tree, and the red hibiscus surrounding the lawn nodded in the gentle breeze.

The other Americans of the Embassy staff were wandering about chatting, the men in dark suits, the women in their prettiest dresses with white gloves. We were going to the Presidency, where I was to present my Letter of Credence from President Kennedy to the President of the Gabonese Republic, M. Léon Mba. Normally an ambassador takes only his Deputy Chief of Mission and perhaps a few other senior officers to this ceremony, but our American staff was so small, and starting an embassy in a new country in Africa was such an adventure for all of us, that I asked everyone to accompany me.

My Deputy, Walker Diamanti, a short swarthy man perking with energy and humor, equally good at negotiating an international agreement and repairing a leaky faucet, was talking to Milly Giblin, the Assistant Administrative Officer. Men were always around Milly, for although tall and angular and no longer sweet seventeen, she had a fetching Irish way. Willie (Adolph) Jones, our Administrative Officer, was as usual explaining something, his victim this time being my gentle and able secretary, Mary Jo Ahlert. Willie, with a French mother and French wife, was bilingual, an enormous advantage in this French-speaking country, and he knew administration inside out. William Mansfield, late of Dartmouth and the U.S. Navy, now our Third Secretary and Vice Consul, was joking with Virginia Greer, our Communications and Records Clerk, and Diamanti's secretary, Colette Welker; Bill could tell stories, tease the girls and write an economic report with equal enthusiasm. This was his first post, and he did so well that he obtained two promotions. Our Public Affairs Officer, Joe Cox, and Norman Baum, who gave English lessons at our Information Center, made up the rest of the staff.

Suddenly we heard the high-pitched, squeaky horns of the President's escort motorcylists coming out from town. When they turned into our rough and rutted driveway they must have cursed, but they arrived in perfect order at the foot of the great steps leading up to our terrace. The riders in black trousers, with white jackets and helmets, crisp and polished, were followed by a car out of which jumped M. Roger Kiavué, the President's Chief of Protocol. He bowed me in and took his place in front beside the driver. The staff got into our Embassy cars, the motorcycles turned round and we sped toward the Palace.

I had been in Gabon less than a week. The house would not

4

be put to rights until my wife came next month. I was in the gray zone, appointed and sworn in as Ambassador, but not yet accredited. I would not be the American Ambassador to Gabon until this ceremony had taken place. I was impatient to have it over so that I could make my official calls and start work.

I had come to Gabon fired by the challenge which Africa offered. When in 1960 much of the continent, including Gabon, had become independent, the United States decided to open an embassy in each new country. This was an opportunity that I could not resist, and I was delighted to receive President Kennedy's appointment as Ambassador in one of them.

International affairs had been my life's work. Thirty-three years earlier, in 1928, I had had the good luck to be accepted as one of the handful of Americans in the Secretariat of the League of Nations. Shortly afterward, I joined the newly-created Bank for International Settlements in Basle. Later I worked with Secretary of State Cordell Hull when he was starting the Trade Agreements Program, and in 1945 I helped to write the Charter of the United Nations. My time since college had been almost equally divided between government work and positions in private business. Before the Second World War I was Foreign Exchange Manager in General Motors, and after the war I spent a number of years in the Mobil Oil Corporation, mainly concerned with the Middle East. No job, however, had caught my imagination as much as my appointment to Gabon. I did not consider myself a political appointee. I was a professional returning home.

We had all studied Africa in our school geographies, then forgotten about it. Like many Americans I knew something of the Arab north from travels and from the Second World War, but the great central mass of Africa, Black Africa, was to me, as to most of my countrymen, just colored areas on a map. It was the province of the colonial powers and played

5

virtually no role in international life. Now of a sudden it had become a troop of independent nations, starting their separate lives. This was 1776 and 1777 for them. What a period to witness! I felt most deeply that the United States had a great opportunity to help these young states and to influence their development.

In the inscrutable processes by which ambassadors are chosen it was only by chance that I was sent to Gabon. If I were to receive any appointment, it would be to a French-speaking country because I had learned that language during the old League days. But there are a swarm of states in French-speaking Africa, and first I was slated for Mauritania. While I would have been happy to have gone to that fabulous land, I was very pleased when the final choice was Gabon, for its extraordinary economic wealth makes it one of the most potentially important states in Black Africa. Remote and almost unknown to Americans, it seemed to offer adventure and all kinds of possibilities for constructive work.

Ceremonial functions in Gabon, especially those in which the chief of state takes part, are conducted with formality and style. Horns blowing, our cavalcade raced through the streets and swung through the Palace gates. M. Kiavué opened my door and I was greeted by M. Louis-Emile Bigmann, the President of the National Assembly, M. Jean-Marc Ekoh, the Minister of National Education, and members of the President's staff. We walked slowly to the entrance where the Honor Guard was waiting—six-foot soldiers with white tunics and long scarlet capes, gorgeous figures reminiscent of the French Foreign Legion. We filed into the room and President Mba walked forward to greet us.

The President's "Palace," as it is called, probably because de Gaulle lives in the Elysée Palace, was formerly the residence of the French Governor. It was a gracious mansion, a small

French château. Its charm lay in part in the great trees that shaded the surrounding gardens; in front there were four rows of magnificent old mangoes stately as New England elms. In time I was to see many of these chopped down to make way for "improvements," but on this first day the Old World atmosphere was undisturbed. The Palace reception rooms where Léon Mba greeted us were high-ceilinged, airy and cool, with gilded molding decorating the walls and set about with formal French furniture.

I handed the President the letter from President Kennedy and said my piece, which was recorded on the Gabon Radio Network. After the President made his reply, we sat down to chat while champagne, whisky and cakes were served.

The President of the Republic of Gabon, then fifty-nine years old, is short with a very bald head and a rubbery face. His complexion is a rather light brown. Within the Fang tribe to which he belongs there are considerable variations in color, but such differences are family and personal and have no significance in African eyes. Of course, there are Gabonese who are lighter-colored because they have a white ancestor. This can usually be told from their features, and it does occasionally affect their standing with other Africans.

Léon Mba is a captivating person. He is a man of the people, earthy, appealing, passionate. His face frequently breaks into huge smiles, his eyes twinkle, and he overflows with genial vitality. He walks with the firm and quick step of a man who knows where he is going. His French is cultivated and graceful. He can speak extemporaneously with eloquence and force, and is a master of small talk. This has never been one of my strong points even in English, and I think that the President must sometimes have been a bit disappointed at my lack of ability to respond to his fast banter.

All but a very few of the younger generation of Gabonese

who achieve high position have had university training in France, but the older ones lacked that advantage. Léon Mba had little formal schooling beyond the elementary grades, but he possessed great intellectual curiosity and had a wide knowledge of the world and its problems. I was often amazed at his grasp of American politics and economics, which he had acquired without ever seeing our country.

African thought processes differ from ours in subtle ways. You have to be careful that your meaning is properly understood, and you must be cautious in assuming that what appears to be agreed is really agreed and will be carried out. Because most Africans appear open, it is easy to delude yourself that you understand them, but underneath their surface there is another plane of consciousness where you cannot enter.

Léon Mba was no exception. Certainly he was a very easy man with whom to do business. He was, moreover, an African with whom a European or an American could feel friendship without constraint: I did. But as time went on I began to see beneath his urbane manner, and what lay hidden was less attractive. He was suspicious, domineering and ruthless.

A major problem for every citizen of Gabon is his adjustment to the French, who seek to control the country. Every man in political life must decide how far he is going to be France's man. Years ago Léon Mba took his stand on this issue: he has consistently been, and is, wholly committed to France. This does not mean that he is a puppet; he is too strong a personality for that. But he is ambitious, and early on he apparently decided that the path to success lay in working with and for the French Government and French business interests. There was in this choice, I am sure, much that was not cynical, for France had done a great deal to help Gabon, and in the years when Léon Mba was coming into power it was the only foreign nation concerned. Although he would doubtless have

8

been successful in politics through his own abilities, it was French support that put him on top in 1957 and helped him to stay there.

Over a long period Léon Mba's policy was a productive one for both himself and his country. But in recent years its fruits have become increasingly sour. As its first President Léon Mba wanted to be considered the Father of his Country; he possessed the ability not only to fill this part but, with the riches of Gabon as his base, to play a significant role as an African statesman. Instead, he allowed himself to be used by France and French business, and, although his policies have given the country and foreign investors prosperity, they have also created political stagnation. Where there should be a vigorous young democracy there are now, except in the small circle of the government, apathy and apprehension.

On this opening day neither the President nor I could foresee the troubles which lay ahead for him or how they would affect our relations. I was charmed by his warm and open manner and looked forward to a pleasant and fruitful relationship. After the ceremony, M. Kiavué with the motorcycle escort took me back to my house.

Poor M. Kiavué, the day had been a great strain for him. The President, probably thinking that no Gabonese was sufficiently proficient in the mysteries of ceremony, had engaged this tall, gangling Haitian as his Chief of Protocol. It was a difficult and thankless job, but M. Kiavué's overzealousness made it harder than necessary. When he came to my office to plan the Letter of Credence ceremony, he said, "Now, Mr. Ambassador, when you leave the President you must walk backwards and make a *'révérence'* [a low bow]." Walker Diamanti jumped up exclaiming, "An American never makes a *'révérence'* to anyone." "Walker," I said, "don't let's take it that way," and I got to my feet and produced a sweeping bow worthy of Cyrano de Bergerac, whereupon M. Kiavué cried, "Oh, no, no, one must not exaggerate," and nothing further was heard of *révérences*.

One day he failed to meet me at the door of my car when I had an audience with the President. A little while later I met him walking on the beach, lonely and disconsolate. "What is the matter, my friend?" I asked. "You remember that day," he replied, "when I forgot your appointment; the President made me stay in my bedroom for a week, and he still refuses to see me." M. Kiavué was a good friend; several times he loaned me his strip of red carpet for our own ceremonies, which I suppose is about the highest mark a Chief of Protocol can give.

My Letter of Credence presented, I was now ready to call on the other members of the Gabonese Government.

Gabon received its independence from France on August 17, 1960. Seventeen African countries gained their freedom that year—nine in the month of August: Dahomey on the 1st, Niger on the 3rd, Upper Volta on the 5th, Ivory Coast on the 7th, Chad on the 11th, the Central African Republic on the 13th, Congo (Brazzaville) on the 15th, Gabon on the 17th and Senegal on the 20th. Africa was a maternity ward filled with lusty infants.

Gabon, like the others all former French colonies, is a republic: La République Gabonaise (the Gabonese Republic) is its official name. The President, as in France, is called *Le Président de la République,* a title to which enormous importance is attached. He is at once the symbol of the state and its chief executive. The other partner in the government is a National Assembly, which, as in France at present, is weak. The judiciary plays only a minor government role. Not long after independence Léon Mba, perhaps copying his hero de Gaulle, rewrote Gabon's constitution concentrating power in his own hands and taking it away from the National Assembly.

10

The government is highly centralized. The executive power wielded by the President extends throughout the country. Although the nine Regions, or states, possess considerable individual personality, they have little measure of self-government. The prefects who administer them, and the subprefects who administer the subdivisions of the Regions, called Districts, which may be likened to our counties, are appointed by the President and are accountable solely to him. Such appointments are made almost entirely from the ranks of the Civil Service.

France gave Gabon a strong Civil Service, an asset in that it promotes effective government administration and a weakness in that it attracts most of the nation's able young men. The great majority of the select Gabonese, who have the advantage of going to France for university and postgraduate training, prepare themselves for government jobs. Few aim to be doctors or lawyers because the courses are difficult and the rewards uncertain, and almost none looks to business because most businesses are French-controlled, and Frenchmen do not give up the good jobs. The Civil Service, which has grown rapidly and which is now staffed entirely by Gabonese, provides the greatest opportunities. The top positions fall to the men trained in France, who form an elite, proud of their rank as administrators.

My wife and I knew well a great number of these officials and their wives. Most were serious, hard-working and competent. A few were playboys, and some of the older men who had not had the advantage of training in France could not measure up, but so far as we could judge most of the Gabonese senior civil servants were doing a good job.

Of course, one's judgment depends on one's point of view. When we first went to Gabon all of the Regions and most of the Districts were run by Frenchmen with a lifetime of experience in colonial administration. With perhaps one or two exceptions the Gabonese who took their places lacked comparable administrative background. A Corps of Inspectors composed of senior officials attached to the President's office periodically checked the Regions and Districts. During our early time in Gabon most of these inspectors still were Frenchmen, who would give the most doleful accounts of their findings. The Gabonese administrators did not keep their accounts up to date; things were being allowed to slide; nothing was getting done. Much of this I am sure was true, but I felt that, as the Gabonese had never before run a government, their showing was really quite good.

The ministers who headed the government departments, the members of the President's Cabinet, were a group apart. All, including the Vice President, were appointed by the President. Among those who were in office when I arrived were several who did not belong to the President's party, holding portfolios allotted to their party when the government was formed. André-Gustave Anguilé, who long served as Minister of National Economy, was chosen because of his technical ability. But most were men who were prominent, because of their tribal positions or for other reasons, in the different Regions. Marcel Sandoungout and Eugène Amogho had strong tribal ties in the Haut-Ogooué, Stanislas Migolet was a power in the Ogooué-Lolo, Vincent de Paul Nyonda was a leader among the Eshira, Pierre Avaro was an important Ouroungou politician from Port-Gentil, and so on. Of all these regional figures, the one with perhaps the strongest position in his bailiwick was the fat and genial Vice President, Paul-Marie Yembit. A leader of the Bapounou, he controlled the southern part of the N'Gounié and through it had a good hold on all of that Region, the largest in Gabon.

Not one of these men, however, had more than local standing. They were strong men in their own states, could win votes

12

there, but not outside. In all the years since Gabon began to develop its modern political life only two men have achieved nationwide political importance. One was Léon Mba; the other Jean-Hilaire Aubame. The political history of Gabon turns on the rivalry and interaction of these two.

Jean-Hilaire Aubame having the portfolio of Foreign Affairs was the first Minister on whom I called. He received me in his rather dreary office on the top floor of the shore-front apartment house that had been converted for his Ministry. Jean Davin, the Secretary-General of the Foreign Office, the Ministry's highest civil servant, was also present. Champagne was brought in—always, with Aubame, G. H. Mumm Cordon Rouge—and we drank to our respective countries and to the success of my mission in Gabon. For the next year and a half I was to conduct most of my work with these two men and their admirable French adviser, M. Etienne Raux.

Aubame was then not quite fifty, ten years younger than Léon Mba, although he looked the older. I found him a handsome man, tall, stiffly straight, dark black, with a deeply lined face and sad eyes. He was quiet, withdrawn, dignified.

Like Léon Mba, Aubame is a Fang born in Libreville, but in all else they are very different. Aubame is more intellectual, more European in outlook. Léon Mba, magnetic, gregarious, earthy, is essentially still a tribal African. For thirteen years Aubame lived in Paris as one of the members representing French Equatorial Africa in the Chamber of Deputies, an experience which shows in his fondness for debate and in his cultivated speech and manners. I have heard him talk with a tremble in his voice of the *"quartier"* in Paris where he and his wife had their home. After Gabon's independence he retained his French citizenship. He has had but one wife and has led a chaste life; Léon Mba has had a number of wives.* Both are

* Under the system of polygamy which prevails through much of Gabon a man may bring into his household a woman, or women, to

13

leaders, but while Léon Mba is the executive who dominates, Aubame is the intellectual who reasons, and at critical moments he is inclined to be indecisive.

The long-standing rivalry between the two was political—each headed a party seeking office and power—but the issue between them was France. While I was still in Washington preparing to go to Gabon, the earliest dispatches from the Embassy indicated this difference. Léon Mba was prone to give France and French business what they wanted; Aubame, while still preserving the closest ties with France, would have cut back some of its preferences and sought more independent policies. For that reason he was distrusted and feared by the French community. They knew that he would curtail their privileges. They knew that he would proceed more rapidly to replace Frenchmen by Gabonese in government positions and that he would insist that Gabonese be pushed ahead into some of the better jobs in business. They knew that he would move against their tight monopolies, insist on more competition, demand better prices for consumers. But as time went on, what counted increasingly heavily against him in French circles was that Jean-Hilaire Aubame made it obvious that he liked and admired the United States—he was pro-American.

As Sir Winston Churchill described himself as "a House of Commons man," Aubame might call himself "a National Assembly man." Parliamentary democracy was what he believed in and fought for, as opposed to Presidential control.

---

whose parents he has paid a dowry, an act which under tribal custom creates certain rights and obligations between the man and the woman, or women. Such women are commonly referred to in English as "his wives," or in French as "ses femmes," but this latter term can mean either "his wives" or "his women." Under customary law they are his wives. Some Gabonese, although possessing several wives in the above sense, may marry one in a Catholic or Protestant church, and she in the eyes of the church would strictly speaking be his only wife.

14

The story of the National Assembly in Gabon is a tragedy. It should have played a role of the highest importance, educating its members in the ways of running a democracy. Advanced training is given to the Civil Service, but no special training is provided for the men—and the few women—who vote the country's laws and furnish many of its ministers, and with no college in the country and few secondary schools, these politicians have little legislative knowledge. A national government, a government possessing modern powers, a democracy that the people control—these are all new things in Gabon. They cannot rest on a Civil Service alone. What better school could there be for the Gabonese people to learn how to make democracy work than the National Assembly?

But, just as de Gaulle has disdained the National Assembly in France, so his imitator Léon Mba has scorned the Assembly. Its sixty-seven members who were elected in February, 1961, were chosen by the government and then voted on as a single list without opposition. The price of nomination was a signed undated letter of resignation. When certain of these deputies showed the courage to hesitate in passing laws that the President wanted, he became furious, and I heard him publicly chastise them and call them to task.

Of the forty-seven members who formed the Assembly of April, 1964, sixteen were elected by voters opposed to Léon Mba and his government, but it was not long before he got all but two of these representatives to switch to his party and give him their allegiance. We do not know the details of this legerdemain, but it was accomplished by a combination of threats against the hesitant and rewards for the pliant. The two men who maintained the positions for which their constituents chose them found themselves in jail. In March, 1967, a new Assembly, also of forty-seven members, was elected, all government men for this time no one opposed dared to run. A National Assembly thus abused is of little value as a lawmaking body or a school in democracy.

The saddest part of this tragedy is that most of the deputies were earnest and sincere. I do not think that I am naïve in forming this judgment of them for M. Claude Cabrol, a Frenchman, who was the Assembly's first Secretary-General and knew the work of its members far better than I, confirmed this opinion. Of the Assembly elected in 1961, I believe that I can speak with some knowledge for I was in Gabon during two and a half years of its tenure. I could give the names of all its sixty-seven members by the Regions that they represented, and I knew most of them personally. If you ask how I can call people earnest and sincere who under pressure switch parties, I can only reply that you do not know the pressure that the President in Gabon can exert—prison is but one of his instruments.

In an attempt to stress the importance of the National Assembly, my wife and I gave a formal reception for all the members every year during the body's spring term. No other embassy did this. In 1963, curiously enough, the President imitated us in entertaining them, but only once. For him, as for many Chiefs of State in Africa, the parliamentary body is only a nuisance.

The opposing concepts personified by Léon Mba and Aubame are not unique to Gabon, but in different shapes are found in many countries. On the one hand are the ideas and interests which emphasize order, obedience, stability, a favorable climate for investment, profits. On the other are the concepts and forces which stress the enlargement of human freedom and the use of government for the people. This is one of the conflicts of our time within the underdeveloped world, and often poses dilemmas for the advanced countries in their relations with the underdeveloped.

Léon Mba prevailed in Gabon and runs the country; Aubame lost and is in jail. The former in his success must how-

16

ever sense some secret doubts while the other, a tragic figure, I suppose is nourished by his convictions. It is not for me to say which would have gained control in the absence of outside interference, or which would give Gabon the better government; such judgments would be improper for an ambassador. But I can observe that the choice was made by France and not by the Gabonese people. In the colonial period, when Frenchmen manipulated Gabon's early electoral machinery to put Léon Mba on top, one might argue that this kind of thing was accepted among colonial powers, but after independence a question so absolutely basic for their country should have been left to the Gabonese to decide.

Léon Mba's government has kept the country, in some respects even more than in colonial days, a happy hunting ground for French investors and businessmen. The result has been good in terms of economic progress, but the cost politically has been high: the country is only nominally independent and democracy has had hardly a chance. If economic progress is the only objective, Gabon could have had that remaining a colony. Other values which independence should have brought have been denied.

The Gabonese like the people in many underdeveloped countries need help. Some must be material: investment in schools, hospitals, roads and the machinery of modern life. But some also—and perhaps the more important part—should be in the moral domain: assistance in creating sound institutions of government, instruction in the operation of democracy, and the teaching of forbearance and self-discipline which government by the people demands. The French have given quite generously in material things and have also taken much in return. On the moral side, it is they who have played the main role in the weakening of Gabon's young democracy. That this is the work of de Gaulle's government, done primarily for French in-

17

terests, is unmistakable. The pity is that the choice did not have to be drawn so sharply. France could have achieved its legitimate objectives in more tolerant ways.

Gabon has been betrayed by France. How this came about is the main story in this book.

kitchen my wife insisted on the prescribed precau-
en we went out to the houses of friends or to restau-
would enjoy everything set before us and ask no ques-
d we were never the worse for that. Perhaps the
hy we had so little trouble is that almost all food con-
the European population, including the personnel of
ssies, comes by ship or plane from France. We did,
drink boiled or bottled water.

produces no meat whatever, except for the occa-
phants and the small game such as antelopes and
killed in the bush. The tsetse fly carrying sleeping
has made it difficult to raise cattle or horses. A strain
resistant cattle is now being developed and a ranch
started in the south of Gabon, but it will be a long
re the householder can buy any home-grown beef. It
be long before he sees a home-grown chicken in the
hickens there are running about every village, but
sisted the innumerable parasites which would kill an
bird in a day, their meat is as hard as an old retread.
d sheep are kept but not cared for. They are killed
ed for special occasions and are tasty, but my wife
m tough.

to interest AID in a chicken program, but was un-
. Except here and there it is not a good country for
Eighty-five percent of Gabon is covered by the Equa-
forest, tall straight trunks bare of branches thrusting
d crowns into the sunlight a hundred feet above the
restry flourishes. The soft mahogany called *okoumé*,
admirably suited for making plywood, has brought
its to French entrepreneurs and investors as well as
for sixty years. What little open land exists is mostly
leached of chemicals and nutrients by the tremen-
fall.

d forests: that is Equatorial West Africa. If you wish

22

II

Gabon: Rain Forest
Equatorial Africa

W HEN I stepped off the plane at Libreville, I had the sen-
sation that I was still in France. The airport looked
French, the bar where I was taken for coffee smelled French,
around me the French language sang in my ears. Loving
France, I felt at once at home and at ease.

On the way into town the hot wind, the blowing palms and
the shacks with Negro children playing in the dirt bespoke the
tropics, but as we drove along the shore boulevard past the
Hôtel de Ville, the shops and the banks, I again had the feeling
of France. Wooded hillsides, white buildings glistening in the
sun, small craft busying about the port: I could have been in
some out-of-the-way part of the Riviera.

Libreville is a cluster of African villages with a French
façade. Commercial offices, apartments and villas line the thor-
oughfares, but in the background thatched roofs nestle among
banana trees. Independence has accentuated these contrasts.

19

Jealous of Brazzaville and wanting Libreville to look the part of a capital city, the Gabonese Government has emphasized its modern aspects and tried to hide its more traditional characteristics. Houses fronting on streets must be constructed of cement in European style, while the old wooden houses with their palm-frond roofs are being torn down. But despite all the recent changes, the quiet of colonial days still lingers in the byways. Streets meander up the hills under old mangoes, cottonwoods and plane trees, with bright patches of bougainvillaea and hibiscus. In all sections blacks and whites live side by side. The division into African and European quarters seen in so many African capitals has happily been avoided here.

On my first afternoon I went to inspect the house that had been rented as the Ambassador's Residence. It was well out of town on top of a low hill with a fine view over the city and the gleaming sea. In the evening I dined alone at the hotel. My waiter told me that the help had been watching out of the windows when I arrived that morning. Several waiters left their places to walk over to my table to shake my hand—always with both their hands clasping mine—and the headwaiter said how grateful he and the others were that I had come to live among them. Guests at the other tables, all white, observed unsmiling.

The windows were open and a strong breeze from the sea flowed through the room. I was perfectly comfortable in my average-weight suit, but later I learned to respect the climate; it is not easy. The temperature is not particularly high, holding most of the time in the upper eighties but with little variation from day to day or between day and night, and with constant high humidity. My wife and I, older and hardened, took it without difficulty, but sometimes new arrivals to our staff would feel poorly for several weeks. Outside an air-conditioned room one was usually wet. After attending a crowded reception I would return home to find even my jacket heavy

20

with water. Africans, I noticed, per
I have seen a fat Gabonese squee
his necktie. Clothes not currently
plies have to be protected against n
place or a closet with a dehumidifi

This, after all, was the tropic
almost on the Equator. Later on
Residence I would point to some
and ask a visitor if he could see th
them. He would squint, and som
would say, "Well, that is the Equ
road to Lambaréné. Bill Mansfiel
the United States there would be
Equator" or "Get your Equator
Gabon forest the spot was unmar

That night there was a storm,
and on each of the next few even
I was about to go out to dinner. I
an umbrella to be had in any stor
pours are so intense, and the wind
such force, that an umbrella is o
the first week of October, just the
son which, with a slight let-up ar
June. Then the rains cease and it
and August, expecting to swelter
selves sleeping under blankets. W
temperature, the forest dampness
whites prefer this season, but for
a difficult time, as the water holes
pneumonia in the chilly nights.

Before I left Washington I wa
cautioned against eating meat not
and other greens that had not be
But soon we lost any nervousnes

21

our ov
tions,
rants w
tions—
reason
sumed
the em
howeve

Gab
sional
monkey
sicknes
of tsets
has bee
time be
will als
shops.
having
Americ
Goats
and ro
found t

I trie
success
farming
torial ra
their br
earth. F
which i
good pi
to Gabo
rocky a
dous rai

Rain

to plant some tomatoes or other vegetables, you must protect the beds from rain and sun for the rain will pound the seeds out of the ground or rot them before they take root, and the sun will kill the tender shoots. This is why there are so few vegetables in the local markets. They take skill and effort to grow. The Gabonese burn the land, which further damages the soil, before planting their annual crop of manioc, their staple, starchy food. The forest is their enemy: with his machete and his ax the Gabonese man spends his life fighting it. Cut, cut, cut all the time, but the burgeoning of tree, shrub and vine is inexorable. The man is worn out, the growth takes over and, as in the desert sands, his traces are obliterated. I said to Léon Mba, "What a shame to cut down these magnificent trees around the Palace!" "You do not understand," he replied. "We have always fought to keep the forest from engulfing us; we have to cut trees down!"

The forest is a reservoir of humidity. Near it, as our house was, a light breeze at sundown would make us shiver even though the temperature was 80°. The jungle abounds in game —elephants, gorillas, chimpanzees, monkeys, antelope, snakes —but is an unhealthy place for man.

The saying is that a Gabonese does not consider himself sick until he has four maladies at once: malaria, filaria, intestinal worms and tuberculosis. And there are quite a few other diseases he can get too. Malaria is endemic: 68 percent of the population have it. With swamps along the coast, many rivers and lakes inland and everywhere the rain forest a breathing sponge, Gabon is the ideal breeding ground for mosquitoes. Whites take malarial suppressants (Nivaquine, Aralen, quinine), yet still can be stricken—as was I. Few Africans bother with these preventatives, for the drugs, although widely available, are expensive. My wife, like many others, bought Nivaquine for the servants and insisted that they take it regularly.

Almost no one takes the suppressant for filaria, but our

Peace Corps boys were given it when living in the bush. This is a very unpleasant disease, but common in Gabon. Flies deposit eggs in the skin that hatch into worms which circulate in the blood and travel through the body. We soon learned to identify the filaria-carrying fly, and also the tsetse fly found mostly along the rivers, but fortunately we escaped their infection.

Disease is one of the reasons for Gabon's extraordinarily small population, only about 475,000. There are but 4.6 people per square mile, one of the lowest densities of any country in the world. Widespread female sterility caused by illness contributes to the low birth rate, but the system of the dowry combined with polygamy is also blamed. The older men who have the money, it is said, can afford the wives while young men cannot. The difficulty with this argument is that the younger men can, and do, father children without creating social problems. The low population and low birth rate are of serious concern to the Gabonese Government, and if the Chinese keep a file on countries which could absorb more people, Gabon must be in it. In area it is not small. Containing 103,-100 square miles, it is almost as large as our New England states plus New York.

Gabon's coastal plain is swampy. Inland the ground rises to a plateau, 1,000 to 2,000 feet, pierced by several mountain ranges, one of which bears the lovely name, the Cristal Mountains. Rugged, slashed by ravines, covered with dense forest, these fastnesses are almost empty of humans but form the habitat of the gorilla.*

Gabon is often called a land of rivers. All the nine Regions

* There is also a very large type of gorilla which inhabits the lowland rain forests along the coast. While we were in Gabon a fine specimen was obtained by the American big game hunter, Frank E. Delano, and its skin sent to an American museum. The event made news for few foreign sportsmen visit Gabon as facilities for hunting have not been developed.

take their names from rivers, of which the most majestic is the Ogooué.* Coming off the plateau they break into rapids and waterfalls. On the Ivindo there are said to be four waterfalls each higher than Niagara, but they are surrounded by such deep forests that they are almost inaccessible and few whites have seen them. It is this drop from plateau to plain which makes the rivers of Gabon, in common with most in Central Africa, navigable for only a short distance from the sea.

The traditional social and political organization of Black Africa is the tribe. The term covers quite disparate groupings. The great tribes of Nigeria—the Ibos, Yorubas and Hausas—resemble separate nationalities; in other places tribes may be small, little more than large families, perhaps closely related to their neighbors and exhibiting slight ethnic differences. Yet differences are there and, as you get to know Africans, you gradually perceive how deep they lie.

Earlier Gabon was inhabited by a conglomeration of small tribes, all Bantu, except for a few pygmies in the forests. In the middle of the last century the Fang, or Pahouins, came from the northeast in a long slow migration from perhaps as far away as the Sudan. These people, then tough cruel cannibals, of other stock mixed with Bantu, forced the weaker, less aggressive groups toward the sea and southward, and took for themselves the area comprising what is today the southern part of Cameroon, the northern part of Gabon and most of Equatorial Guinea. This invasion gave to Gabon its current ethnic, tribal and political character.

Now all the country north of the Ogooué and west of the Ivindo is Fang except in the triangle formed by Libreville, Lambaréné and Port-Gentil. Here with their backs to the sea,

* That fabulous character Trader Horn performed his incredible exploits up and down the Ogooué, and we were shown a house at Lambaréné where he is purported to have stayed.

and among the lakes and marshes surrounding the river, half a dozen of the older tribes, all small, held on, but the Fang are still gradually encroaching. One can see this process today in Libreville: the northern parts of the city are solidly Fang, the center houses a mixture of tribes, while the south along the waterfront is still the home of the original M'Pongwé. In and around Lambaréné the Fang are pressing against the Galoa.

The Fang tide stopped at the Ogooué. The south of the country contains some thirty-odd tribes, some large such as the Bandjabi and the Bapounou, others very small such as the Pové. Compared to the Fang, these tribes appear similar, but compared to each other they exhibit surprising differences. The Mitsogo, for instance, are scrappers, the Bandjabi gentle and amenable. Before the colonists brought order, raids and wars were never-ending, and the suspicions and hatreds still poison the body politic. Tribes in Africa are an anachronism, and with the coming of the nation-state their importance will gradually decrease, but it will be many years before their differences disappear. In the meantime, the problem a national leader faces is to make them to lie down together.

The tribe is the big family. When I left the house of the Subprefect of N'Dendé to drive to M'Bigou, his wife said to me, speaking of the wife of the Subprefect there, "Say hello to my sister." When I reached M'Bigou, I said to the Subprefect's wife that I brought her word from "her sister." Then I discovered that their only tie was that both were Fang, a tribe which numbers 150,000.

Within the tribal family are the individual families. No matter what happens, a Gabonese can always find shelter among his own people. In his own village there is always a place for him, a house to sleep in, food and care, and safety. Time does not matter: he can stay a day or the rest of his life. The city African holds his ties to his village, for if he should lose his job that is where he will go. If he has enough money left, he will take a bus, otherwise he will walk—distances on foot mean little; along the way he will pick bananas from the trees and travelers are rarely refused food. Home is his refuge; there he will always be welcome. After we left Gabon our cook, Grégoire, and our gardener, Jean-Pierre, to whom we were so devoted, returned to their faraway villages.

In the family, the senior member—the father, the older brother—is responsible. A Gabonese who had visited the United States and had made a most favorable impression here called on me looking distraught and told me that he was in great trouble. A younger brother who had a job in a government office had been selling government property and keeping the money; the amount was large, over 100,000 francs ($400), and unless it could be made good he would go to jail.

"Seventy-five thousand francs," my friend said, "is all I have," perhaps hoping that I would help with the balance. "Why must you put up all this money?" I asked. "After all it is your brother who did this, not you." "You do not understand the African way," he replied. "No one will blame him; it is I whom they will blame if I do not find the money, because I, his older brother, am responsible for him." With the coming of modern ways, pension systems have been established for the Civil Service and others. But the social security for the masses still rests with the family.

In the Gabonese family the girls attract attention. Many are pretty. Especially among the southern tribes their winsome simplicity and affectionate nature make them most appealing.

As public lodgings can be found in only a few places, a traveler of any importance will be put up by the headman of the village or, if it is an administrative center, by the Prefect or Subprefect. He will receive the warmest hospitality, which will often include a courtesy that may seem strange to us but which is natural in its setting. After dark an African village is

27

locked tight, the cooking fires are out, there is no light, no sound. For almost twelve hours the Equatorial night will drag on, a long time in the solitary darkness, and so traditionally it has been the right thing for a thoughtful host to do to offer his guest, if single, a girl to beguile him. The girl will by no means be one of mean account; on the contrary she will belong to the host's household or come from some neighboring family. She will probably be one of the highest in her class in school, and she will regard it as a compliment to be chosen for this assignment.

The age when girls are available is about fourteen to sixteen. Later they will be married. Rare is the girl who does not have at least one child before marriage, a child who will be the oldest and a fully accepted member of the family that will follow. A girl who has produced a child possesses evidence that she is not sterile.

In the late afternoon of the first day of my visit with the Subprefect of Médouneu, a reception was given for me. It was out of doors in a glade beside a small river. There must have been a hundred people present. A transistor radio played music; girls passed food and drinks. One with a swirling skirt, long legs and a saucy face commanded general admiration. I said to the Subprefect, "You introduced me to that girl, but I have forgotten who she is." "Why," he replied, "that is the daughter of one of the most important men in the community," and then he added, "I have arranged for her to sleep with you while you are my guest." "That is most thoughtful of you," I said and continued to circulate.

After a while I began to feel very tired. I had been up at five that morning to catch the plane; since arriving I had been on the go every moment. All of a sudden I felt drained of strength. I went to the Subprefect and said, "About that girl, I am very tired. Perhaps, don't you think we might start tomorrow night rather than tonight?" Thus I thought to postpone the matter and deal with it tactfully the next day. He hesitated a moment, then said, "Why, Mr. Ambassador, it is of course as you wish, but her father I am afraid may be offended; he will think you do not like his daughter—and you, the American Ambassador!" Then I saw that this was more than a private matter. I have the greatest affection and respect for the charming young women of Gabon.

Gabon, like all Black Africa, is a Tower of Babel. Each tribe has its own speech. Until the French came and imposed their language the different tribes could not communicate with each other, which perhaps is why their few contacts consisted largely of raiding and fighting.

The inhabitants of the Libreville–Lambaréné–Port-Gentil triangle—the M'Pongwé, the Benga, the Galoa, the Seké, the Ouroungou and some others—speak variations of a common tongue, the Miené. Among the assortment of tribes in the south some speak related languages, so that a person in one tribe can get the drift of what a man in a neighboring tribe is saying. But in the same area villages exist side by side where the languages are totally different.

After breakfast you can leave Lambaréné where Fang and Miené are spoken, drive south through Fougamou, the center of the Eshira who have a different language, and arrive for lunch in Mouila where most of the people are Bapounou who speak yet another tongue. Waiting at a ferry crossing I got out to talk to the people standing around. There were three or four houses on either side of the road. To my amazement I found that the people on one side were Eshira, on the other side Fang. Not more than fifty feet separated them, but they could communicate with each other only in French. I judged that talk across the road rarely took place. A little Eshira boy pointed suspiciously saying, "Those are Fang over there." In this way they lived, year in and year out.

29

Not only is the multiplicity of languages remarkable in so small a country but also the fact that no one of them developed a written form. So there is no history, no knowledge of the African past beyond memory embellished by repetition.

A storyteller of renown lived about forty miles to the west of Médouneu, and during my stay there the Subprefect and the Deputy arranged for him to give a performance for me. It began quite late on a very dark night in a cabin lit by a few oil lamps. He was an elderly, dignified man, indicating by his demeanor that the things he had to tell were important. He donned a headdress of feathers, and twanging a haunting pattern on a metal-stringed instrument chanted his story or ballad, called in Fang a *Mvette*. Half a dozen young men sat about beating a staccato accompaniment with sticks on hard wood. I had a yellow pad and pencils for I wanted to take notes. Whispering in my ear, the Deputy interpreted the Fang in French while I scribbled. The storyteller went on and on. The pace quickened, and the enthusiasm of his accompanists and the neighbors who had crowded into the room mounted to a pitch. After three hours I was exhausted and gave up; the storyteller stopped after a bit. Had I not weakened, he would have kept going till dawn.

The French discourage the tribal languages, which may in the long future die out. Only the little band of American missionaries of the Christian and Missionary Alliance work against this trend. They assign a missionary permanently to a certain tribe, where he learns the language and translates into it such portions of the Bible as have not already been done. We visited missionaries who lived among the Eshira, Bapounou, Bandjabi and Massango. One attractive, dark-haired girl was quartered in a remote village of the Bandjabi where she was working translating the Book of Revelation into their tongue, Indjabi. As I find Revelation difficult in English, I wondered what those simple mountain tribesmen would make of it. I write this in-

30

tending no criticism for these devoted missionaries have done much to promote goodness and kindness.

Because Gabon, a coastal country, was accessible and the colonists were there so long, it became the most Christian of all of France's Black African possessions. About 50 percent of the population is Christian: 40 percent Catholic, 10 percent Protestant. There are only a handful of Muslims. The remainder are still animists, that is people who perceive spirits in the world around us: the trees, the leaves and the brooks. Fetishists, whom the irreverent sometimes call witch doctors, know how to deal with these spirits and are men of great importance in their villages. Ritual, semisecret societies such as the Bwiti and the Mwiri found in most parts of Gabon also have mystical aspects. Gabon's old native art, the fashioning of masks, is related to animist beliefs.

Prior to colonization the Gabonese did not build cities. Libreville, now with fifty thousand people, and Port-Gentil with twenty thousand, were created by Europeans. The African lived in villages which might consist of no more than the four or five houses of a single family. The average village contains fifteen to twenty houses and only a few have more than five hundred people. Some villages periodically move. The surrounding land becomes exhausted, the women have to go farther afield for food until the distance becomes unbearable; then the village seeks another location where the men clear fresh land and build new dwellings.

The houses, or huts, are usually constructed of thin straight poles lashed together; some have siding of rough boards, some are covered with bark, and in many the chinks between the poles or boards are stopped with mud. The roofs are a thatch of palm fronds or banana leaves. The floors are of beaten earth, sometimes covered by reed mats. Most villages have little formal arrangement, but among the Fang and the Mitsogo there

31

are customarily two rows of huts facing each other separated by a court of hard earth.

At night the only light is from kerosene lanterns and the cooking fires, which in the cool summer season are made indoors. The wood is burned on the floor, filling the room with acrid smoke which blackens the walls and roof before escaping through the thatch. I have visited in huts where the smoke smarted in my eyes so that I had to step outside, but the Gabonese stand it red-eyed and often coughing. Piped water in the villages is unknown, the women carrying the day's needs in pails or jars from the nearest stream. Nor is there sewage disposal; the surrounding forest suffices.

The villages where the French established their administrative centers, the headquarters of the Regions and the Districts, developed into modest towns. The largest are Lambaréné, Mouila and Oyem, each with a population in the neighborhood of four thousand. The residence and office of the prefect or subprefect, the school, the gendarmery and the houses of the French are built of whitewashed cement with red roofs and spacious verandas. In the smaller towns they are grouped around a central square in the center of which is a flagpole where the national flag is run up each morning to the accompaniment of a bugle. For the rest, these towns, like the villages, are composed of native huts sheltering among the palms and banana trees.

Lambaréné, like Libreville and Port-Gentil, has running water and electricity, and public lighting is planned for some of the other centers. Otherwise the administrative centers are dark at night, only the houses of the prefect or the subprefect and one or two others having a few faltering bulbs supplied by a pounding diesel. In a prefect's house water may be poured into a barrel on a platform at roof level from which it will trickle down to a basin in the house. Yet, visiting in these houses, we were always made comfortable.

Most of the villages now are along the roads or on the rivers where the colonial administration encouraged their growth for ease of control. Roads did not exist before the Europeans built them. The women would carry anything that had to be moved. When a man went to hunt, he traveled the forest trails, or the rivers by pirogue. Some of these trails have now become roads. The few main ones are broad and reasonably good in all weather, but most are little more than dirt tracks, in many places just two ruts with grass growing between, treacherous if not impassable during the rainy season. In the more remote areas we would drive all day without meeting another vehicle. On Peace Corps business Dick McDaniel, Don La Voie and I went three hours south from M'Bigou beyond the Louetsie River, a part so remote that even the President had never visited it. Along the way the people rushed out of their huts to stare at us, and we learned that not one vehicle a month passed that way.

Over the next three years my wife and I were to know this country well. We visited almost all of it by plane or jeep. Driving in the forest can be monotonous, but as our eyes became adjusted we saw much that was beautiful—the sweeping rivers, the mysterious lakes, the mountain views. Gabon's flag has three equal horizontal stripes of green, yellow and blue. The green, the Gabonese say, is for their forests, the yellow for the sun and the blue for the sea. Broken only by the silver strands of rivers, the great rain forest cloaks rolling land and mountains. From an airplane you look down on deep velvet pincushions, broad parasols, traceries of lace, in every shade of green with patches of gray and yellow and an occasional red plume topping a majestic *okoumé*. Above strides the golden Equatorial sun, outsized, burning. And off the long coastline the blue Atlantic laps white beaches. Green, yellow and blue.

Gabon has a long tradition of hospitality. Foreigners were

33

always welcome to its shores, particularly by the gentle M'Pongwé of Libreville. *"C'est un bon petit pays,"* the French fondly say—"It is a good little country"—and the Americans who have lived there, I think, with but few exceptions, would agree. It is a country where one soon feels at home. We did.

CHAPTER

III

The Setting in Which the
United States Opened Its Embassy

THE United States Government decided at the end of President Eisenhower's Administration to open an embassy in each of the new African countries, a policy which has been continued by Presidents Kennedy and Johnson. Consequently today we have an ambassador accredited in thirty-six of the thirty-nine independent nations of Africa, and an ambassador actually resident in thirty-five.* Conversely each of the thirty-six states has an ambassador accredited in Washington and most have an ambassador residing there. No country other than the United States has adopted this policy. It has proved a wise one. Whether we did much or little besides, it evidenced

---

* One ambassador is accredited to both Senegal and Gambia and lives in the capital of the former, Dakar. We had an ambassador accredited in the Brazzaville Congo, but in 1965 he was withdrawn due to certain difficulties experienced by the personnel of our Mission. Ambassadors have not yet been named to Botswana and Lesotho.

our interest in the nations of Africa, established our influence and assured a steady exchange of ideas.

When I arrived in Gabon I found the resident Diplomatic Corps small indeed. Besides France and ourselves only the Republic of China had a representative in Libreville. This man, Leao-Tchoung-Kin (who was of less than ambassadorial rank), did an excellent job conveying his country's policies and won general support for its cause. Both he and his wife became good friends of ours.

A number of other states had ambassadors accredited in Gabon, but these men were responsible for other countries as well. The Belgian, British and Israeli ambassadors lived in Brazzaville, the Danish, Dutch and Japanese in Léopoldville, the Canadian in Yaoundé, the Swiss in Lagos, and so on. Periodically they would come to Libreville, would call at our Embassy to exchange information and we would entertain them at the Residence. Later Belgium placed a chargé in Libreville, and Germany and Spain sent resident ambassadors.

As soon as I had presented my Letters of Credence to President Léon Mba and had been to see M. Aubame, I went to pay my respects to M. Jean Risterucci, the High Representative and Ambassador of France. A short, vivacious Corsican, he had great strength of will, wisdom and charm. Having been the last Governor (Chef de territoire) of Gabon prior to independence, he possessed an authority which the Gabonese, including the strong-minded President, respected and which his two successors, whom I knew, could not match. The political stability which prevailed while he was there I later realized rested in a good measure on him: it ended a month after he left. My relations with him were of the best. He was never too busy to talk to me at length about Gabonese history and politics, and whenever I sought his cooperation I received it to the full.

His responsibilities were large. Not only was he concerned

36

with the several hundred French administrators and technicians working in Gabon; he also had to keep an eye on the five thousand-odd nonofficial French men, women and children living in the country. He said to me that he was a sort of father confessor to all of them.

Gabon is a biracial society, but in a different sense from many other African states. The French—there are only a handful of whites of other nationalities—did not settle on the land * and raise children to grow up feeling that Gabon was their country, as did the *colons* in Algeria, the Boers in the Transvaal, or the English in Kenya and Rhodesia. Instead, although a man might live for years in Gabon, he did so as a government or company employee. He and his family spent their summer vacations back in France and they looked forward to "going home" when he retired. The whites in Gabon, therefore, as generally in the countries of Black Africa that had been under France, did not create the same political problems that are found in the "white settler" countries. But their importance is still very great.

Gabon's association with France extends over some 125 years. The treaties signed by Bouët Willaumez, the commander of a French naval vessel, with Kings Denis and Louis on the Gabon Estuary in 1839 and 1841 were made peacefully; and the penetration of the country by de Brazza after 1875, and its gradual occupation, although accomplished with soldiery, involved little real force. With isolated exceptions, the Gabonese tribes accepted the colonizing power meekly.

By the time of independence this history had been transformed into a myth which neatly fitted the pattern of tribal thought and emotion. The country had not really been a colony;

* In part this was because the climate and soil in Gabon are not attractive for farming, but also because the legal system instituted by the French protected the Gabonese from the alienation of their tribal lands.

the association with France had been voluntarily entered into and freely maintained. The French were the big brother, the Gabonese the little brother. No other country, even African, stood in such close relationship to Gabon. To the Gabonese the French were more than friends; they were "our brothers."

France had done much to earn and hold this affection. In the capital, out in the countryside, wherever we went we saw the work of France and of Frenchmen: schools, hospitals, administrative buildings and roads. Almost everything in the country above the primitive level of the African village was built by the French or came from France. And everywhere we heard the French tongue, which under Gabon's constitution is not simply an alternate, but the country's only official language.

The French Government and French business work together in a compact system. The fuel that makes it run is French Government aid, which year in and year out pays the salaries and other expenses of a host of Frenchmen—administrators, financial experts, agricultural advisers, engineers, doctors, teachers, judges, to name only a few. It also finances all manner of capital projects and economic and engineering studies, and buys equipment from bulldozers to hypodermic needles. French aid is not only large but admirably carried out. The many projects that I observed seemed well selected and effectively and tastefully executed.

I was also impressed by the personnel which France provided. To run its enormous colonial empire France had to recruit well-qualified people, give them varied training and make life overseas attractive to them. The administrators who helped to operate the central government and administered the Regions and Districts were men of stature, competent and experienced. Some were still in Gabon when we arrived, mostly men near the end of their careers, who with their wives had given a lifetime of service in Indo-China, North Africa or here

38

in Black Africa. They were an impressive lot: efficient, objective, disinterested. They worked for the good of the country and the people to whom they were assigned, and they worked for France. The technicians, too, I thought were generally of high caliber.

The other part of the picture is French business. There are many large French enterprises in Gabon. Perhaps of the greatest political importance is the Compagnie des Mines d'Uranium de Franceville (CMUF). This is controlled by the French Government and provides France with her only outside source of uranium. But there are as well the manganese company, COMILOG; the oil exploration and producing company, SPAFE; the great forestry concerns; the big road-building company, CEGEPAR; the construction companies; the trading houses and the banks. And there are also many small businessmen and women: the butcher, the baker, the candlestick-maker, not to mention the fishmonger, the restaurant owner, the garageman and the coiffeur. All of them, large and small, are busy sending money back to France, the big concerns for their shareholders, the smaller people so that they can buy a villa on the Côte d'Azur and retire as soon as their pile is made. All are ardently French and have a passionate sense of proprietorship in Gabon.

The French forestry concerns use Caterpillar and Allis-Chalmers equipment because these are better than French makes, but, for the rest, industries in Gabon buy their equipment, and French trading concerns their wares, almost exclusively from France. Gabon is small, but the thirteen countries of Black Africa that are within the French system, with a population of some 36 million, provide French manufacturers with a market which, although poor, is almost three-quarters as large in numbers as that of France itself.

Thus French businessmen sending wages and profits home, and producers in France who enjoy safe and high-margin markets in Gabon, are the beneficiaries of a system fed and kept functioning by French aid. It is a form of closed circuit: the French Government puts money in, while French businessmen and French residents of Gabon take it out. If some French tax-payers grumble at the high cost of the government's programs, there are a host of other Frenchmen whose interest is to sup-port those programs, so the system is politically viable and weathers attacks with little difficulty.

In the process the Gabonese have benefited greatly. They have been provided with a safe foreign market for their prod-ucts at prices not infrequently above world prices. They have, in addition, shared the great heritage of French culture. When I made my formal call on the Minister of National Educa-tion, M. Jean-Marc Ekoh, he introduced me to a Frenchman, M. Paul Chatenay, who held the high rank in the French educational system of "Inspecteur d'Académie." He, I soon learned, and not the Minister, had the effective power in edu-cational matters in Gabon.

The Minister of Education's office was separated from the adjoining office by a partition that did not go entirely to the ceiling, and in this room sat his French administrative assist-ant, who could overhear everything that the Minister and his callers said. Not long after our first meeting M. Ekoh asked if he could call on me, and when he came to my office he ex-plained with emotion that, devoted as he was to France and grateful for all she was doing, he felt at times smothered by French control. The Minister who followed him, M. Vincent de Paul Nyonda, was content to leave the character and qual-ity of the national education to France and confined himself largely to housekeeping tasks.

Under one of the so-called cooperation agreements the French concluded with their African possessions, France is given large responsibility for education. This responsibility is taken with the utmost seriousness. France has reserved to herself the molding of the minds and the intellectual and cultural development of "her Africans," and the thoroughness and sincerity with which she has carried out this task lie at the heart of their devotion and loyalty. The French Government channels an important part of its aid to this work. And I was impressed that the Gabonese Government devotes some 17 percent of the national budget to education. The Catholic and Protestant churches also run schools throughout the country, which exist side by side with the state schools. The churches receive Gabonese Government support, and the curriculum and teaching in all schools come under the supervision of the Inspecteur d'Académie and his staff.

In the primary schools all instruction is in French. In Gabon 80 percent of the children of primary school age are in school. Out in the countryside many walk miles and miles each day; some come from so far that they cannot return to their homes except on the weekends, living during the week with friends or relatives. Only in the most remote forest areas does one find a few children who are not in school and do not speak French.

Secondary school education is a more recent development. It was insignificant before the late fifties, but it is now expanding. Higher education is provided through scholarships to universities in France—also a part of French aid. Some students of less promise are sent to Dakar or Brazzaville. Free supplemental training in France is also given to outstanding Gabonese administrators and civil servants. The teaching staff in the secondary schools is recruited abroad, almost entirely from France, while the primary school teachers are Gabonese. Altogether the work of the French Government and of Frenchmen in educating the Gabonese represents an immense effort.

The curriculum, particularly in the secondary schools, can be criticized for being too greatly concerned with French history, French literature and French thought. The world is shown revolving around France. Relatively little attention is given, short of postgraduate work for the selected few who get to France, to practical matters such as economics, business administration or government. When Etoughe Joseph, the Sub-prefect of Médouneu, was staying with me, he took a scholar-ship examination for a two-year course in France. I asked him to show me one of his papers and found to my surprise that while it called for an essay discussing the thought of Alphonse Daudet, it did not ask a single question relating to the admin-istration of a subprefecture. Many Gabonese in government administrative positions and in business start off poorly because the education they have received has not prepared them for such tasks. Notwithstanding this, my wife and I thought that the results of French education in Gabon were remarkably impressive.

Its effect was, above all, civilizing, which has been France's objective. Children display a deportment that puts American children to shame, young people handle themselves with re-serve and grace, while the older men, particularly those who have been to France, express their ideas with logic and dignity. The beautiful and accurate French language, and the refine-ment and distinction of French culture, have been France's greatest gifts to her Africans. I never failed in my travels in Gabon, particularly in my frequent talks to school children, to tell them how fortunate they were in receiving these gifts, and it was always my pleasure to pay tribute to France for the spirit and effort she brought to this great work.

Education is one of the happy aspects of France's relations with Gabon, but it is by no means the full picture. Other char-acteristics of the relationship are less admirable, particularly French involvement in Gabon's political life. When I first met the Gabonese ministers, each had his French adviser beside him, and during the first year or so of my service when I called on a minister to transact a piece of business his French adviser was usually present. This seemed to me a natural and proper thing. The Gabonese had just assumed the responsibility for running the government and the former colonial power was helping the newly appointed ministers while they learned their jobs. The character of a minister's decisions, of course, was influenced by these advisers, but they were seasoned colonial administrators (in several cases they had been the ones who had previously run the ministries), and their role, obviously helpful, I thought did little to prejudice the effective independence of the new state.

But when it came to Gabonese political life, the French did more than just advise. Here it was plain that France was playing a political role of her own.

In my briefings in Washington I had studied what I could about the political history of Gabon, but very little was available. When I arrived in Libreville, I found the Embassy staff anxious to share the information that they had gleaned and as interested in "talking politics" as was I. No part of an ambassador's education in the affairs of the country to which he is sent is more important, since out of this knowledge of the past he must interpret what is taking place and try to forecast the future.

News and information are not available in Gabon as they are in the United States. Although the President of Gabon and the ministers occasionally make a formal announcement, they seldom hold press conferences. They are rarely subjected to questions, and apart from official handouts there is no current record of what is happening. Occasionally a foreign correspondent will visit the country to write a particular story, but inquisitiveness about politics and government is discouraged. Keeping informed about current events, sifting fact from rumor, requires diligent and discerning work even when one is on the spot. Learning about the past is even more difficult.* The Gabonese have no written language, so they have put nothing down. French records are fragmentary and scattered. So far as I know, there is no written source where one can find an authoritative account or interpretation of political history. In part you have to form your conclusions by talking to as many people as possible who lived through the events you are studying.

In Gabon modern political forms were laid on top of the traditional family and tribal organization. The people who inhabited this vast area of steaming forests and infertile savannas had developed only the most localized and simplest of associations. There is no record of any government of strength or any civilization such as existed at different times in other parts of Black Africa from Mali to Zimbabwe. Living in small groups isolated from one another, speaking many different languages, the people on this Equatorial coast had little need of organization and authority wider than the family and village, or the clan ** living in a few neighboring villages. Traditionally each family or clan was governed by its chief, who, although he counseled with the elders and with the fetishists or witch doctors, possessed practically absolute power. When there was public discussion, it was only advisory; the politics and parties familiar in the West were unknown.

Colonization did not change this order. The colonists, while using African chiefs to manage village and tribal affairs, placed on top of this simple African organization an over-all administration. It was when the first steps were taken toward bringing

* Brian Weinstein, in his scholarly book *Gabon: Nation-Building on the Ogooué*, M.I.T. Press, 1966, has assembled a considerable amount of historical material and an extensive bibliography.

** I found this word "clan" (a French word as well as English) frequently used by Gabonese to describe a grouping larger than a family but smaller than a tribe (or "race," to use the French term).

Africans into this wider government that political activity was born and political organization became needed.

This, practically speaking, began in 1946 when Gabon had its first elected legislature in which some of the places were filled by Gabonese, and also became entitled to send representatives to institutions of the Fourth Republic in Paris. Jean-Hilaire Aubame was elected in that year a member of the French National Assembly, a seat he held until 1959. In 1947 he founded Gabon's first political party, the Union Démocratique et Sociale Gabonaise (UDSG). Paul Gondjout, who had been elected to the legislative body in 1946, was elected in 1949 to represent Gabon in the French Senate. In 1954 he organized the Bloc Démocratique Gabonais (BDG), to which he shortly attracted Léon Mba.

Until 1957 Aubame and the UDSG consistently won at the polls. In that year elections were held for the members of the Territorial Assembly. The BDG won eight seats; the UDSG, nineteen; and various independents, ten. Aubame for years had enjoyed French intellectual and liberal support, but in 1957 French business interests in Gabon, lead by the powerful forestry concerns, apparently concluded that Léon Mba was their man. His political ability must have influenced them in his favor, but what doubtless counted most was his willingness to play ball with them. With their help and contributions Gondjout persuaded all ten of the independent Deputies to sign up with the BDG. Despite this feat the BDG still had only eighteen seats to the UDSG's nineteen. So Gondjout and his French friends induced three French members of the Assembly, who had been elected by the UDSG, to switch sides. With the majority they provided, the BDG formed a government under the French Governor as provided by the Loi Cadre, and not surprisingly, each of these three men turned up as a minister!

From then on, the BDG was the dominant party in Gabon. Its control was shared by Léon Mba and Gondjout, with the

45

former constantly increasing his power. Léon Mba claimed that Aubame was interested primarily in the Fang and would pay inadequate attention to the interests of the southern tribes, and that if he came to power the country would be in danger of coming apart on tribal lines. This charge Aubame ridiculed.

When Gabon gained independence, on August 17, 1960, Léon Mba, who had been the Deputy President of the Council of Ministers under the French Governor, became President of the Republic. Gondjout was President of the National Assembly.

Then came the Battle of the Constitution. In 1958 France had given Gabon a constitution which divided power between the Legislative Assembly and the Executive. With independence some revision was needed. Would the change place more authority in the President's hands, or would the President continue to share his power with the Assembly? This issue, so important in the political life of France, was reflected in its colonies. Léon Mba of course was for the former, while the great majority of the deputies naturally favored the latter. Léon Mba wanted to force the issue, but his French advisers counseled him to give in a bit in order better to advance. So Léon Mba announced that he was for the parliamentary constitution, whereupon it was voted.

It was short-lived. A month later, in November, Léon Mba dramatically accused Paul Gondjout of plotting to poison him. Declaring the state to be in danger, Léon Mba imprisoned Gondjout, dissolved the Assembly and ordered new elections. Gondjout's younger brother, Edouard, and René Sousatte, the head of the small Parti de l'Unité Nationale Gabonaise (PUNGA), were also imprisoned but were soon released.

Being imprisoned in Gabon can take different forms. One of these is to send a man to a remote village where he is kept, in secrecy, under tight house arrest. This is not always as rigorous as it sounds for he may be supplied with all the whisky and beer he can drink, and all the girls he wants. The purpose is not so much to be nice to a former political colleague whom one has decided to dump as it is to undermine his will to continue resistance, to lower his sense of personal dignity—in short, to deprave him. Gondjout was "imprisoned" in this manner for some sixteen months, but he proved too tough a character to be undone.

Some time after his release and return to Libreville, I invited him to come to the Residence for a drink; I felt it important to see what manner of man he was and to hear his stories. I found him carefree, ebullient, amusing and apparently none the worse for wear. During the final months of his detention he had been kept in the government-owned hunting lodge at Booué, an attractive house on a high bluff overlooking the Ogooué, a gorgeous location. My daughter and I were the first visitors to be put up there after he left.

To go back to 1961, after getting rid of Paul Gondjout, Léon Mba was in a position to call the tune. Under pressure from M. Risterucci, he agreed to form a Government of National Union with M. Aubame's party, the UDSG. The UDSG, however, was to be very much the junior partner. Of the sixty-seven seats which it was decided that the National Assembly should have (a large number for a country with a population then of 450,000), only some twenty were given to the UDSG. A single list was constructed and duly voted on February 13, 1961. At the same time Léon Mba, running as the only candidate, was elected President of the Republic for a seven-year term. His first act was to have the National Assembly adopt a "presidential type" of constitution placing almost total power in his own hands. The text was prepared by his French advisers. The French business interests had won. Aubame and his colleagues, who favored a more independent policy for Gabon, were locked into a government that would be run by Léon Mba.

The government which Léon Mba then named contained four UDSG members: M. Aubame as Minister of Foreign Affairs, M. François Mèyè as Minister of Finance, M. Jean-Marc Ekoh as Minister of National Education, and M. Eugène Amogho as Minister of Public Works. These were the ablest men in the Cabinet apart from M. André-Gustave Anguilé, the Minister of National Economy. This government, often referred to as the Government of National Union, lasted for almost two years, until February 19, 1963. It was a good time in Gabon. A spirit of national unity prevailed, and one had the sense that people were pulling together to make something out of this potentially rich little country. French guidance was still unquestioned, but it did not appear excessively heavy-handed and its constructive aspects appeared to me generally to excuse its possessiveness.

This was the setting into which the United States moved to place its Embassy in Gabon, and this was the climate prevailing during the first year and a half of my term as Ambassador.

CHAPTER

IV

An American Ambassador in a
New Country

To cover the many new African nations before ambassadors could be selected and sent out to each, our government assigned several countries to one man. Ambassador W. Wendell Blancke, accredited in Congo (Brazzaville), was asked temporarily to take charge also in the other three republics that, with the Congo, had formed French Equatorial Africa: the Central African Republic, Chad and Gabon. He presented his credentials to President Léon Mba in December, 1960, four months after independence, and continued although resident in Brazzaville to represent our country in Gabon until I came at the start of October.

Willie Jones arrived on March 16, the first of the permanent staff. Walker Diamanti followed within a few days to act as Chargé d'Affaires, then Bill Mansfield, Milly Giblin, Virginia Greer and Colette Welker. The previous fall Loy Henderson, the Deputy Under Secretary of State for Administration, had visited a number of the newly independent countries, and even earlier Alan W. Lukens had been to Libreville to locate accommodations, but in these young African capitals housing was hard to find at any price, so the first few weeks were spent living and working in a hotel.

Shortly afterward the American Embassy opened in a rather down-at-the-heel, two-story house across the street from one of the most popular French bars in town, "Le Petit Bidule." There we spent the first two years until Willie Jones cleverly discovered that a French bank was closing its Libreville office. The Department bought the property, a handsome structure on a large plot of land on the shore boulevard, where the United States Embassy now stands.

The staff were tucked into houses and apartments scattered through the town. Air conditioners sent from the United States were installed in the bedrooms, various small things were done to make the places more livable, and when my wife and I arrived everyone appeared to be housed in moderate comfort. It took a long time to get screens, so in the evening when the lights were on, the living rooms were filled with crawling and flying insects of every size and shape, but in time Washington gave us the money and we were able to have screens made. In the small African posts these things are important for people spend most of their free time at home. It is too hot to walk in the streets, there is nowhere to go in a car, Libreville has no concerts, no parks, and only one movie house. It does, however, have miles of pleasant beach, which all year round provided our chief diversion.

An American ambassador's work in these new African nations differs considerably from his life in the more developed countries. He cannot be a detached observer. If he is doing his job properly, he will soon find himself deeply engaged.

An ambassador is the personal representative of the President of the United States, not to a foreign nation or government, but to its chief of state. The relationship is a personal one. It is an ambassador's job, therefore, not only to bring to his work the objectivity and competence of the professional civil servant, but also to reflect the essence and style of the man whom he represents. I was particularly conscious of the latter serving as I did both Presidents Kennedy and Johnson.

An ambassador's work covers the entire range of relations between the United States and the country where he is accredited. He must conduct current business between the two governments, he must establish his influence, and he must obtain information. He is on duty twenty-four hours a day. Our office opened at 7:30, and from then until bedtime there was seldom an idle moment for any one of us. Reporting takes a large share of everyone's time. We had to send our cables through the public facilities, which, even with the reduced night rate, were expensive. Jones would get them to the telegraph office, and if I wrote a cable as long as a page, he would rush up to my room saying, "Mr. Ambassador, we don't have enough money in the budget for cables like this." So I would often write long dispatches, but when I returned to Washington I found that almost no one had read them. The volume of cables alone coming into the Department is so great that you have to read like the wind to go through even a selection of the day's "take" from just your own geographic area.

In a small post it is difficult for an ambassador to delegate work. I found that I had to attend personally almost every meeting with a minister or high official, for if I sent my DCM or some other member of the staff, he would be asked, "Where is the Ambassador, is he ill?" Above all I wanted to make sure that no official in this new African country would feel slighted or think that I would not put myself to trouble for him. My deal, regard their opponents as traitors and are extremely critical of the slightest contacts with them. A diplomat manifestly cannot have contacts with people who are plotting revolution, but a distinction must be made between them and people who are simply dissatisfied and would like to see change within the framework of established order. And with the latter the problem has different degrees: it is one thing to avoid association with a known opposition leader; it is something else to shun contacts with all persons not supporters of the regime.

The third of my circles embraces the general population, and it is here that the work of an American ambassador in a new country differs most from that in an old established nation. The American Ambassador to Great Britain, for instance, does not, cannot, concern himself with the whole British people, but it is precisely this which our ambassadors in Black Africa must do. In Gabon the government and its known dissenters in the capital represented but a fraction of the population. With virtually no media of communication it was impossible to know how closely these men reflected the thoughts and feelings of the people. I considered it important, therefore, to get to know the men and women in the street and out in the villages. The nation was, and still is, in its infancy. Other countries would not be slow to work such virgin soil could they get the chance. Surely the United States ought to make the most of its opportunity to win the minds and hearts of the whole people.

The tools an ambassador has are the men and the money that Washington gives to him.

Closest to him is the embassy staff, personnel from the Department of State. A Deputy Chief of Mission, an Administrative Officer, and a junior Foreign Service Officer acting as Economic Officer and Vice Consul made up the complement of my Embassy, in addition to communications, general services and clerical personnel. Occasionally the Department would always sufficient to establish American influence, either with the leaders in the capital or with the mass of the people in the towns and villages throughout the country.

In these circumstances, I believe, our most effective tool is the spirit that an ambassador is able to communicate. This is something that Africans are quick to grasp. Because few can read, and perhaps because animist beliefs are widespread among them, they are extremely sensitive to spiritual forces. So my wife and I constantly worked to give the Gabonese some understanding of what the United States stands for, and we sought, by our demeanor and conduct, to exemplify our country and our people.

Picture a nation such as Gabon. There are some men and women who have gone through secondary school and a handful with higher education, but most of the people, scattered over a large area with primitive communications, know little outside the narrow confines of their forest clearings. All are aware that their country is now independent, but there is little conception of what freedom means and what it involves. Even among the educated there is small understanding of how to go about making democracy work. The American ambassador must, it seems to me, regard it as a principal part of his job to help these people, by spiritual as well as material aid, to use their freedom creatively. The former colonial power will have launched the young country with certain democratic forms but the people's hold on freedom is in fact very fragile. To help them to find the resources within themselves to build their nation must surely be one of the purposes of our relationship with them.

From the day I arrived in Gabon until the day I left, my door at the office as well as at home was open to any Gabonese, from members of the government to the poorest laborer, who wanted to come and see me, no matter what the purpose. And many came: some for scholarships to study in the United States

57

(which I did not have), some for advice on this subject or that, many to ask for help of one kind or another, many to pay their respects, and some just to talk with the American Ambassador. In a larger country one could not see so many people, but I found it possible; it took time, but was never a burden.

In Black Africa travel is about the only means an ambassador has to extend his influence outside the capital. The best way is by road, for this enables one to be seen by, to see and to speak with many people. It is imperative to allow ample time. I never succeeded in planning a trip which allowed really enough time except the week I spent in Médouneu, and there I could have used two. I always had frequent opportunities to speak to groups: at the village center, at a reception for the village "notables," at the schools. In one place I was asked to come into a hall where people had gathered from far and wide, and I talked to them and answered questions for three hours.* Wherever we stopped, the people were anxious to show all they had: the school, the church, the administrative buildings, the gendarmery station. In the little villages where there were no public buildings they invited us into their homes and always offered us something, palm wine to drink with them there, or an egg or chicken to take away. Often I sat inside dark huts, the smoke of an open fire making my eyes smart. Time means nothing. You must not hurry.

Being an American, representing and interpreting America, is a great source of strength in the large part of the world that has known colonialism. Our country stands in the eyes of the

* After each of our trips I would make a report, oral or written, to the President. I gave him a written report of this meeting, telling him that I had urged the people not to wait to be made rich by their country's manganese, oil and iron, or by handouts from Libreville or by foreign aid, but to work harder themselves. I found that when you talked to the Gabonese straight from the shoulder they like it. The President sent me a most gracious and friendly reply. This was September 16, 1963.

Africans for the goals they seek, liberty and opportunity. An American does not take a cynical view of the Africans' capacity to govern themselves and eventually to solve their problems. We do not question or deplore their independence because some of their affairs are less well administered now than in the colonial period. We have faith that they will find their feet, and that they will demonstrate the character and stamina to move forward. Also—and this I think is important—when an American encounters radical young persons, he is not afraid that they will frustrate *our* objectives in their country. Instead, his concern is how he can help them to attain *their* objectives, which will most often be found to concern human dignity and a better life. Thus he establishes an identity of interest with them, and as that is achieved there is no need to worry about *our* objectives.

This is what I call the Philosophy of the Ambassador. Its appeal is in the realm of the spirit. Its effectiveness can be enormous.

A most striking illustration was given after the death of President Kennedy, when there was an incredible outpouring of grief and affection in Gabon, as throughout Black Africa. I had been in Washington when the tragedy occurred, and returned to Libreville some ten days later. When I called on the Vice President, M. Yembit, he said, "When my children heard the news they would not eat all day." The President of the Supreme Court, M. Aubame, said, "He is a martyr for the blacks." Many letters, some with poems, came to the Embassy. A most touching one reached me from our former Congolese chauffeur, Bernard. "I cry for our Chief," he wrote. Services in Protestant churches, and Masses, performed in all parts of the country, were packed, as if the Gabonese felt that they had lost one of their own leaders.

This is a classic example of the power of the spirit. The essence of President Kennedy's appeal was that the Africans felt he was for them; the poor trusted him, the young caught his spark. The benefit to the United States was incalculable. Part of his appeal, to be sure, sprang from the fact that he was President, and it was accentuated by his death, but I believe that in a measure all Americans can reach into the minds and hearts of the peoples in the underdeveloped countries, and particularly those who are young. This in my opinion is the wider task of an American ambassador in such countries.

All these things, I fear, appear better on the clean printed page than in what we actually accomplished, but they are what we tried to do.

V

American Interests and Roots in Gabon

WHEN he told me that President Kennedy was considering appointing me Ambassador to Gabon, Governor Williams, the Assistant Secretary of State for Africa, and his deputies Wayne Fredericks and Henry Tasca, praised my fortune as Gabon is one of the wealthiest of African states in natural resources. You are being given, they said, a country where there is a good basis for economic development and where there are important American business interests. Adlai Stevenson also congratulated me because Dr. Schweitzer's hospital was at Lambaréné in Gabon and I would have the opportunity to get to know that great man.

American private investments in Gabon are larger than in any other of the fifteen countries of Black Africa that were formerly administered by France except Guinea where they are of approximately the same magnitude.* The most important today—it may be overshadowed in time by the iron of Belinga—is that of the United States Steel Corporation in the Compagnie Minière de l'Ogooué (COMILOG). Their mine at Moanda is said to have the largest reserves of high-grade manganese in the Free World. U.S. Steel owns 49 percent of this company, having in it an investment of over $60 million. The remaining 51 percent is in French hands. As none of the French shareholders is a manganese user, the major part of the production is shipped to the United States.

Before going to Gabon I visited the headquarters of U.S. Steel in Pittsburgh to learn about this enterprise, and soon after arriving in the country I flew to Moanda to see it. The location, in a country covered mostly by dense forests, is pleasing: rolling, open uplands like the south downs in England. The airstrip is laid on top of manganese, and the roads in the concession, made of manganese ore, are a shiny black. It was fascinating to watch immense bulldozers push aside the few feet of overburden to expose the thick layer of ore. After crushing and washing this is loaded in buckets swinging on an aerial cableway called a *téléferique*, for transport some forty-five miles to M'Binda in the Congo. From there it is carried by rail to be loaded on ore ships at Pointe Noire.

During my years in Gabon I visited Moanda several times, receiving always the most gracious welcome from the resident executives, all of whom are French, U.S. Steel acting as technical adviser. The most notable occasion was the formal inauguration of production in October, 1962, when many distinguished personalities were present. I shared an automobile with General Sizaire, the commander of French forces in

* The figure includes the Malagasy Republic. I use the word "administered" because Cameroon and Togo were not French colonies, but were administered by France under United Nations trusteeship.

62

Equatorial Africa, whose successor, General Kergaravat, was to play such a dramatic role in Gabon in 1964. It was the first time I heard President Léon Mba make a chauvinistic speech.

The other outstanding American interest is that of Bethlehem Steel in the Société des Mines de Fer de Mékambo (SOMIFER), which holds the concession to the iron ore deposits at Belinga, where there are believed to be approximately a billion tons of very high grade ore, one of the richest known reserves in the Free World. By dint of some very determined bargaining Bethlehem Steel obtained a 50 percent participation. The other shareholders are steelmakers and financial interests in the several countries of the Common Market. The investment so far is small, representing only prospecting, engineering and administrative expenses, but when production begins, a very large investment by SOMIFER, perhaps some $150 million, will be required.

I had spent an informative and pleasant day with Bethlehem Steel in Pennsylvania, and soon after my arrival in Libreville, Peter Telfair, the resident director of SOMIFER, came to call. I was to have a lot to do with Peter during my years in Gabon, and my wife and I became very fond of him and his wife Frances. Peter Telfair was SOMIFER. It was he who a decade earlier had walked into the forest north of Mékambo and reported to Bethlehem on the fabulous deposits of iron ore; and it was he who played the major role in establishing the American interest in the face of very keen competition by the French Government's Bureau des Mines.

We were Peter's guests at the mining camp in Belinga and also at his house in Makokou where he had located the SOMIFER office. Belinga is about sixty miles up the Ivindo River from Makokou. No road or commercial air service reached it, so Peter took us on the river in two large motor-powered pirogues, a five-hour trip. My sister Caroline, who was visiting us from Vermont, and Milly Giblin came along. The river was full and swift, and reflected the great trees on the banks so sharply that we could not tell where water ended and land began. It was a trip of unparalleled beauty. Now and then we would pass a Bakuélé village and occasionally another pirogue, but otherwise we were in solitude. Peter and Frances were perfect hosts, and it was a great relief to get away from the humid heat of Libreville into the fresher, cooler air of the mountains. SOMIFER and its problems, particularly how the ore was to be brought to the Atlantic, were of great concern to our Embassy.

COMILOG and SOMIFER are immensely important in the Gabonese scheme of things. Although Gabon's other natural resources—wood, uranium, oil, gold—exceed those of many other African nations, manganese and iron are the products upon which the Gabonese base their future. With such wealth under their soil, they look forward to the time when Gabon will need no foreign aid from any source and when its standard of living will have reached an acceptable level in comparison with the West.

These hopes in large measure rest on the United States. If they are to come true, we must continue to buy large quantities of Gabonese manganese at satisfactory prices. And iron production must be started, which depends largely on the attitude of Bethlehem Steel and the ability of the Gabonese Government to find the $120 to $140 million that will be needed to build the railroad to carry the ore to the sea. As the American interest is half of the total in the concession-holding company, the Gabonese expect that at least half of the railroad money will be raised by the International Bank for Reconstruction and Development in the United States and by American public and private lenders.

Besides its utility, the railroad will be a symbol of modernity, and the Gabonese have their hearts set on it. I was very much alive to the dangers, as well as the opportunities, that this situation held for our relations with Gabon. I worked with the Minister of National Economy when the Gabonese Government made proposals and reports to Washington so that these were presented in a business-like manner, but I cautioned him, as well as the President, that the large sum they hoped to obtain from the United States, $60 to $70 million, was by no means certain.

Furthermore, from time to time I drew the attention of the President, the Minister and others to the inconsistency that existed between their hopes for United States financing and their treatment of American imports. "How can you," I asked, "discriminate against American goods in favor of France, and then think that the United States will be enthusiastic about financing your projects?" They tried to pretend that the two things were separate, but I am sure that they understood very well the close connection. They were prisoners of the French system of restrictive import and exchange control.

The manganese and iron-ore holdings of United States Steel and Bethlehem Steel are the predominant American investments in Gabon, but there are others. Mobil Oil and Texaco market petroleum products, and both may be able to participate in a refinery being built in Port-Gentil. Between 1959 and 1962 Mobil Oil devoted considerable effort and money to finding oil, but without notable success. An American chemical company has obtained certain rights from the Gabonese Government to build a plant for the manufacture of explosives and agricultural chemicals. More, I think, might have been done to help Americans find other investment opportunities in Gabon had the staff of the Embassy been slightly larger, for it takes time and effort to uncover and develop possibilities. Perhaps the American banks now represented in Libreville may be able to help in this direction. The Bank of America, the Morgan Guaranty Trust Company and the First National City Bank of New York have recently become part owners in three Gabonese banks.

Foreign investment, which pays good wages, provides health services, trains and educates local workmen and divides the profits of the enterprise fairly with the country in which it is located, is of inestimable benefit. The manganese, the oil, the iron ore under the ground of Gabon are worth nothing until produced, processed and brought to markets. This can be done only by private capital from the developed countries where the need for these products exists. American private investment in Gabon provides one of the brightest hopes for the future of the country.

As our investments in Gabon are of mutual benefit, so is our trade. The United States stands in second place, after France, both as a buyer of Gabon's exports and as a supplier of its imports. The amounts, even for our large economy, are not negligible; in 1965 our purchases amounted to $20.1 million (the largest item was manganese) and our sales to $7.4 million (primarily forestry and mining machinery). Through the long colonial years the Gabonese knew few goods but French. The importing houses were French and drew their supplies from France, as is the case today. French administrators and technicians encouraged and fostered the use of French products. Goods could, and can now, be bought from France without restriction, but Gabonese wishing to buy American products face greater handicaps at present than they did when Gabon was a colony.

When I arrived the year after independence, imported goods were subjected to revenue taxes, which were the same regardless of source. There were no customs duties. This was the case also in Congo (Brazzaville), the Central African Republic,

Chad and Cameroon. On July 1, 1962, these five countries, which were then in the process of forming the Equatorial Customs Union, surrounded themselves with a customs tariff known as the Common External Tariff. The duties imposed were additional to the revenue taxes, but they did not apply to goods from France or from the other countries in the European Economic Community. As these other nations had only a small trade with Gabon, the beneficiary for practical purposes was France. The supplier that was hit was the United States.

I know from the talks that I had with President Léon Mba that this was no idea of the Gabonese Government. (Moreover, it was not something to which Gabon was bound later by the Yaoundé Convention, whereby the colonies of France, and certain other countries, became associated with the European Economic Community.) It was plain that the step had been engineered by the French technical advisers (M. Jacques David in the case of Gabon),* who would not have taken this coordinated initiative without behind-the-scenes guidance from the French Government.

The figures speak for themselves: in 1965 we took 21.8 percent of Gabon's exports, France 46.2 percent, but France supplied 58.5 percent of Gabon's imports while we sold only 11.7 percent. If nondiscriminatory conditions can be restored, imports from the United States should increase to the benefit of the Gabonese and ourselves. We can be sure that the Gabonese and their sister peoples will not indefinitely allow these restraints to curtail their freedom to buy in whatsoever markets of the world they wish.

* M. A.-G. Anguilé, long-time Minister of National Economy of Gabon, and M. Jacques David are co-authors of a book just published (by Editions Paul Bory, Monaco) called *L'Afrique sans Frontières,* in which they try to explain the common External Tariff and its discrimination.

When Gabon started its independent life in 1960, the United States was virtually unknown; there were in fact very few Americans in the country. On my first trip, replying to a toast after dinner in N'Dendé, I said that I was sure that everyone in the room had seen an elephant but that not a single one had ever before beheld a representative of the American Government; they roared, showing that I had hit the truth.

Some missionaries of the Christian and Missionary Alliance, a sect distinct from the Presbyterians who had worked earlier in the north, had been in the south of Gabon since the 1930's. They established six or seven mission stations and numbered perhaps thirty souls, counting wives and children, but their purpose was to convert Gabonese to Christianity and they refrained from accenting the fact that they came from the United States. Had they done otherwise, their residence in this French-controlled land, never easy, might have become impossible. Beside them, only two Americans, Peter Telfair and his second, Paul Geiger, were permanent residents in Gabon when the American Embassy opened. American exporters to Gabon did not have American agents but sold through the established French importing houses. For a period at Port-Gentil there were a few Americans from Mobil Oil and their drilling contractor. And there were occasional visitors, such as Mrs. Preminger to Dr. Schweitzer's hospital, and engineers from U.S. Steel on COMILOG business. That was all. Among Gabonese the number who had been to the United States could be counted on the fingers of one's hands. Perhaps the first had been Jean-Marc Ekoh, who came to our country in 1954, visiting Hyde Park where he met Mrs. Roosevelt.

I found, however, a widespread knowledge that Americans had had important contacts on this coast in an earlier period. When President Léon Mba accepted the letters accrediting me as Ambassador, he said that by this action President Kennedy "has sealed the warm friendship which has existed continuously between Gabon and the United States since the arrival of the first American missionaries on June 22, 1842, 119 years ago." Louis Bigmann, the President of the National Assembly, who was born and lived all his life in Baraka, received me in his house with tears in his eyes saying, "The Americans have come back to Baraka." It is an extraordinary fact that in what is now this most French country both the first Protestant missionaries and the first Catholic missionaries were American. The first school was started by Americans. And the first white man extensively to explore the interior was an American. These early relations were widely and affectionately remembered, and they gave us some slight political foundation.

On June 22, 1842, a little band of Presbyterians sent out by the American Board of Commissioners of Foreign Missions in Boston settled at a spot on the Gabon Estuary called Baraka—now a part of Libreville. They founded a mission station and a school, and a short time later brought over the boards sawed to measure in New England for a church which remains today the center of Protestant life in the capital. The same boards, now weathered by a hundred years of sun and rain, still resound on Sunday mornings to the familiar old hymns, but sung in the Miené language and in Fang. The location was fraught with difficulty. The murderous climate decimated the missionaries, as the many gravestones of Vermont marble in the little cemetery behind the church attest. And the natives, used as intermediaries in the purchase of ivory and ebony, and in the traffic in slaves seized in the interior and kept here in stockades awaiting ships (as the name "Baraka" indicates), had been perverted and weakened by alcohol and formed an unpromising congregation.

In the following years other missionaries of the ABCFM opened missions in the forest villages and in 1876 established

69

their first station on the Ogooué.* For fifty and more years these courageous men and women worked civilizing the tribes, teaching them about God, settling their quarrels, treating their sicknesses. As the French administration extended its control, they found their positions becoming increasingly difficult. In 1890 the Evangelical Church of Paris, at the instance of the colonial administration, took over the direction of the Protestant missions in Gabon. One by one the remaining Americans left until the last of this early company departed for Ebolowa in the Cameroon about 1913.

Although a century and more have passed, one often comes upon reminders of these early dedicated Americans. One day I went to help a Peace Corps group establish themselves in N'Toum where they were to build a school. The Ministry of Public Works has a yard there where it keeps materials and equipment for maintaining a section of the road. I walked over to it and found the manager, an elderly Gabonese, who introduced himself as Mr. Bushnell. "Bushnell?" I said, surprised. "Why, I know a Mrs. Bushnell in New York, but how does it happen that you, a Gabonese, have that name?" "Oh," he said, "there was once an American missionary named Bushnell who was very kind to my family, so we took his name." On my return to my office I found that a Rev. Albert Bushnell had been a missionary of the ABCFM in Gabon from 1844 to 1877. Our present Mr. Bushnell was so pleased to have the American Peace Corps boys in N'Toum that he invited them to set up their tents on the lawn in front of his house, and he

* In *My Ogowe,* Neal Publishing Co., New York, 1914, Dr. Robert Hamill Nassau recounts the experiences of his many years in charge of the missions on that river. He must have done great good, but a modern reader is amazed at the unrelenting zeal with which he brought the stern religion of John Knox to the blacks. He was particularly strict about Sunday observance. The book breathes a deep love for the country and its people, and an intense devotion to duty.

loaned them one of the yard buildings for meals and recreation.

The Catholic Church now runs a large and excellent secondary school, the Collège Béssieux, named after Monsignor Jean-Rémi Béssieux, who had come to Libreville as Apostolic Vicar in 1844. He is commonly thought of as the first head of the Catholic Church in Gabon, but, in point of fact, he was preceded by an American. In 1842 Pope Gregory XVI named Monsignor Barron, who had been Vicar General in Philadelphia, to be the first Catholic Vicar in West Africa, with his seat in Libreville and a vicarate extending from the Sahara south, excepting Angola, to the Orange River. Monsignor Barron, after seeing his missionaries die one after another, became discouraged and returned to the United States.

Paul B. du Chaillu, a fearless Bostonian, was one of the earliest and greatest of West African explorers.* In 1856 he made his way through the swamps along the Río Muni and into the Cristal Mountains to find and learn about the Fang. After returning to Libreville du Chaillu worked his way up the Ogooué from Cap Lopez, exploring the area between the lakes and Setté-Cama, then pushed south into the plain of the N'Gounié and beyond. This was about twenty years before Savorgnan de Brazza made the first of his three expeditions which led to Gabon's acquisition by France. The largest range of mountains in Gabon, in the southeast, are named for du Chaillu, but many think he was French and some pamphlets printed in France refer to him as a Frenchman.

An exclusive colonial policy ended American association with Gabon and kept the country closed to our people for over half a century. This negative state of affairs obviously had to be changed. As an independent nation Gabon would make contacts with the world beyond France, it would begin to form its

* *Explorations and Adventures in Equatorial Africa* by Paul B. du Chaillu, London, John Murray, 1861.

own opinions and take positions on matters of concern to us. What kind of society it developed, and the place that this young state took in the world, concerned us greatly.

The United States has a number of objectives in Africa, many of which touch Gabon. We wish to see African states adopt policies consistent with ours. We wish to maintain access to their raw materials. We wish to trade with them, buying their goods and selling on nondiscriminatory terms in their markets. We wish to have access to African ports and air space. And we wish to maintain on African territory our communications and space-tracking stations and other installations which are important to science. We seek our objectives by explanation and persuasion, never by pressure.

The essence, however, of our country's policy in Africa and hence in Gabon, as defined by both Presidents Kennedy and Johnson, is that we seek to help the Africans. We do not try to use them for our political purposes or for economic gain. On the contrary, we are working with them to strengthen self-government, to create conditions of economic and social opportunity, to build a modern Africa. Our particular economic and political interests which I have mentioned have their places in this relationship, but all are subordinate to the overriding aim of helping the Africans to achieve their vision of Africa.

We try to conceive of our help as something positive and many-sided. We know that we must assist the Africans to overcome the obstacles they face in economic development, education and health. We know also that we must give them moral leadership and support. We owe it to them as well as ourselves, when elections are falsified, when there is obvious graft, or when democratic processes are flouted, to make sure that the impression is not given that the United States condones these abuses. There are also occasions when we can help by advising, doing this with restraint and moderation. So that Africa may catch up with the modern world within a tolerable length of time, we must try to make use of opportunities to accelerate the existing momentum for constructive change. These are the main features of United States policy toward the new states of Black Africa, as I understood it and tried to carry it out in Gabon.

CHAPTER

VI

AID

I KNEW when I went out to Gabon that aid would be my most important business. I was to represent the United States: mature, developed, wealthy, a nation of almost 200 million people; Gabon was young, poor in everything but undeveloped resources, a nation of under half a million. The essence of our relationship, at least for a number of years, would lie in the help we could give them, help over the whole range of their needs: finance capital, equipment, technicians, health care, education and moral leadership.

From the start to the end of my service in Gabon I made aid my personal business, yet the results for the Gabonese, and for me, were disappointing. It was inevitable that the amount of our aid should have fallen below Gabonese expectations, but the record ought to have been better than it was. The whole process was not well handled, placing our country in an unfavorable light. The delays, the frequent changes in policies and personnel and the red tape came as a sharp surprise to people who had expected legendary American efficiency. My experience was not unique. My brother ambassadors in other African countries had similar disappointments and frustrations, and the State Department's files contain pleas and urgings, not just from me, but from many others. I shall tell the story as I lived through it.

Since Léon Mba was in Paris during the first week in October, 1961, when I stopped there on my way to Gabon, I arranged to call on him at the Gabonese Embassy in the Rue des Belles Feuilles. Mr. Donald C. Bergus, a First Secretary in our Paris Embassy, went with me. Even if we had not known the number, we could not have missed the house, for half a dozen Africans were talking on the street in front. Inside a man lounging in a chair pointed for us to go upstairs. On the small, second-floor landing, as on the ground floor, a number of Gabonese were standing, some arguing, some idling, all apparently there because the President was in town. It was not a particularly dignified setting, I thought, for a chief of state.

We asked where the President was; someone pointed to a door. We knocked and a droopy figure appeared, took our cards and closed the door again. As there were no chairs, we sat on the stairs leading to the floor above. By and by the door opened a crack and a little face peered out at us and said, *"Entrez."*

Until you become accustomed to them, you do not identify black faces as readily as white; many seem alike, and it is easy to confuse one man with another. The blacks, I have heard, have similar trouble with white people. I had seen pictures of the President—in fact, his photograph was right before us on the wall—but neither Mr. Bergus nor I was sure of the face at the door. Once in the room, our doubts disappeared.

As this was not a ceremonial meeting—that would come later in Libreville—our talk was easy and straightforward. Only a few pleasantries had been exchanged when the President brought up the subject of aid. His opening was blunt,

"What aid are you bringing us?" he asked. I gave a general reply, saying that of course we wanted to be helpful, but I was rather annoyed to have this matter thrust at me during the first five minutes of our meeting. I was impressed, however, by Léon Mba's earnestness and sincerity, and by the simplicity and directness with which he spoke. There was no suggestion of begging or of asking favors. He said that Gabon was a new and small country and, although it had potential riches, its people were very poor; the United States, the big brother, was the strongest and richest nation in the world. "We have to look to our friends, including the United States, for help," he said.

A few days later in Libreville I made my courtesy calls on the ministers of the Gabonese Government, accompanied by my Deputy Chief of Mission, Mr. Diamanti. Without exception, every one of them asked me for aid: the Minister of National Economy, for various development projects; the Minister of Public Works, for road construction and maintenance equipment; the Minister of Health, for medicines and hospital equipment; the Minister of Agriculture, for farm equipment; the Minister of Waters and Forests, for help in reforestation; and so on through the list.

I had brought no instructions from Washington on how to meet this situation, so I returned to my office and, like Mary, pondered these things in my heart. One point was obvious: at that particular moment in little Gabon, I was at the center of the stage. The Gabonese are oppressed by the backwardness of their country and the wretchedness of all but a few of their people. The educated know what the uneducated sense—that to pull themselves up they must have foreign aid, and a lot of it. They saw what French help over the years had accomplished, and even the ignorant knew that the United States was far richer and more powerful than France. I realized with dismay that I was Santa Claus—without instructions and with an empty pack.

76

This was the middle of October. In the early summer a survey team from the aid agency had made a flying trip through Equatorial Africa, including Gabon, for a preliminary appraisal of the situation. Their time in each country being limited, they could do little more than set down some impressions and toss off a few suggestions. But one thing they did accomplish: they whetted everyone's appetite. That the United States would send, not just one man, but a whole delegation to Libreville to find out what the Gabonese wanted was surely evidence of great things to come. Such was the background when I sat down with a yellow pad to think out what I would say to Washington.

It seemed clear that for the welfare of the Gabonese and the reputation of the United States we would have to do something, and the sooner it could be started, the better. Also, I thought that I stood more chance of getting action from Washington if I kept my recommendations modest. Mr. Diamanti, Mr. Mansfield and I discussed all the proposals that had come to our attention, weighing them against three standards: how much good they would do for the people of Gabon, how much recognition they would achieve for the United States and how much they would cost. On October 30, we got off our dispatch recommending ten projects. It was a good list: we had something for almost every minister, and we made our selection so as to benefit different parts of the country. All our proposals were for grants, and we envisaged a total outlay of about $500,000. One of our ideas was to have the Peace Corps build schools, but then we were thinking of something smaller and simpler than what ultimately took shape.

Aid has to be fitted to our government's fiscal years, which end on June 30. The proposals that we had put forward applied to the Fiscal Year 1962. This did not mean that the aid in question would have to be given, or even started, by that date, but only that by June 30, 1962, the projects would have to be approved by both governments and the funds obligated. We then discovered that the preliminary program for Fiscal Year 1963 had to be sent off by December 31, so we prepared another report consisting largely of an extension of our FY 1962 proposals. This report should have been simple, but in fact it required a tedious amount of work, for we had to set it out in that incredible jargon in which the Development Agency delights. With Saturday and Sunday work, the job was done on time, but I could not help thinking how much less clear and forceful it was than the statement in simple English we had sent off in October.

We then sat back and waited—and nothing happened. The ministers who had talked to me so hopefully in October by January began to look at me rather wonderingly. The French watched in cool detachment. "You must realize," I told people, "that the United States has many responsibilities and Washington has many things to attend to." But from my staff I could not hide my surprise and chagrin.

In March I was summoned to a meeting in Lagos with a high-level group from the Agency for International Development, led by the competent Mr. Edmond C. Hutchinson, who had just been appointed Assistant Administrator for Africa. Also present were the American Ambassadors to Brazzaville, Bangui, Fort-Lamy and Yaoundé. We learned that the new team directing the Agency were stressing two policies. They strongly favored loans over grants and they were interested, not in the political value of aid, but in concentrating it in those countries where they saw a significant potential for rapid economic development. This latter policy practically knocked out the Brazzaville Congo, the Central African Republic and Chad, countries with few known resources. But it opened the door to Gabon. Hearing from me of its riches, the AID group waxed enthusiastic. I was told to forget about my previous recommendations, which apparently had hardly been read, and asked to send Washington information on loan possibilities. A strong

AID mission then starting on an African tour was instructed to stop in Gabon to look into the wonderful things I had described.

Not long afterward, this mission arrived in Libreville. It was a seven-man team, all senior officials, led by Arthur W. Mc-Glauflin, whose death the next year was a great loss, not only to the Agency, but to Africa. Visitors to foreign parts, I had observed, often wasted time and wore themselves out dashing from one appointment to another, so, in order to enable our guests to learn the most about Gabon and to judge the quality of the men who ran the country, I sat the mission down in our Residence to which I invited the various ministers to come and speak their pieces. The ministers were well prepared; one after another they presented their requests, and without exception they made an excellent impression. It worked: the mission departed enchanted with Gabon. If its members were rather vague about the aid Gabon might receive and the projects they thought good, they were strong and clear on administrative steps. We were promised an AID mission with a top-flight director, something only the important countries got. My wife, my staff and I were delighted. What we did not realize was that this was our high point, and that from there the road would wind downhill all the way.

In Libreville there was an atmosphere of expectancy and confidence in the great United States. Surely now great things would begin to happen. But after the AID mission left, silence again settled down. At the end of June, on the last day of the fiscal year, by dint of nagging at Washington I was authorized to sign two agreements: one for the Peace Corps to build schools, the other to make a study of improving Libreville's water system. In August the AID Director came, the genial and enthusiastic Mr. Bertram B. Saymon, but he brought no aid, only plans relating to the organization he was to have, their housing, vehicles and so on.

Then, with the autumn, the atmosphere gradually changed.

The small African countries, and particularly those which had formerly been French colonies, learned that Washington was moving toward the position that there would be little aid for them; American efforts would be concentrated in a few African states, such as Tunisia and populous Nigeria, where it was hoped that a real impact might be made. Gabon, despite its development potential, would not be included. Mr. Saymon, who had been planning for a staff of fifteen Americans, was told that he would have to make do with three or four.

The details of our disappointments filled my days. Plead as I might, in cables and letters, my words fell on deaf ears. Having been asked at Lagos to submit proposals for loans that would contribute importantly to economic development, I had sent Washington four worthwhile projects. It is instructive to note what happened to them.

One was for $303,000 to buy American tractors and bulldozers for an *okoumé* reforestation project that would provide the raw material for a paper pulp plant. Getting it started was a matter of some urgency. The McGlauflin mission liked the idea. M. Anguilé, the Gabonese Minister concerned, asked for a grant. Mr. McGlauflin indicated that if the Minister would agree to a loan he, McGlauflin, believed that he could secure approval for it in the current fiscal year, that is within the next two months. To our dismay, no word whatever came from Washington for six months. Then, in the fall, I was instructed to inform M. Anguilé that the Export-Import Bank would entertain an application for a seven-and-a-half-year loan at 5¾ percent. The Gabonese Government snorted at this and got French equipment with a grant from the French aid fund.

The fate of another of my proposals has never ceased to amaze me. At Kinguelé about ninety miles from Libreville on the Mbei River there is a waterfall that would be ideal for a modest hydroelectric works. The Gabonese proposed to use French grant money for the local currency costs, chiefly tunnels and buildings, and to procure the generating and transmission equipment in the United States if AID would provide the financing, which would amount to about $4.5 million, on AID loan terms. A more advantageous deal for us could hardly be imagined. For almost a year this possibility remained open to us while I urged Washington to accept it. Finally Washington held out the prospect of an Export-Import Bank loan at 5¾ percent for a twelve-to-eighteen-year period. On these terms Gabon was not interested. Then a new and tougher French Aid Director, M. Paul Theeten, arrived in Libreville. Not long afterward he came up to me during drinks before a dinner party and said, "By the way, Darlington, on that Kinguelé project, we will take the equipment too." I could only reply dejectedly, "I am hardly surprised."

The third of my projects was a new water system for the capital, Libreville, that would supplement the city's wells, which were quite inadequate during the summer dry season when for weeks at a time water would be turned on for only a few hours a day. The new system would provide an abundant supply from a nearby river for a cost of about $2.5 million.

Initially I was successful. Washington authorized me to sign a project agreement with the Gabonese Government under which the United States agreed to make an engineering study. When you contract to make a study, it is hard to avoid the implication that after it is finished you will seriously consider financing the project itself, and this, despite my caveats, was what the Gabonese expected. As the atmosphere in Washington toward the smaller African countries cooled, AID began to drag its feet. A technician was sent over to talk about the study, and then, after months of waiting, we were informed that the survey would take at least another two years—one year having already gone by—and that when the study was completed it was highly unlikely that the United States would have any interest in financing the work. Hearing this, the Gabonese said

81

that they could not wait that long without a definite commitment and preferred to look to some other country. I then had the unpleasant task of signing another document with the Gabonese Government releasing us from the obligation to make the study that we had assumed.

My fourth project was the railroad which would bring iron ore from Belinga to Owendo on the coast and open up a large area which was now almost inaccessible. Because this venture would be a major economic and social asset for the whole country, I included an analysis of it, not for action as the start of construction would be many years off, but so that Washington would be informed. Now in the spring of 1967 plans for the railroad are progressing, and it looks as if AID may be able to participate in its financing, but this prospect, far in the future, did little to help at the beginning of 1963. The position then was that my current loan proposals had come to nought as had my earlier recommendations for grants. A year and a quarter of hard work had been put in with no result. Fortunately by this time my wife and I were friendly with all the Gabonese ministers; our good personal relations, and their generous recognition that I had done my best, softened their feelings of dismay at the wondrous ways of the United States Government.

There was nothing for us to do but to go back to grants. Now the distinction between grants and loans in an aid context is rather artificial. A grant is a gift. But a loan on the terms AID was then using—forty years with no interest for the first ten and less than one percent thereafter—may not be very different. Gabon with its resources is perhaps an exception, but loans to states as poor as most in Africa are may be scaled down or forgiven before forty years have passed. Except for a few projects where the revenue created can be pledged, the loan technique used with such countries seems to me to be little more than a device whereby the donor, calling himself a lender, fools himself. These thoughts were in my mind when

Mr. Hutchinson in Lagos told us of AID's enthusiasm for loans, but I said nothing; when you want money, you don't argue with the bank.

Our AID Mission Director, Mr. Saymon, worked up proposals for a number of small grants, some revisions of ones we had submitted in 1961, some new. An old hand in bureaucratic technique, he took two trips to Washington, where, by buttonholing and arm-twisting, he secured approval for one project, then another. Things began to look up. In March the first group of Peace Corps Volunteers arrived and with them a number of trucks and scout cars, the first American aid apart from the independence gifts to reach Gabon. As 1963 wore on other items came. But I found that even after a grant was agreed to some six to nine months elapsed before the goods arrived. Procurement was amazingly uncertain as well, for when the goods were unloaded from the ship we often discovered that they were different in make and type from what had been requested.

I have a story to tell in this connection which may be unfair because it is extreme. In 1960 as independence gifts the United States presented to the people of Gabon a truck equipped as a medical dispensary and a jeep fitted to show movies. Fifty thousand dollars had been obligated, but when the vehicles were delivered, it was found that only about $45,000 had been spent. To use up the rest of the money, Washington decided to make a personal gift to the President of a fine American automobile. The Embassy was asked to inquire what kind of a car the President would like. He said, a black one, not a hard-top which he already had, but a convertible that he could stand up in during parades. The automobile came in October, 1961; it was a superb Lincoln Continental, but a cream-colored hard-top. I presented it; Léon Mba expressed gracious appreciation, even pouring a bottle of champagne over it; but I noticed in the following years that it rarely left the garage.

Mr. Saymon had been with us a year when we received word from Washington that Gabon was to be made a "delegated post." This meant that there would no longer be an AID Mission, but that instead the AID Administrator (Mr. David Bell) would delegate his authority to me and I would be directly responsible for all projects with the help of whatever staff the Development Agency might leave me. Our missions in other former French colonies were to be treated similarly. In January, 1964, therefore, Mr. Saymon left and I carried on with an AID staff of two men and a secretary. Fortunately these men, Mr. Fred C. Bruhns and Mr. Rodolphe Ellert-Beck, were excellent, so I felt confident that we would be able to manage. But Washington does not stay put for long. A few months later the astounding advice came that all AID personnel, without exception, were to be withdrawn. I was to handle all AID matters with my small Embassy staff and the occasional help of visitors from Washington who would look in from time to time. Again, this applied to all the countries of former French Black Africa. A more nonsensical arrangement could hardly be imagined. Of course it did not work, so after about a year AID sent back one man, who first had the title of "AID Liaison Officer" and is now called "AID Operations Officer."

Thus in the space of about four years we went through six administrative stages:

a. No AID personnel
b. An AID Mission with a Class 1 Reserve Officer as Director and a staff on paper of some 15 Americans
c. An AID Mission with an actual staff of 4 Americans
d. A Delegated Post with 3 Americans
e. No AID personnel
f. One AID Liaison or Operations Officer.

These administrative changes, along with the shifts in policy I have described, were confusing and discouraging not only for us but, more importantly, for the Gabonese ministers and officials with whom we were working. We tried to put the best face on things that we could, but our performance did not increase United States prestige. We had inundated the Gabonese with talk, but apart from the shining work of the Peace Corps, the aid they actually received from us was small.

I admired the way in which France handled its aid. The French Mission of Aid and Cooperation in Libreville is a small group, but it directs a program many times the size of ours—some fifty-three times as great in the present year, 1967. The procedures are straightforward and simple. I observed them with envy. The Libreville Mission worked up what it considered should be the program for the following year. The official from the Paris ministry responsible for aid, the Ministry of Cooperation, would come to Gabon and stay for perhaps three weeks, during which time he and the local people would agree on the various projects. During our years this was always M. Michel Fiemeyer, who had the advantage of continuity which our changing personnel from Washington did not possess. When he took the agreed recommendations back to Paris, the Minister's approval still remained to be obtained, but the program was substantially settled. How simple! Our constant churning involved much more work for a much smaller result.

In the years when I was Ambassador our aid to Gabon ranged between $239,000 and $798,000; now in 1967 it is to be $300,000. French aid ran between $9 and $9.5 million a year; now in 1967 it is about $14.3 million. Germany underwrote a section of road for $2.5 million. Some assistance in rice growing was received from the Republic of China. From independence through 1965 $22,440,000 was obligated by the European Development Fund for assistance to Gabon. Aid has also been received from the United Nations Technical Assistance Programs, the U.N. Special Fund and UNICEF. I mention these other aid sources and the amounts which some of them have provided merely as reference points. What we should do depends on our attitudes toward the underdeveloped countries and our relations with Gabon.

United States aid to Gabon is shown in the following table. It is complete except for the independence gifts, costing approximately $50,000. As the figures are those of the Agency for International Development, they do not include the expenses of the Peace Corps. In the appropriation made by Congress for Fiscal Year 1967 $300,000 is planned for Gabon. The $300,000 for Fiscal Year 1968 is the amount included for Gabon in the Administration's aid request sent to Congress on February 9, 1967, except for such multilateral participation as there may be.

Our aid in the five years which have been completed, FY 1962–FY 1966, totaled $3,062,000, an average of $612,000 a year.

By far the largest project has been the Rural School Construction done jointly by the Peace Corps and AID. Volunteers are trained, sent out, maintained and directed at Peace Corps expense; they are furnished, also at Peace Corps expense, with some small items of equipment and some vehicles for their personal mobility. But it is not the Peace Corps' business to pay for the construction materials—stone, sand, cement, lumber, nails, roofing, paint—or the trucks, gas and oil to haul them. This is an AID function that AID accepted as one of its projects for Gabon. The original program under which 29 schools and 72 teachers' houses were built (AID Project 003) cost $882,000. On the second program, Phase II (Project 025), $588,000 is to be spent. These two amounts represent 48 percent of the total that AID has spent or committed in these first five years in Gabon.

It is helpful to divide the other areas of AID activity into four categories: roads, health, agriculture and training. Of these, roads have claimed the largest sum, $512,000 (Project

UNITED STATES AID TO GABON

Project Number	Project Title	FY 1962	FY 1963	FY 1964	FY 1965	FY 1966	Operational Budget FY 1967	Congressional Presentation FY 1968
000	Technical Support	$ 14,000	$ 34,000	$ 48,000	$ 5,000	$ 4,000	R	R
003	Rural School Construction	225,000	275,000	236,000	118,000	28,000		
004	Animal Husbandry		26,000	—	—			
005	Road Maintenance		137,000	375,000	—			
006	Mechanics Training School		35,000					
007	General Participant Training		37,000	14,000	4,000	68,000	R	R
008	WHO Health Planning Assistance		100,000					
011	Improvement of Health Services		45,000	—	50,000	65,000	$ 50,000	$ 50,000
018	Assistance to Vocational Education Improvement					115,000	200,000	200,000
019	Pilot Farm Equipment		—	125,000	—			
023	Technical & Feasibility Studies		—	—	—	4,000		
024	Special Self-Help & Development				1,000	48,000	50,000	50,000
025	Rural School Construction (Phase II)				509,000	79,000		
026	Improvement of Mineralogical Services				85,000			
027	Assistance to Ministry of Education				13,000			
028	Port-Gentil Reconnaissance Survey				—	40,000		
029	Assistance to Agricultural Production				—	100,000		
	TOTAL	239,000	689,000	798,000	785,000	551,000	300,000	300,000

R = These two items in 1967 and 1968 will be included in a regional budget.

005), mostly for heavy maintenance equipment. Health projects ranked second with $260,000: $100,000 (Project 008) financed a study of Gabon's health situation by the World Health Organization; $110,000 (Project 011) was spent on vehicles for doctors and hospital generators; and $50,000 (Project 011) was given for two motorboats to carry doctors and medical supplies to villages on the rivers and lakes. Agriculture accounted for $251,000: the two largest allocations being $125,000 (Project 019) for equipment to clear lands for some government experimental plantations, and $100,000 (Project 029) for sprayers and trucks to aid cocoa producers. Training has taken $238,000, of which $123,000 (Project 007) was devoted to participant training (the sending of some Gabonese for short training trips abroad, mainly to the United States) and $115,000 (Project 018) was used to equip an electrical workshop in the technical training center in Libreville.

This is the record of the aid which our government has committed to Gabon in the five fiscal years beginning July 1, 1961, and ending June 30, 1966. American aid has actually been arriving in Gabon since the spring of 1963. What has it accomplished? How may it be judged? It is of the utmost importance to give a fair and balanced answer to this question.

American aid as authorized and appropriated by Congress is primarily for the purpose of economic development, health and education being considered as contributing to that end. Our various projects undoubtedly have furthered economic development in Gabon, but their effect, in total, must be judged small because the amount is so small. $3,062,000 spread over five years would hardly make much of a splash in the economic development of an American town. As the vast oil revenues of the Middle East have shown, even very large sums of money poured in over a number of years do not rapidly overcome nationwide underdevelopment. The self-congratulatory statements that come out of Washington about the important contribution we are making to economic development may be valid in certain parts of the world, but heard in Libreville and in most of the smaller countries of Black Africa they make our critics smile and embarrass our own people.

From a social viewpoint our aid to Gabon has accomplished something. The children and teachers in the light and airy Peace Corps schools are better off than before, and various people here and there have been given employment and have had their lot somewhat improved, but again the effect has been small because the aid has been so small.

In my opinion the main value of our aid to Gabon has been political, in the best sense of that term. So often, in the villages of the back country as in the towns, men and women would crowd around us asking, "You will help us, won't you?" Their simplicity, their eagerness and their trust in me as the representative of the great United States were deeply moving. I would reply: "Yes, we are doing this," or "I have just signed an agreement for that," and I would enumerate some of the programs that we had started and some that we were planning. Always I stressed that the aid was from the American people to the Gabonese people, not just a transaction between two governments. We could sense a remarkably personal response. I was always careful not to promise anything in reply to the many requests and pleas made to me, and then I found that this did not matter particularly; what was important was the knowledge that America was doing something for Gabon. To witness these reactions of faith in the United States was a very satisfying experience.

For the government and the educated few our aid, small as it was, represented a counterweight to France. With our help, and some small amounts also from other nations, the Gabonese could feel that they were not wholly dependent on that very possessive power (and the European Development Fund, which in Gabon and its sister states is French-controlled). To all walks of Gabonese, United States aid was psychologically important.

For us likewise it had psychological or political value. When other peoples perceive that we have a genuine interest in their welfare, they will be drawn to us and sentiments and relations engendered out of which grow trust and a willingness to follow our leadership. An ambassador's hand is greatly strengthened when he is able by concrete aid measures to demonstrate his country's interest. Also, at the level of day-to-day operations an ambassador to an underdeveloped country finds aid invaluable. Frequently I had to go hat in hand to the Gabonese Government with some request. Sometimes it was for a parcel of government-controlled land that the Embassy wanted for a building, sometimes to overcome an import restriction, sometimes in the interest of an American investor, or sometimes for a vote in the Assembly of the United Nations.

"Just buying their votes," I have heard people say, but this is such a superficial reaction. Each one of us, every day, is doing things for other people without thinking of getting something in return. Yet it is only natural that our interest in their welfare will result in their taking a favorable attitude toward the things we want. This, as I understand it, is the essence of politics, which is why I term this aspect of aid "political." Governments and nations respond in the same manner.

When Jean-François Ondo was Foreign Minister, I was instructed by Washington in one week to urge the Gabonese Government to vote in the United Nations to approve the World Court decision that peacekeeping outlays were to be treated in the same manner as ordinary expenses, and to continue U.N. troops in the Congo for a further six months. The first of these requests was difficult for the Gabonese because France was one of the main defaulters in the payment of peacekeeping charges. The decisions were to be taken at a Cabinet meeting, and I was in some doubt despite my best efforts in persuasion that they would go as I wanted. It so happened that I had just had some aid discussions with the President, and I had also talked with the Foreign Minister about the locations of Peace Corps schools in the Woleu N'Tem, which pleased him as this was his home Region.

The evening before the meeting I was sitting at home when the phone rang. It was Bonjean, Ondo's son, who said, "Father would like to speak to you." "Fine," I replied. "Shall I come over to your house?" "No, Father will go to yours." In a few minutes the Minister arrived, and we sat on the terrace under the stars while he said, "The President has authorized me at the meeting tomorrow to propose that both of these questions be settled in the way you want. I just thought that you would like to know." I went to bed that night blessing our aid. Buying votes, nonsense! Warm human relations with practical support, yes!

My judgment of our aid to Gabon, in sum, is this: its economic effect and its social effect have not been great, but its political value has been considerable. However, even politically there were limits, as is shown by the fact that our influence—which on this issue was very closely keyed to the level of our aid—was not enough to prevent the imposition on July 1, 1962, of discriminatory duties on imports from the United States. This discrimination in favor of France and the other countries of the European Community exists to this day.

Our total foreign aid, within which our aid to Africa must be related, is not in my opinion consistent with our economic position in relation to that of the underdeveloped countries. Without massive foreign support young nations such as Gabon, notwithstanding their resources, cannot progress toward a modern standard of living at an acceptable rate. The problem is not only economic and political, but also, in my view, a moral one. I would suggest that the right measure of aid would be the amount required, in combination with other appropriate policies and taking account of aid from other donors, to check the present condition in which we become more prosperous while the underdeveloped world falls further behind.

The inadequacy of our aid to Gabon and to many countries, in terms of amount and the way in which it is handled, stems from a defect which is basic, namely, that Congress is involved in all the multitude of details. Each year the aid program has to run the gantlet of four Congressional committees, first for authorization and then for appropriation of the funds, in both the House of Representatives and the Senate. Each of the four committees holds hearings where top officials from the Agency for International Development (as well as from the Department of State) must submit to interminable questioning, not simply on policies and objectives, but on every little point that a Congressman or Senator may raise about any particular project. The Assistant Aid Administrator for Africa, Mr. Edmond C. Hutchinson, on one occasion was obliged to testify before one committee for twenty-six consecutive days, not a little of the time subject to hostile criticism and ridicule.

Placed in this situation, our AID administrators can hardly be other than timid. Their Washington staff is swollen in order to prepare the vastly exaggerated presentations and further presentations that the Congressional committees arbitrarily demand; while in the field, where the work has to be done, many posts are understaffed. The temptation is created to procrastinate, to delay endlessly in making decisions, and then to turn down a proposal lest approving it lead to trouble with Congress. The strongest recommendations from the field are disregarded if a doubt is raised on this score. To meet the views of Congressman X or Senator Y so that their vote can be obtained, the whole aid operation is burdened with legal requirements, regulations and inflexible policy positions which render it next to unworkable.

I had to contend with a number of these in Gabon. One

Congressional stipulation was that we could finance a project only if no other "Free World financing" were available. This meant that we had to by-pass many good projects while accepting the dogs. Take, for example, the Libreville water system or the Kinguelé hydroelectric equipment. It was apparent from the start that if we did not want to support these programs, they would not go begging; the French or the European funds would take them, which is precisely what happened. But these are limited funds, so once monies were allocated for the water system and hydraulic equipment, other less interesting projects would be turned down. We could then take them because no other Free World financing was available. Thus we placed ourselves at a disadvantage. In general, a better policy for the United States would be to make up its mind whether it wished to take a position in the development of a certain country, and then to choose the very best activities possible.

I found that the Export-Import Bank was considered a Free World source of funds, so, before AID could agree to a loan, it had to make sure that the Bank would not take it. If the Bank were interested, then AID would be shut out. That is precisely what happened to my reforestation and hydroelectric projects, but Eximbank loans are not aid in the sense in which it is sought and needed by the very poor countries in Africa. In my opinion, it is bad economics, bad politics and bad morals for us to propose to countries such as Gabon short- and immediate-term loans at high interest rates. Countries in Gabon's position not only cannot but must not be allowed to finance their long-term economic development on such terms.

Another requirement which is unrealistic with small countries such as Gabon is called "self-help." Under this theory, as it was applied during my term as Ambassador, Gabon had to contribute 20 percent of the cost of any project that we decided to support.

Just a few days before the end of June, 1962, a cable came

from Washington authorizing me to sign a project agreement (a "Proag") under which AID would put up $225,000 to get the Rural School Construction project started. There was no explanation why the amount was $225,000; it was just a figure, but the Proag draft that came over the wires included a paragraph asking the Gabonese Government to commit itself for $56,250 (20 percent of the grossed-up total). I had not heard of this requirement, and I foresaw that it was not going to be an easy one to explain to the Gabonese, who certainly were not aware of it. I told the Foreign Minister, M. Aubame, over the phone that I had to see him urgently, and I gave him an idea of the problem. Arriving at his office, I found that he had summoned the Minister of Finance and the Minister of National Economy. I sat down in the middle of the sofa, the three ministers sat on chairs around the coffee table facing me, and I began to talk.

"Gentlemen," I said in effect, "I am most happy to be able to tell you that my government is prepared to agree to give $225,000 to start building schools in Gabon, but it wants you to contribute $56,250 or 20 percent of the combined amount. More money doubtless will come from us later and you will be asked then also to contribute your share. I do not know when the work will start [the Peace Corps Volunteers were not to arrive for another ten months], nor do I know how many schools you will get for your money, or how much you will ultimately be called on to put up. But, gentlemen, have faith in the United States and I assure you that this will turn out all right. One more thing: the decision must be taken at once for the Proag has to be signed the day after tomorrow [the 30th] since it is the end of the fiscal year."

It was a difficult moment. The Minister of Finance said that he did not have the sum in his budget, the Minister of National Economy said that France never made any such condition with its aid, and, further, he could think of plenty of things that

94

Gabon could do with $56,250 of its money that were better than schools. In the end they took the proposal on faith and the Proag was signed, but I am sure they felt, as I did, that this was a strange way to do things.

I always had trouble with the self-help requirement, particularly with the money for school construction. The Gabonese Government at that time was not as enthusiastic about building rural schools as we were. Each time that I went to talk with the government to get them to put up their 20 percent for the ensuing period, I found them reluctant and I had to wheedle and persuade. Thus our proper roles were reversed; instead of being the giver I was the asker, and Gabon's appreciation of our aid was reduced because the ministers felt that they were being pressed to devote more money than they wanted to this particular activity.

Of course it is only proper that the countries to which we give aid should do all they can to improve their own situations, but we can bring pressure on them in ways other than by the formula I had to apply. This is a concept carried over from our experience in aiding European countries, where there were considerable reservoirs of local capital on which to draw. In the desperately poor infant states of Africa it is not appropriate when rigidly enforced.

A basic change is now being instituted in our foreign aid. We are attempting to channel much of it through regional and other international bodies. At first this idea was put forward in order to give our aid a "new look" and make it more acceptable to Congress. Now it is Congress that is pressing the Administration in this direction.*

* A report that has not been made public, prepared for the President by the Honorable Edward M. Korry, then our Ambassador to Ethiopia, gave support to this change, but his reasoned and balanced conclusions are being used by some to press regionalism further and faster than I believe he intended.

95

No one denies that Africa's economic development will be furthered to the extent that there can be integration between countries in the various regions. Such opportunities as our aid program offers in this direction should be taken. But to state that henceforth certain high percentages of our aid must be extended through international bodies is unrealistic. Such bodies simply do not exist. Neither the Organization of African Unity nor the Afro-Malagasy Common Organization have the capability to handle aid, nor could they easily develop such capability. The Economic Commission for Africa is a non-operating, planning organization. The East African Common Services Organization has operated in only a few countries and its future is in doubt. Perhaps the African Development Bank or the regional development banks that are being created might perform some services in connection with loans, but banks are not a suitable instrument for handling the planning and executive functions connected with the extension of American aid.

Some of the proponents of this idea argue that it will "take the United States out of politics" in the countries we are aiding. What this means is unclear, but it is not necessarily advantageous. I had an experience illustrating the point. In 1963 AID gave Gabon $100,000 to finance an over-all study of the nation's health by the World Health Organization. I did not favor the idea, for what Gabon needs in health is not more studies but more action: more doctors, medicines, clinics. Any number of practical steps that we could have taken were obvious, and I had recommended several to Washington, but they were turned down. The people who run AID in Washington, however, wanted to finance this study and our AID Director, Mr. Saymon, persuaded me to agree, saying, "Take what you can get." The U.N. agency perhaps was attractive to AID in that it provided a buffer, making the expenditure relatively safe from Congressional criticism. WHO entrusted the study to a retired French Medical Corps General, Marcel Bonnaud, an excellent choice, and early in 1965 he produced a fine report which I hope will be of some benefit to Gabon. My point here is that for Gabon there were better ways in which AID might have spent the $100,000 had Congress not been breathing down its neck. And for the United States the expenditure brought next to nothing. The Gabonese Minister of Health graciously expressed his appreciation, but his thanks took only two and a half lines in a long preface which he wrote for the report. The number of Gabonese who know of the report or that the United States paid for it could probably be counted on your fingers. As a general matter give me bilateral aid; there is where the United States gets leverage.

The crowning blow has now fallen. In the most recent amendments to the Foreign Assistance Act Congress limited the number of countries which could receive U.S. "technical assistance" (the AID term for grants for development purposes) to forty; the number which could receive "supporting assistance" (grants which do not have to meet the development criteria) to eleven; and the number which could get development loans to ten. With all the underdeveloped countries that there are in the world little Gabon cannot place in these restricted numbers. So United States bilateral aid to Gabon is now being "phased out," as can be seen from the meager amounts of $300,000 provided for FY 1967 and FY 1968. After June 30, 1969, there will be none. Perhaps I should not say "none," for in the last couple of years the Ambassador has been given by AID a small fund which he can disburse largely at his own discretion; it is now suggested that this be increased to $200,000, which would be all the bilateral aid that the United States would provide to Gabon in any single year.

Gabon could still receive aid contributed by the United States through regional or other international organizations; it could still receive United States aid given toward a "multinational program" in the sense that that program has another recipient nation besides Gabon; and perhaps (although this is not yet clear) it could receive United States aid given toward a multinational program in the sense that that program has another donor nation besides the United States. An example of the latter would be the proposed road from Lastoursville to Franceville if the U.S., France and Germany, say, all chipped in. Whether U.S. aid to such a road would fall within the intent of Congress, and hence be legal, would become more doubtful if each donor were to build a separate third of the road rather than contributing a third of the cost of the entire road. In this manner Congress adds complexity after complexity to our foreign aid program.

The purposes of this abracadabra are three. The first is to compel United States aid in the direction of regional development. The second is to put pressure on other donor nations to give more; as France is giving to Gabon this year $14,300,-000 and the United States only $300,000, I am sure this effort will be appreciated. The third is to concentrate United States aid in the countries which have the greatest capacity for rapid development, meaning the ones among the underdeveloped which are already the farthest advanced. There is equal logic, and more heart, in doing just the opposite.

The first countries we plan to wash our hands of are the small African states which until recently were European colonies. No one who knows the political realities will consider this wise. Africans, particularly the young, resent the condition of neo-colonialism and want to reduce the degree of their dependence on their former masters. They hope to develop relations with other countries—and aid, the forerunner of trade, is the best way to open the door. They know, also, that they need massive foreign capital and technical assistance. Not only is it cruel to say to countries like Gabon, "You are too small for us, you must look to France (or Great Britain)," but it is bad politics in terms of our own interest. The struggle for Africa knows no sleep; it is going on as intensely in the small countries as in the big. I know of no greater mistake we can make than to let any country, no matter how small, feel that it is not important to us.

I have tried to describe some of the inadequacies and short-comings of our foreign aid, its policies and procedures, as I lived with it in Gabon, trying to get a program started and then to carry it forward. Our Ambassadors to the other countries of francophone Black Africa had generally similar experiences. Chopping and changing every year to please Congress, burdening the program with restrictions to please Congress, giving it periodically a new look to please Congress, and every few years reorganizing the Agency keeping its personnel in perpetual apprehension to please Congress: it is impossible to conduct our foreign aid program effectively in this manner.

Foreign aid is an extremely important matter. It is one that will be with us into the days of our children and our children's children. It is imperative that we learn how to do it better. The United States, in my opinion, will not handle its program satisfactorily until it can be conducted by the Executive Branch under broad Congressional authorization. This view must not be interpreted as a criticism of Congress; the legislature, operating through its various committees, is simply not organized to handle the enormously complex details of foreign aid.

President Johnson recently took a modest step in the direction of executive control by requesting the Congress to authorize a total program in terms of money for the five years, 1967–1971. In doing so he hoped to continue the steps taken by Congress in 1961 and 1962 on the recommendations of President Kennedy when it gave multi-year authorizations for some development loans. The essence of the problem, however, lies not in the authorizations but in the appropriations. Ways will have to be found to appropriate moneys for aid purposes for periods longer than a year. Admittedly this is difficult, but it could be done.

Because I had a part in it, I cannot help but think of what was accomplished some thirty years ago in the tariff field. The two situations, of course, are different, but they have some important traits in common. Congress traditionally had occupied itself with all the details of the tariff, with results that were deplorable. People said, "Congress will never give up its right to tinker with the tariff." But Cordell Hull thought otherwise; he recognized that the situation had to be changed, and with President Roosevelt's support he succeeded in winning the passage of the Trade Agreements Act on June 12, 1934. None but his disciples believed it possible, and even after the Act was on the books few thought that it would last. But it did last, and executive tariff-making is now so firmly established that we wonder how we ever put up with the old Congressional logrolling system. Someday something similar will have to be done in foreign aid if our performance is to measure up to our interests and responsibilities.

VII

The Peace Corps

THE largest and most successful aid project that the United States has launched in Gabon has been in constructing schools in conjunction with the Peace Corps. During my visit to Paris before proceeding to Gabon I consulted M. Fiemeyer, who was responsible for France's aid. I told him that we hoped to start a modest aid program which would supplement his, and I asked him if he had any ideas as to useful small-scale projects that I might look into. He said, "Why don't you build some primary schools, and some simple houses for teachers?"

I was well aware of how sensitive France is about education in its former colonies. The French distrust foreign, and particularly American, participation in the educational field, fearing that this might dilute the purity of their culture and weaken their influence. "Building schools and houses," M. Fiemeyer said, "will not conflict with our work; on the contrary, it will help us, for in many small villages in Gabon classes are now being conducted in disreputable shacks, and the houses are often so poor that we have great trouble getting teachers to go out into the bush." "All right," I said, "I'll look into it."

In Libreville the French Ambassador, M. Jean Risterucci, and the Director of the French Aid Mission, M. Gérard Wattel, confirmed that the building of primary schools and teachers' houses would be a very useful project. The Gabonese Government was not slow in showing its interest. In my first meeting with the Minister of National Education, M. Jean-Marc Ekoh, he made a plea for this aid, pointing out that France was responsible for education in Gabon but did not build primary schools, leaving this for the Gabonese Government with whatever help it could get. The government had an extensive school-building program, but its money had to cover many other things.

The Minister handed me a memorandum listing seventy-one towns and villages where primary schools and teachers' houses were particularly needed. At the end came the catch: the government had sought prices from local French building contractors and found that each school would cost some $32,000 and each house $5,000, making a total for 71 schools and about 200 houses of over $3,000,000. This was way beyond anything the United States would consider. Moreover, a large share of the money would have to be spent in Gabon, coming under the heading of "local currency costs," which, because of our balance-of-payments problem, had to be avoided like the plague.

I had all but concluded that aid in school building was not for us when my Deputy Chief of Mission, Mr. Diamanti, tossed out the suggestion, "Why wouldn't this be a good project for the Peace Corps?" The idea quickly developed: Peace Corps Volunteers, working with Gabonese, would do the building; simple machines could be brought in for making mud blocks; framing and roofs would be of wood and other local materials.

We became enthusiastic. We knew that many Peace Corps projects were in teaching or technical training, work for which

102

college graduates were preferred. Here was one tailored for the noncollege Volunteer; surely that should appeal to the Peace Corps. So we included the proposal in our first dispatch to Washington on aid, and I wrote a personal letter to Sargent Shriver. We were off.

The idea apparently pleased Shriver, after which there was never much doubt that it would ultimately be approved. But there were many difficulties and doubts to be overcome and many delays. At an early point it was seen that the material required went considerably beyond the modest equipment which the Peace Corps provides to its Volunteers for their personal needs, so the Agency for International Development had to be interested and its support obtained. AID was skeptical, but we kept up the pressure, as did Shriver, and after considerable balking they agreed to cooperate. In this way the schools became the first project, and one of the very few, in which the Peace Corps and the Agency for International Development have worked together. Both have been pleased by the joint effort, the Peace Corps because it increases what they can do, and AID (after some early doubts) because it provides a project which another agency has the main responsibility for administering.

The first group of Volunteers, thirty-five in number, arrived in Libreville by the regular morning plane on March 21, 1963. The Minister of Education, then M. Vincent de Paul Nyonda, welcomed them, and the distinguished French Inspecteur d'Académie, M. Marcel Vitte, also gave them a warm greeting. Then after breakfast they drove out of town to their first camp, at Owendo.

Setting up camp is something that Americans know all about. We had rented for $40 a month a large and somewhat dilapidated barracks built by the RAF during the Second World War on a lovely promontory overlooking the placid waters of the estuary. In no time the boys had fixed their cots and mosquito nets, spread out their duffel, and made the place quite like home.

Getting started building the schools, however, was a different matter. The first location given us by the Ministry was a hamlet not far from Libreville called Okala, where a schoolhouse with two classrooms and two teachers' houses were wanted. The Volunteers had put up a similar school during their training period in the Virgin Islands. The architect, Marshall Erdman, a successful builder from Madison, Wisconsin, came to Gabon to help get things under way. But neither he nor they had any conception of the difficulties they would encounter.

Sand and gravel and stones (called "laterite") were needed so that the Volunteers could start on the foundations. Sandy McCaw, a girl and the only field officer the Peace Corps Representative then had, telephoned the Gabonese Government and asked if they would have a delivery made at the site on Monday morning. A most polite and agreeable official replied, "Of course"—an African does not like to say no to you—but on Monday Sandy and the Volunteers waited and waited and nothing showed up. That morning they learned their first lesson: in Gabon one does not call and order something; one goes out and finds it if one can, and then tries to fetch it oneself.

The Volunteers dug the necessary sand themselves and loaded it on trucks at the seashore; later in the interior they had to cart it from streams and river beds. They shoveled the gravel out of banks and sifted it through screens they made themselves. They transported the laterite stones from wherever they could be picked up or pried out. "Scrounging," we termed these operations. And they often had to obtain a permit from some local officials to work a particular stream or gravel pit. I was called on daily to help during this period. The French were a bit shocked to see the American Ambassador running around looking for sand, gravel, stone and lumber.

Gradually these early difficulties were surmounted, and the schools started to go up: after Okala then at Akok, N'Toum and Kango, each with three houses. The usual primary school in Gabon has three classrooms, expected to accommodate about a hundred pupils. Each room requires one teacher; hence we usually built a teacher's house for each room in the school.

The buildings were quite primitive by American standards: just the three bare rooms, each about 24x30 feet, partly open on the sides. There were none of the facilities that we usually consider essential: no closets, no running water, no toilets, no canteen. Far from having some milk and crackers in the morning, the Gabonese schoolchild has nothing to eat even in the middle of the day unless he lives near enough to walk home. Sometimes a mother will provide a piece of manioc or a banana to be carried to school, but this is the exception. For toilets the children as well as the teachers use the surrounding grass and bushes, which seem to do well enough thanks probably to the heavy rains that occur almost daily throughout the academic year.

The school designed by Marshall Erdman was more solid than we had originally conceived. Mud bricks and pole framing were ruled out as not up to the standard that the United States should exhibit in its first Gabonese buildings. Our work had to compare with the many structures put up over the years by the French, which were generally solid, serviceable and reasonably attractive. So we built in stone, cement and lumber, and our schools and their accompanying houses are good-looking as well as substantial.

This represented very much more of an effort than we had foreseen. A French contracting company would have used white foremen overseeing Gabonese labor. The Peace Corps is not a construction outfit. Our Volunteers were able-bodied boys, but few had had any building experience. Moreover, they were not supposed to act as foremen bossing gangs of natives, but instead to work side by side with the Gabonese in a cooperative effort.

That the Volunteers succeeded in getting schools and houses built so well and in such good time is a great tribute to them and to the United States. Everything was difficult. Supplies and building materials had to be trucked to the site by the boys themselves on abominable roads. The round trip sometimes could take a week. The Gabonese had to be shown how to do even the simplest tasks. The Volunteers lived in small tents, roasting in the daytime and often getting soaked in the nightly downpours. They were constantly bitten by insects. They had no running water. When dusk fell, as it does at about 6:30 the year round on the Equator, the village closed down, doors shut, the natives went to bed; there were no drugstores, no movies, no lights. Yet the schools and houses went up one after another, as they are doing to this day.

At points all along Gabon's one main road, running from the Cameroon south to the Congo, groups of Volunteers have worked. Everywhere their trucks and their blue scout cars became familiar. One would come upon their camps and schools every few miles. In the Libreville area at Okala, Akok, N'Toum and Kango; in the south at Fougamou, Mandji, Moudouma, M'Boukou, Mouila, N'Dendé, Moussambou, Makongonio and Mimongo; and in the north at Abam-Eba, Mvane, Assok-Begué, Alene, Zanangoué, Bikodom, Nkolayap, Melep and many other places.

The last of the Volunteers—there were two groups numbering fifty-six at their peak—who had worked on this first school-building program left Gabon in September, 1965. Forty Volunteers for a second construction project arrived in October of that year, and thirty-five were sent to sites in the three

Regions of Ogooué-Ivindo, Moyen-Ogooué and the Nyanga. Instead of putting about ten Volunteers on a school and completing it in a few weeks, the present plan is to assign only two, or even one, and to use more Gabonese. Thus twenty-one schools are now in the course of construction, but they will be finished slowly. The Volunteers spend about four to five hours a day on their schools and devote the rest of their time to community development. They help the people of the village to build better houses, to start a school vegetable garden, or to attach a pump to bring water so that the women will be spared the labor of carrying it.

"Les Américains" are known from one end of the country to the other. And everywhere they are favorably known, not only for what they have built, but for their openness, sincerity and warmth. Important in the eyes of the Africans has been the absence of any racial or class feelings. Moreover, I believe there has not been one unpleasant incident since they first arrived in March of 1963.

I visited many groups while they were at work and was pleased to see how sensitive the Volunteers were, how *"gentil,"* toward the Africans. At the outset the boys were inclined to do most of the work themselves because it was easier than explaining across the language barrier, but as time passed they learned how to involve the Gabonese so that the villagers thought of the schools as something they had built themselves with the help of their American brothers.

It is a wonderful record! The Volunteers deserve great praise, but they must share it with Bill Wilkes, a retired Marine Corps colonel, who headed the entire operation and daily disposed of a swarm of problems with energy, skill and tact. Great credit also goes to Dick McDaniel in charge of Field Operations and his wife, Nan, and to the devoted and indomitable Sandy McCaw. And, of course, Marshall Erdman, the imaginative architect-builder, will always be remembered in Gabon.

107

The man appointed by the Gabonese Government as its liaison with the Peace Corps, M. Athanase Bouanga, has proved a staunch and helpful friend.

In these small African countries, where it is important that what we are doing be known not just to the governments but to as many people as possible, projects that use Americans in person are highly effective. A piece of equipment given by the United States will probably be identified as American if the local person who sees it stops to think about its origin, but no one has to think to recognize an American boy or girl. And when they are seen doing hard physical work, which the French colonialists saved for the blacks, they have a striking impact.

The Peace Corps was reluctant to have the aid aspect of the building project stressed. Its officers and evaluators, who periodically visited us from Washington, had to be handled with great care. Their chief concern was in personal relations and community development. For some time I had a running battle with the Peace Corps because I insisted that the schools be built according to a schedule and with a certain speed, whereas those who ran the organization in Washington regarded these objectives as rather irrelevant. But at the start of the program, when everyone was watching us and there was a lot of skepticism among French contractors as to whether our Volunteers could actually put buildings up, it was necessary to produce. Also the Gabonese Government was paying 20 percent of the bill and wanted to get schools, not just a dose of idealism. Later, after the program's success had been established, I argued that the heat could be taken off, and this is the way it has turned out.

Sometimes it seemed to my wife and me that in their dedication to the proposition that the Peace Corps' purpose was to create friendships between Americans and people in the underdeveloped countries, the Peace Corps administrators in Washington underestimated what it took to make possible such relations. You had to have some specific activity that the Americans and Gabonese could do together. That something was provided by the hard physical labor and the shared satisfaction of creating a building. We found that when men toil and sweat together for a common objective, it ceases to make a difference that some are white, some black; that some speak English, some Fang; that some are Gabonese and some Americans.

Our Rural School Construction Project was unique. Teaching is a usual Peace Corps activity, and the Peace Corps supplied some teachers to Gabon. Like her French-speaking sisters, Gabon desperately needs English teachers. France cannot supply enough, and many of those whom she does send speak our language with a strange accent. Recognizing this, France has been prepared, although not with great enthusiasm, to admit some American and British cooperation. I remember a day when the Minister of Education, M. Ekoh, pleaded with the British Ambassador and me to send him English teachers. The next autumn Great Britain sent two, but I could get none out of USIA besides the one we already had who conducted English classes at our Cultural Center.*

When later we learned that the Peace Corps was willing and able to provide English teachers, we applied for some, and in September, 1963, received twenty, mostly young women. Sixteen taught English, four taught typing, shorthand and accounting, and some of the men also coached in sports. They were attached to official, Catholic or Protestant schools, some in Libreville, others in Port-Gentil, Lambaréné, Oyem, Mitzic, Minvoul, Bitam and elsewhere. They worked hard and well,

* This man, Mr. Norman Baum, a contract teacher supplied by USIA, was first-class. Competent in French and skilled in the art of teaching, he had a personality that drew students to him. For reasons I could never understand, USIA let him go. I strongly opposed this step, but, although an ambassador is supposed to have great authority, my recommendations and pleas fell on deaf ears in USIA, Washington.

and they brought to the Gabonese a somewhat different approach to education than the more formal methods of the French.

In the school year 1964-65 there were again sixteen Peace Corps Volunteers in Gabon teaching English, and in 1965-66 there were ten, five of whom transferred from construction work because of the acute need for English instruction; this year, 1966–67, there were seventeen. Four Volunteers have continued teaching secretarial skills.

Some people argue that what Africans should have is training in mechanical tasks—how to service a truck or mend a hoe—and that education in the arts, including foreign languages, is wasted if not harmful for the mass, who will have no opportunity to use it. This idea apparently has gained some acceptance in the Peace Corps for in February, 1967, it disclosed that it was "phasing out" a large share of its English-teaching in French-speaking Africa, including Gabon. It will provide teachers only for the few secondary schools which carry students into advanced grades, and there are, I believe, but four of these in Gabon. This change in policy I consider a mistake. In the formerly French countries of Africa there are no programs in the schools in which Americans can take part except English-teaching. It seems a pity to eliminate ourselves from it. The young of Gabon will not welcome our decision.

This is the story of the Peace Corps in Gabon. The teaching was good, the school construction exceptional, among the best things that our country did. My wife and I took immense satisfaction in helping start these projects, and had a great deal of fun with them too.

VIII

The Deteriorating Situation

THE first part of our stay in Gabon had been a good period for the country and a constructive and happy one for us. The political stability and favorable economic prospects had enabled us to stimulate increasing American interest in Gabon. We enjoyed in most respects cordial cooperation from the French. My wife and I had made many friends and seemed to have won general confidence. But even during this period incidents occurred which pointed to underlying weaknesses and problems.

The most significant political event was the bloodletting in September, 1962, when the Gabonese fell on the Congolese minority within the country, maiming and killing many and driving out most of the rest.* This catastrophe helped create the emotional background for further mistakes. To the French it acted as a warning bell of the troubles that independence made possible. And it sowed doubts in my mind as to the

---

* Described by my wife in Chapter XXI.

validity of my assessment of the maturity and stability of the Gabonese Government and the correctness of the image of the government that I had tried to convey to Washington.

Also in this period the French Government made plain its determination not to loosen the reins of economic control. Over the years of colonial rule France had developed many techniques for exploiting its possessions, using their resources and markets, limiting their freedom of action, for France's exclusive benefit.

The main instrument was exchange control. All thirteen countries of Black Africa, like Gabon, within the French franc currency area prepare annual programs of imports from the non-franc area countries. In the past these programs had to be submitted to France for approval. The formal submission to France is no longer required, but each country's import schedule and foreign exchange requirements still have to be discussed with Paris. The arrangement is made to sound informal, but it is operated in a highly restrictive manner.

As France has accepted responsibility for the stability, and the convertibility through the French franc, of the CFA franc used in these countries, it is natural that France should have a certain control. But the degree of control in fact exercised is large and predatory. Instead of providing these states with an allowance of foreign currencies above the amounts they themselves earn, as a strong Western country might be expected to do, France takes part of their exchange earnings for the benefit of the metropole. This is the old colonial practice which is now quite rightly termed "neo-colonialism."

The system bears particularly harshly on the dollar earnings of these states and limits their commercial relations with the United States. Exports to the United States are almost twice as large as imports from us. If such invisibles as Embassy and Peace Corps outlays are added, the dollar earnings of the area are more than double the dollar expenditures. Since the flow of capital is chiefly from the United States to Africa, it is evident that France, far from aiding these states to diversify their purchases, is providing them with substantially fewer dollars than they would have if they managed their own currency affairs. The difficulty of their doing so is recognized, for the dollar surplus is mostly in the hands of the Ivory Coast, the Malagasy Republic, Cameroon and Gabon, while the other states are in deficit. Nonetheless it is obvious that the procedure, insofar as currency management is its objective, could, with equity, be operated in a manner which would give these countries much more freedom in developing their economic relations.

Aside from currency management, the French use licenses to shape their former colonies' foreign purchases to France's own advantage. Not only are total imports into each country from outside the franc area limited, but many individual items are subject to fixed maximum amounts while minimum amounts are set for the same imports from France. Items treated in this way throughout the area include such characteristic United States exports as automobiles, radios, refrigerators and air conditioners.

One of the Embassy's jobs was to intervene with the Gabonese Exchange Control in behalf of American interests. One case on which I worked shows how tight the system is. Mr. John A. Parliman, the Chairman of the Christian and Missionary Alliance (the American missionary group in Gabon), wanted to import a Dodge. It was being provided by the parent organization in New York, so that no money had to be paid out of Gabon. But Mr. Parliman's request was turned down, because the car had not been entered on the import program that was established before the start of the year. After all his pleas were rejected, I took the matter up with the Director of the Exchange Office, M. Walker-Deemin, who told me that he was powerless to authorize the entry of the Dodge, as it was not on the list agreed upon in Paris. He suggested that the parent organization buy and provide a French car, but this I refused. To get the Dodge admitted I had to make a personal call on, and write a follow-up letter to, the Minister of National Economy.

While France attaches high importance to her "mission civilisatrice," she is equally interested in French business. So long as she continues her high aid levels, she will expect correspondingly high levels of exports and profits. Any significant intrusion of other countries into the economic life of the area encounters resistance. Notwithstanding provisions of the Convention of Association favoring other members of the European Economic Community, there is little evidence that France is prepared to share the economic advantages of her private hegemony in Africa even with them.

This situation, of course, was fertile ground for business monopolies. The import houses, that is the big stores, regularly ordered a slightly smaller quantity than they knew the market would take, so they could always sell their goods at a premium: their volume was not much less than its potential, but they could do what they wanted to with prices.

As is natural in the capital of a new country, Libreville was in a boom. New buildings, government and private, were appearing on every hand. The half-dozen French construction firms had a field day. As there was no real competition among them, the prices they charged were astounding, particularly when one considered how little they paid their labor. And the work they did was often shoddy. When you complained, the contractor would hold up his hands and lay all the blame on his shiftless Gabonese labor. Labor was anything but efficient, that is true, but after watching the system for three years, I was convinced the real difficulty was that the jobs were both mismanaged and milked.

When the Peace Corps was building its first school, Willie Jones reported that the big contractors in the city, all of whom were French, some the subsidiaries of Paris firms, were up in arms. I telephoned the head of the builders' syndicate and said that I would be happy to meet with his members. A meeting was set up; a few of the contractors were understanding, but most were grim-faced. What did the United States mean, coming into Gabon, taking business away from them? Patiently I explained that this was a project intended to help Gabon, done by volunteers, and that only a few rather minor buildings were involved. We ended with handshakes all round, but I could see that their basic resentment remained unchanged.

All French businesses were protected by the powerful Chamber of Commerce, which made sure that its members were not disturbed by newcomers. There were only two or three electricians, only three metalworkers, only one baker, and so on down the line. What means were employed to keep others out I do not know, but they worked. There is a story, for which I cannot vouch but which is widely told, that one day a French baker turned up determined to start a second bakery; he was given a million francs ($4,000), put on a boat back to France, ticket paid, and told not to return. In earlier days the Gabonese, not being familiar with Western ways, or goods or prices, I suppose took all of this as a matter of course, but this state of affairs is passing. I observed a growing realization that they were being "taken" by the French businessmen.

Among the many nice things that Léon Mba has done for business is the control of labor. Unions are weak, since potential leaders are bought off with government jobs or sent out of the country. And then there is the law fixing minimum wages. I hired laborers for the Peace Corps, so I know what the rate then was: 79 cents a day! This law ostensibly protects the workman, but in fact it aids the employers, for the figures it sets are of course maximums as well as minimums.

Graft we saw grow by leaps and bounds. French aid seemed to be well administered, so I would assume that the projects which it financed were clean. But the Gabonese Government has a large excess of revenues over operating expenditures, so it is able to sustain with its own funds a capital budget greater than the aid in capital projects received from France. The temptations to which those in the highest offices were exposed were immense, and it is common knowledge that the resistance of many, commendable in the first year or so following independence, later broke down. The stories are legion as to how much this Minister and that, and others as well, put in their own pocket, on the construction of such-and-such a building, or on the furnishings in government houses, and so on. One cannot know these things for sure, but a number of the ministers I believe were above such practices.

Sometimes a French civil servant rebelled against the system. One day the Director of Public Works, the highest Frenchman in the Ministry of Public Works, refused to sign a falsified payment voucher. He was told that he must sign, and again he refused; then he was ordered out of the country and was not even allowed to wait for the next commercial flight, but was flown in a military plane to Douala within the hour. The other parties to these shoddy operations were always French, the Gabonese businessmen being too small and too poor to play in this league. All of this was generally known to the young intelligentsia, who saw that money belonging to their government was being drained off into private pockets.

It was not simply that there was graft. The evil was deeper than that. The state at the time of which I am writing was corrupt, and the principal agents of its corruption were the large forestry interests and other French businesses which had long been the main support of the regime. In 1965 they gave a convincing demonstration of their power. Private French interests were discovered buying up land along the route of the big iron-ore railroad that had just been traced by Foley Brothers. The Director of the National Planning Office in the Ministry of National Economy drafted a decree making the land along the right of way government property; the President refused to sign the decree and cashiered the Director.

I have devoted space to this aspect of the role of French business in Gabon because it is important to an understanding of Gabon's government and the country's relations, through the Elysée, with France. If some French businessmen in Gabon did not approve of all that went on, they kept still, for they were part of a tightly organized group and most in one way or another were beneficiaries of the system. Willie Jones, responsible for remodeling the new Embassy and for maintaining our other properties, had excellent relations with the French contractors and suppliers, although he was constantly struggling with them. The contacts that my wife and I had, almost entirely social, were until near the end of our stay quite agreeable. Sometimes an amusing incident would occur.

The telephone rang in my office. Would I come to see the President? I went. A young elephant had been caught at a forestry operation and had been offered to Léon Mba with the suggestion that it might be an appropriate gift for President Johnson. After expressing thanks, I said that I would be surprised if President Johnson did not already have all the elephants he wanted, in fact, with our prolific zoos the United States had become an elephant-exporting country. This may have slightly exceeded the truth, but I thought it was in a good cause. Of course I had to inform the Department and shortly received a reply saying, "Try tactfully avoid accepting elephant," signed Rusk. Just then Léon Mba's secretary came on the telephone and said, "Vous savez, Monsieur l'Ambassadeur, le petit éléphant est mort" ("the little elephant is dead"). What happened, most likely, was that the workmen at the lumber camp ate it.

The gradual deterioration in the moral climate in Gabon discouraged and saddened us. The Gabonese are impressionable people, wise in many ways, but inexperienced. Although many deplored the erosion in character which they saw robbing them of the bright promises of independence, the quality of life in Gabon, starting from about the time of the Congolese riots, steadily declined.

Excessive glorification of the chief of state has been a common plague in French Africa. It is a carry-over from the undisputed position of the village chief; it is also an obvious aping of Charles de Gaulle. Because he is considered the architect of independence, de Gaulle has been regarded in much of French Africa as a god, particularly by the chiefs of state who came to power under his tutelage. Of these none was more admiring, more devoted, than Léon Mba. My colleague, the U.N. Representative, one day laughingly observed that when in doubt as to how to act, Léon Mba would ask himself, "What in the circumstances would de Gaulle do?" The proper course then became crystal clear, leading not infrequently to inappropriate and ludicrous results. Even the old fence in front of the Presidential Palace had to be torn down and replaced by one of immense black spikes topped with gold—of course horribly expensive—but just like what de Gaulle has at his Palace in Paris.

As time passed, Léon Mba became increasingly autocratic. He was convinced that the members of the UDSG were scheming against him, and that for his own safety and the good of the country the government should contain no one except members of his own party. So the Government of National Union was broken, M. Aubame and the other members of the UDSG were forced out, and their places were taken by BDG stalwarts.

The action, as is widely known, took place in the Council of Ministers, where the Vice President, M. Yembit, a BDG member, presided. His first move was to propose that for the good of the nation all political parties be eliminated and a single new party created. As this idea seemed fair enough, and

118

as the President wanted it, M. Aubame of UDSG and M. Sousatte of the PUNGA both agreed to it. Then came the question of a name. The following morning M. Yembit appeared with a list of eleven names, all related in one manner or another to that of the BDG so that the choice of any one of them would have given the impression that the BDG had taken over. This meeting broke up, the members unable to reach agreement. The next day M. Yembit came saying that the UDSG and PUNGA members should join the BDG or resign. M. Aubame, all his party colleagues, and M. Sousatte refused, taking the position that if the President wished to put them out for having done their jobs poorly, that was one thing; but they would not resign in a political squeeze play. The crisis lasted from January 27 until February 19. Throughout this period the President never appeared and refused to see his Foreign Minister or even to answer his letters.

At the end of the crisis the President convoked the Diplomatic Corps and the leaders of the business community and announced that he had decided to reorganize the government so that it would contain only members of his party. I sat in the front row not ten feet away from him, and as he spoke I noticed that, although it was not a particularly hot day, the sweat was rolling down his face into his collar, and I thought, "This is a worried man."

M. Aubame was forced to resign as Minister of Foreign Affairs, and Jean-François Ondo was appointed in his place. His selection surprised me, for I had not realized that he was a candidate for the post. But apparently I concealed my feelings well, for the next time I met his wife, Pauline, she astounded me by saying, "When I heard the news of my husband's appointment, my first thought was, 'How pleased Mr. Darlington will be.'" Ondo proved a good Foreign Minister, but after little more than six months he was replaced by Joseph N'Goua, who also had a short term. Then after a hiatus following the

119

coup d'état the position was given to Pierre Avaro. With each of these three men I had excellent personal relations and was able to conduct our business agreeably and successfully, but no one of them equaled M. Aubame in experience or competence. During this time two excellent Frenchmen, who served as advisers to the President, gave restraining advice which went unheeded. Soon afterward, both resigned and returned to France.

At the height of the crisis I tried to get the new French Ambassador, M. Paul Cousseran, to urge the President not to lose sight of foreign opinion, but he begged off on the ground that he was only forty-one against the President's sixty-one and therefore did not feel able to talk to him in those terms. I personally tried to point out to the President that a serious government crisis (particularly after the Congolese riots five months earlier) might spoil the image of a well-ordered, stable country that we had endeavored to create in Washington and lessen the prospects for American aid. The President, however, was not receiving callers and his French secretary would not put me through on the telephone, so I gave my message to her. What I said was clear enough, but I believe the meaning was changed when it was passed on to the President.

After the crisis things gradually settled down, but within the diplomatic community we all felt that a serious mistake had been made. Luckily the country was still running on the momentum of colonial administration. The government, although considerably less effective than it had been, did not function too badly; the presence of many French advisers gave it continuity. The worst tensions were relieved when the President appointed Aubame President of the Supreme Court, a position of high rank though of little power. He also made Gondjout President of the Economic and Social Council, another elevated post which possessed only such significance as the President chose to give it.

The problems of governing the country became increasingly

concentrated in the President's office. Being quick and intelligent, he did not brook mistakes in his subordinates; one error and the minister or functionary was removed and sent to a lower job. Out in the country the prefects and subprefects were being moved about or dismissed with increasing frequency. After one of our trips when I had seen how unsettling this practice was to the Gabonese who were trying to cope with jobs which were quite new to most of them, I asked the President why he did it. He replied, "To give my men experience," but as time went on it became obvious that the real purpose was to prevent his administrators from having any opportunity to gain a local following. The result was that Léon Mba did more and more of the work himself, to a point where he was up half the night.

Although President of the nation, he was still concerning himself with little personal problems in the manner of a village chief. One day when I went to call on him I found my French secretary in his waiting room. Rather put out that she was not at the office, I said, "What are you doing here?" "Waiting to see the President," she replied. That afternoon I summoned her and asked, "Did you see the President?" "Yes," she said. "What was it you wanted?" "I went to ask him to call in my husband [a Frenchman who ran a butcher shop] and tell him not to divorce me." "Did he say he would?" "He didn't say." Later I learned that the President had in fact given this advice to the husband, but it was not followed, for a few months later my secretary was divorced.

A by-product of the political deterioration which I particularly regretted was that the President, with his fears and his work load, devoted his attention almost exclusively to domestic matters. I had urged him to attend the General Assembly of the United Nations and to visit our country. Late in 1962 he had tentatively indicated that he would do this the next autumn, and as 1963 advanced we talked about it several times. I had also hoped that he would play a larger role in African affairs. But in August of 1963 Fulbert Youlou was overthrown in the neighboring Congo, in part because he had pressed too hard toward a one-party state. At just that moment a Congress of the BDG was meeting in Libreville to fasten tighter one-party rule on Gabon. Quickly it changed its tune and came out with meaningless resolutions, but the President was apprehensive, and he called me to say that in the existing conditions he could not leave the country. It was a pity. He had the ability and the personality to play a useful role in international affairs.

Then in December, 1963, Léon Mba made the same mistake that he had committed the previous February, when he broke the Government of National Union. Stirred up by tale-bearers, he determined to move a second time against Aubame who, rather imprudently, had passed his days at the Supreme Court discussing with callers the President's shortcomings. All of a sudden he was accused of circulating a scurrilous tract against the President.

Tracts seem to us an ineffectual and slightly reprehensible way of publicizing a grievance, but in Gabon, as in many other African countries, they are commonplace. You run off your message on a mimeograph machine and during the night drop the copies on the sidewalk in front of stores, embassies, hotels and so forth. The reason and justification of tracts is that the government-controlled paper will print only approved material. Some tracts are well prepared and are signed; most are anonymous and more or less scurrilous.

It was one of the latter that Aubame was now accused of fathering. A Gabonese clerk at the French Embassy was reported to have said that Aubame had bribed him to run it off at night on the Embassy's mimeograph machine. Whether or not all this is true we do not know. Most people laughed at the story. The President, however, acted immediately. Even though he himself had named Aubame President of the Supreme Court when Aubame was already a Deputy, Léon Mba now submitted a bill to the National Assembly declaring the two positions incompatible; in other words, Aubame could be one or the other, but not both. The Assembly passed the bill, but with seventeen members voting nay.

Léon Mba apparently expected that Aubame would keep the high-paid and honorific job of President of the Supreme Court and resign as Deputy, but Aubame, whose life had been devoted to his party and who has a deep sense of obligation toward his many followers, did the reverse. The President was frustrated. He had given Aubame the court job to keep him out of politics, but Aubame continued to be politically active. The move to get Aubame to resign as a Deputy had failed; and the seventeen who had voted against the President's bill were UDSG members. Faced with this situation, and in order to prevent Aubame from using his position as a pole of political attraction, the President on January 16, 1964, dissolved the National Assembly and decreed the election of a new body.

The conditions that were announced for that election show how a government can so arrange matters that the opposition is excluded. The country was divided into forty-seven new election districts in place of the sixty-seven that existed before. (Since we no longer will have to make room for opposition members, the President explained, we can do with fewer seats, which is good economy.) No one who had held an appointive office within a recent period could be a candidate, a provision which prevented Aubame from even running. But for appearances' sake the opposition was not banned entirely. Any group or party could run candidates, but not singly; it would have to put up a full list of forty-seven to stand against the government's list, or else none. Each candidate had to make a deposit of 40,000 francs (over $160), so the cost of putting forty-seven candidates into the field would be over $7,500 without considering campaign expenses. The general expectation was that none but the government party, the BDG, would have the money (or the guts) to enter so many candidates.

Then occurred an incident which illustrates the type of pressure that an American Ambassador is under in these new countries. On January 23, the chauffeur of one of the opposition leaders came to my office and delivered his master's card inside double envelopes. The message read: "Mr. Ambassador, I would like to meet with you as soon as possible and in strict privacy." I thought a moment and decided that this was not a request I could refuse. Not only had this man held high positions, but he was a good friend of the United States and also a personal friend. I told the chauffeur that I was agreeable, and the man returned to say that his master would be at my home that night at nine.

Earlier in the evening I met him at a reception at the Residence of the German Ambassador. Then I went home and waited, alone, my wife and the servants having retired. A dilapidated "quatre chevaux" rattled up the driveway, a somber figure got out and the car immediately drove off. He mounted the steps, not in the stiff white collar and white shirt that he had been wearing earlier, but dressed in a dark turtleneck sweater. At night an African wearing no white is almost invisible. I did not particularly like this disguise, or his use of the old car, for it made the visit look conspiratorial.

He talked of the election, saying that the opposition was prepared to put up a candidate in each of the forty-seven districts, and he was sure they would win, but they did not have the money for the deposits and other expenses. Would I help? This campaign, he argued, should interest the United States, for the opposition was fighting for democracy against a man who was increasingly assuming the role of a dictator. The United States had acted in other countries to save democracy; would it not do so here? When I told him that the United States could not possibly do what he wanted, his disappointment was painful. He let me drive him back, but before we reached town, motioning me to stop, he slipped from the car and disappeared, invisible, into a clump of bushes.

According to the evidence available to the Gabonese Government and to the several embassies in Libreville, including the French with their abundant sources of information, there would be no other list of candidates on election day than that of the government party. The country was calm. The people, so it appeared, accepted the way Léon Mba did things with that resigned obedience which the African accords to his chief, or simply ignored what was happening in the political field, about which they knew so little. In any event the President's position seemed secure.

IX

The Coup d'État
February 18-20, 1964

MONDAY morning, February 17, 1964, Henry Stephen, who had succeeded Joe Cox as our Public Relations Officer, and I left Libreville on the Transgabon flight for the south. We were going to N'Dendé to take part in the opening ceremonies of the school built by the Peace Corps at nearby Moussambou, the birthplace and home of the Vice President, M. Yembit. The ceremonies were held there for that reason, but they inaugurated also three other schools built by the Peace Corps in N'Dendé itself. Henry and I hoped that in the course of the trip we might be able to obtain information on the forthcoming elections.

The first stop was Lambaréné, where there is always a considerable wait. We went to the airport cafe and sat at a table with a French adviser to the President who was just completing a tour of the nine Regions and who told us that he found the country calm. A correspondent of Agence France Presse who joined in confirmed that this was his impression also.

Since the plane stops at N'Dendé only once a week, Peace Corps Volunteer John Murphy met Henry and me with a car at Mouila. Before starting the drive we went to the residence of the Prefect, M. Jean-Robert Fanguinovény, where his wife as always gave us a delicious luncheon. Her husband was away campaigning with the Vice President. She told us that, so far as she knew, throughout the Region things were quiet.

At N'Dendé in the late afternoon I called on the Subprefect to pay my respects, then spent the night at the house of Dr. Newell Augur, the Peace Corps doctor, and his pretty wife Tenny. Tuesday morning I got up early, planning to drive the hour and a half to Lébamba, where I was told that the Vice President, returning from campaigning in the mountain villages farther east, was spending the night. I knew that he would appreciate the courtesy of my meeting him there and driving back with him to Moussambou. Just as I got to the N'Gounié ferry I saw the Vice President's party appear on the other bank. The boat was on my side of the river, so I parked my car and walked aboard.

Because the water was very high that day, it was unusually difficult getting the cars on board. Two long planks were stretched from the bank to the boat. I thought M. Yembit would let his chauffeur drive over this uncertain arrangement and then walk on himself. But no, he took his accustomed place in the back seat of his Mercedes and the driver started up the steep incline, a swarm of local citizenry, many standing in the water, struggling to hold the planks in line. Halfway up, what I was expecting happened, one plank moved and the rear wheel under the Vice President slipped off. He did not so much as change expression. A number of hands and straining arms then lifted the axle with M. Yembit's pasha-like weight and pushed the automobile the remaining way onto the ferry.

Crossing over he told me that he was very tired. The campaign had been difficult, since he had been heavily questioned as to why many members of the previous National Assembly had been dropped from the new list. "But now that I have talked with them" the Vice President concluded, "everything is all right." This was the first evidence I had had of disquiet in the country. On the way back to Moussambou we stopped at each little cluster of houses. M. Yembit got out of the Mercedes, shook all extended hands and after a brief exhortation would pull some crumpled bills out of his pocket and give them to the two or three senior people and as many others whose clamoring he could not escape. Having been a minor campaigner myself in New York, I was interested to see how it was done by the Vice President at his high political level. No wonder, I thought, that he is exhausted!

At Moussambou there was a stellar assembly of Gabonese officials and a large crowd. The children of Moussambou and N'Dendé were drawn up in ranks before the school. The Vice President spoke, followed by the Minister of Education, M. Nyonda, and Mr. Wayne Flesch, the Peace Corps Volunteer leader in charge of the group that had built this school. I had been billed as giving the main address, so I talked for about twenty minutes, telling the children how fortunate they were to be receiving their education at the hands of France, how pleased the United States was to be able to help by giving them this school, and then exhorting them to work hard, because their country's future rested in their hands. Embellishing this point, I said that twenty-five years hence (by using a far-off date I intended to keep my comment nonpolitical) when Léon Mba and his colleagues had retired, the children of today would be in charge. Little did I realize that some hours earlier the President had been seized and that he and all of the members of his Cabinet except the two who were standing beside me were locked up!

128

At 12:15 John Murphy drove me back to Mouila. On the other side of the Mouila ferry, Peace Corps Volunteers Hyland and Brandstetter pulled alongside in their jeep and yelled, "Léon Mba has been seized and is in prison." "Are you crazy?" I yelled back. "No, no kidding," they replied. We drove at once to the Prefect's house, where Mrs. Fanguinovény confirmed the news. My first reaction, I must confess, was subjective: what will Washington think of my reporting? Later I learned that no embassy in Libreville, including the French, had been wiser than we.

All flights, we were told, had been canceled. How to get back to Libreville? On a chance I had Murphy drive me to the airport, where we waited. A few minutes after the scheduled time a black speck appeared in the sky. It was our plane. The pilot said that since his flight originated in the Congo it had been permitted to come in, but he expected that he would not be allowed to go the whole way to Libreville. We made Lambaréné without receiving any new orders. There the plane was boarded by the crestfallen adviser to the President who the day before had reported that all was calm. The pilot told me that he expected to receive orders in the air to end his flight at the next stop, Port-Gentil. I replied that, if so, he should say that he had aboard the American Ambassador who had to return to the capital that night. At Port-Gentil the pilot informed me that the flight had been stopped but that I had been given permission to hire a Cessna and continue to Libreville. The pilot of the Cessna was anything but happy to take this job for he did not know what conditions he would meet. It would be dark before he could get back to Port-Gentil and the southern horizon was black with storms. Henry and I, however, persuaded him and were climbing into the little single-engine plane when the French adviser ran up. "Please, Monsieur l'Ambassadeur, take me with you." We agreed and were later shabbily repaid, as the reader will see.

I met a general in the French Air Force some time later in Brazzaville. "It was I," he said, "who gave the order that you could come in." This, of course, I knew, but his candid statement gave emphasis to the anomaly of the situation. The American Ambassador accredited to the government of a supposedly independent country was graciously allowed to enter the capital of that country by the order of a French general!

In the early hours of Tuesday, February 18, the First Company of the Gabonese Army under Lieutenant Valère Essone, seized the President's Palace. There was no shooting; no one was hurt. The few gendarmes on duty were told that this was just a military exercise.

The persons who were accused of engineering this remarkable exercise were, besides Essone, Lieutenant Jacques Mombo (assigned to the gendarmery), Second Lieutenant Daniel Mbéné (also assigned to the gendarmery) and Second Lieutenant Ndo Edou. The very few persons involved and the secrecy of their planning were the key to its success. Only during the final evening, February 17, did Lieutenant Essone, I understand, make up his mind to participate, a decision which was crucial for he had command of a company. Apparently on the spur of the moment he called out his troops, telling them that they were to go on normal night maneuvers.

These men were junior officers who lived with the troops. The senior officers were quartered in pleasant houses in town and, as events showed, were out of touch with life in the barracks. As part of our duties we had kept in constant touch with the senior officers as well as with the French colonel and his staff who were in over-all command, and my reports to Washington reflected what they told us, namely that the Army was entirely loyal to President Léon Mba. I offer no excuses for our failure to be better informed.

When Essone's troops entered the Palace gates, the lieutenants went up to the President's quarters where they forced him at gun point to sign his abdication and announce it in a statement which was repeated over the radio the next morning. In his apartment not far away Albert Bongo, one of the President's assistants, heard some noise and telephoned Mr. Bigmann, the President of the National Assembly. Bigmann rushed to the Palace and seeing the soldiers said, in effect, "What is going on here?" Whereupon they opened the gates and grabbed him.

When dawn broke, word was spreading that the President had been seized. The revolutionists then proceeded to round up the ministers one by one and take them to the Army barracks for detention. The Minister of Foreign Affairs, Joseph N'Goua, was able to alert the French Embassy before he was picked up. The French Ambassador got a message through to General Kergaravat, the Commander of French Forces of the Second African Zone at his headquarters in Brazzaville. As the morning progressed all the other important figures in the Léon Mba government were seized and taken to the barracks, with the exception of André-Gustave Anguilé. Our understanding is that the revolutionists left him free hoping that he would join them, but somewhat before noon he gave himself up asking to be detained with the others.

Calling themselves "The Revolutionary Committee," the four lieutenants ran things by themselves during the morning. Perhaps they intended to keep power in their hands for some time. Perhaps they thought that they could imitate Colonel Christopher Soglo, who with some brother officers had recently seized the government in Dahomey, running it for upwards of a month before withdrawing in favor of civilians of their choosing.

France had not intervened in Dahomey, or in Brazzaville in August, 1963, when the government of the Abbé Fulbert

131

Youlou was overthrown. The insurgents obviously did not take into their planning the possibility that France would act here, and did nothing to hamper such intervention. During that first morning they easily could have arranged street demonstrations to give the appearance that they enjoyed popular support; and they could have parked a few bulldozers and trucks on the airport runway, making it more difficult for the French to bring in their troops. But with their revolt an off-the-cuff affair, these things had not been thought of.

The first contingent of French troops, about fifty, arrived from Brazzaville at 10:50 A.M. and took over the Libreville Airport. The commanding general announced that they had come only to protect French lives and property, and no effort was made to eject them. Later one of the officers told me that, being so few in number, they were well aware that their position was precarious. Had the Gabonese Army moved against them, they could have been mauled. Why did the lieutenants of the coup not give such an order? Having received their military training in France, perhaps they were reluctant to fire on white French soldiers, and doubtless they realized the futility of offering military opposition to France.

What they did—if I correctly interpreted their actions—was to adopt a political expedient. They turned to M. Aubame as an experienced political leader who had lived many years in France, hoping that he could arrange matters with the French. So, in the early afternoon of that first day, M. Aubame was brought to the Presidency, where he formed a so-called "Provisional Government," drawing to it Paul Gondjout, Jean-Marc Ekoh and Eugène Amogho, and a number of young intellectuals, including Philippe N'Dong, the editor of Gabon's literary review *Réalités Gabonaises;* Philippe Maury, Gabon's one actor; and Dr. Chambrier, the only Gabonese graduated as a physician.

132

M. Aubame was not able quickly to establish contact with the French Ambassador, but this made little difference for the Ambassador was not in a position to influence the course of events. French policy was being executed through the military zone commander, General Kergaravat, who received direct orders from President de Gaulle, which appear to have been, quite simply, to find Léon Mba and put him back in power. Wishing to have ample force at his disposal, the General called for reinforcements from other French military posts in Africa. During the evening and through the night troops poured in— white French soldiers, and black soldiers of the French Community. They came from Bouar in the Central African Republic and from as far away as Dakar in Senegal. These latter were brought by planes larger than the Libreville runways were designed to take, and they had to land in the dark in a heavy storm. The build-up continued until some six hundred French troops were staged around the airport.

Before dawn these forces moved into the city and along the shore boulevard right in front of our Embassy to the barracks on the far side of town, where the members of Léon Mba's government were confined. With the coming of daylight, about six o'clock, the barracks were attacked. The Gabonese defended themselves bravely but were no match for French soldiery supported by aircraft.

My wife and I sat on the terrace of the Residence in the clear morning light watching four French planes circling round and round and on each circle diving on the barracks, machine guns spattering. There was a steady rattle of fire from the troops, punctuated by the booms of small cannon. After about two hours the barracks fell. Eighteen Gabonese soldiers were killed and one French soldier. The number of casualties among the civilians living in the area was never disclosed, but it was generally believed that they were quite high, for the straw and corrugated-iron roofs on the huts in the neighborhood offered little protection against the hail of bullets from the planes.

Throughout the day bands of shouting Africans ran this way and that in the streets; military vehicles carrying troops dashed about; desultory shots were heard. We kept the door of the Embassy locked, with all American personnel inside.

The radio station held out for a time, but then capitulated without force being used. Aubame and the other members of his Provisional Government were holed up in the Palace, which was shortly surrounded by French troops. Toward the end of the afternoon, after negotiations with the French Ambassador and French military representatives, they were persuaded to return quietly to their own houses. What assurances they were given for their future personal safety it would be interesting to know. The *coup d'état* was over, and the empty Palace awaited the return of the man whom de Gaulle favored.

When the barracks fell, the ministers of Léon Mba's deposed government were released, but he was not among them. He had been spirited away early the previous night on the orders of Second Lieutenant Ndo Edou. Since Ndo Edou had since been killed, no one knew to what place Léon Mba had been taken.

Afterward we learned that he had been driven off in the charge of a noncommissioned officer and two soldiers. Their destination was N'Djolé, but a heavy storm forced them to seek shelter in a village. In the early morning they set out again, his captors then deciding to take him, not to N'Djolé, but over the easier road to Lambaréné. Several hours after they arrived, perhaps having heard over the radio what had taken place in the capital, they decided to return. In the late evening they were met at the Kango ferry by a search party under a French officer and were escorted back to Libreville. An *opéra bouffe* story.

Back in the Palace, the President seized the radio and vowed vengeance on his enemies. Hearing this, some of the members of the Provisional Government (not M. Aubame) in the morning sought asylum in our Embassy, but as they faced no immediate physical danger we felt obliged to ask them to leave. Before long they all found themselves in prison along with the lieutenants, French soldiers acting as their jailers.

Early the next morning, Thursday, General Kergaravat left his headquarters, presented himself at the French Embassy where he saluted the Ambassador, said, *"Mission accomplie,"* and turned on his heel and left. From the time when the General arrived in Libreville Tuesday morning until Léon Mba was restored to his Palace Wednesday night, less than forty hours had passed. How the French Ambassador had been treated by his government during this period must surely be one of the remarkable stories of diplomacy.

Paul Cousseran was not a career diplomat. He had come to Gabon a year earlier with the reputation of a brilliant young administrator. Following Jean Risterucci, who had been the last colonial Governor and first Ambassador, Cousseran's position was not easy. He filled it well. Young, athletic, possessing an easy and warm personality, liberal in outlook, and with a charming wife and five young children, he symbolized a possible new relationship between France and Africa.

When I reached our Embassy the morning of the intervention I was told that M. Cousseran had asked the other members of the Diplomatic Corps to come to his office. I found him with a gray face and a stubble of beard, obviously having been up all night. He told us that he intended to tell Léon Mba as well as Aubame, Gondjout and the others that they must sit down at a round table and work out some way of organizing a government in Gabon which would represent all political factions. There must be free elections, fairly organized, to a new National Assembly. The tension which had cursed Gabonese political life since February, 1963, must be ended. The Ambassador expressed the belief that he possessed the personal authority with each participant, and sufficient leverage over each, to force sensible compromises toward these ends. He also said that the French Government did not insist on restoring Léon Mba to power and certainly did not want to see him operate the repressive type of government of the past year. On the other hand, the French Government insisted that discussions for a political settlement could not begin until Léon Mba was again free and able to take part.

I was delighted to hear these expressions, with which I was in entire agreement, and I told the Ambassador that he would have my full support in working toward the objectives he had outlined. The others present spoke similarly. We were not then aware that M. Cousseran was voicing simply personal sentiments and that he was not expressing the intentions of the French Government. He would, of course, not have acted in any way contrary to his government's wishes, so I can only conclude that the stories which soon circulated throughout Libreville, that he was temporarily out of touch with Paris, were correct. His was a brave initiative, and I admired him for taking it. Probably he was so convinced, as was I, of the rightness of his policy that he assumed it would be that of his government also.

On leaving the French Ambassador's office, I exchanged a word at the door with M. Aubame, who was coming in. Later in the day M. Cousseran told me that M. Aubame had assured him that Léon Mba would be brought back unharmed. After the coup this same expectation was echoed by the Archbishop, Monsignor Jérome Adam, one of the grand old Frenchmen of Gabon, who said to me that France could better have achieved its objective by negotiation than by force—Aubame would have seen to it that Léon Mba was safely returned.

M. Aubame, consistent with his character, gave his trust to

the French Ambassador. In quietly leaving the Palace that afternoon and returning to his own house, I am sure that he took comfort from the Ambassador's hopes of promoting a new government of national union. Léon Mba was later very critical of Cousseran for having had contacts with Aubame.

That night the President gave his vindictive speech. After hearing it on the radio in the morning, I went immediately to the French Ambassador to express my surprise. The authoritarian tone, and the President's statement that he would seek out his enemies wherever they might hide and bring them to punishment, did not sound like a good start toward binding up the nation's wounds and creating a spirit of national harmony. Why had not the Ambassador intercepted the President and prevented this from happening? Later I found out why.

From the time when General Kergaravat arrived at the Libreville Airport Tuesday morning until he left forty-eight hours later, the poor Ambassador was cut off from his government. The Elysée communicated directly with the General. According to stories current in Libreville at the time the Ambassador more than once drove out to the French military headquarters at the airport asking, "Are there no messages for me?" and was told that there were none. The French Ambassador it was later apparent did not know at the time what orders Paris gave to the General, he did not know what de Gaulle's policy was toward Léon Mba, and when the French military delivered the President back to the Palace, Cousseran had no opportunity to impress his point of view on the President before he spoke.

My colleagues, and in particular my Deputy, Mr. William Courtney, were mystified and irritated. We felt that M. Cousseran was not being frank with us; in fact, we wondered if we were not being deceived. Later, when we learned of his predicament, those sentiments gave way to feelings of sorrow.

137

His government certainly treated a fine man with scant consideration.

In the minor international uproar which followed their military action, the French Government was at pains to argue its legality. The French Minister of Information, M. Alain Péyrefitte, in a long statement following a meeting of the Council of Ministers in Paris on February 26, said, "The intervention in Gabon was the result of an appeal made by the legitimate authorities for help against a handful of armed putschists."

Under the agreements which Gabon and her sister states entered into with France on gaining independence, they could call on her for military aid for national defense. President Léon Mba and a few other favored chiefs of state, it is understood, obtained supplementary secret agreements with General de Gaulle's government saying that they could call on France also to save them from being toppled by internal movements. A formal request in writing to France was in fact made from Libreville by M. Yembit, acting for the fallen government, but it is interesting to note that this was not done until well into the next day, Wednesday, more than twenty-four hours after the French attack at Baraka.

We know what the Vice President's movements were after I left him on Tuesday at 12:15 P.M. The fact that his appeal to France was made after all the troop movement and all the shooting were over may raise questions in the minds of some as to just how legal the French Government's action was. If it was not legal, then I suppose it would have to be called an act of international aggression.

The reasons why de Gaulle intervened are not hard to see. Many things conspired to make Gabon a special case. Of all France's former African possessions, none was more French at heart. Nor was any dearer to France, since for half a century it had given handsome profits to French businessmen and investors. No other state possessed the uranium that de Gaulle needed for his *force de frappe,* with which he planned to make France "independent." Léon Mba was a factor too: a magnetic personality, devoted to France, he held a special place in de Gaulle's esteem. Also, the particular time when this coup occurred had a bearing. In January, 1963, Sylvanus Olympio in Togo was murdered, in August Fulbert Youlou was ousted in Brazzaville, and in October Hubert Maga was upset in Dahomey—all countries under French influence. Now in February, 1964, came Gabon, the fourth. Seen from Paris, the time had arrived to put a stop to this sort of thing.

It is more difficult to say why the coup was attempted. Each of the lieutenants was reported to have had a personal grievance related to assignments or promotions, but that could be only part of the reason. Perhaps more important was dissatisfaction among the troops with Gabonese society under Léon Mba. A young American graduate of Princeton who was doing some work for the Evangelical Church, suggested this to me. On returning to Libreville after several months spent in that trackless expanse of river and lakes between Lambaréné and the sea, he said that if trouble came it would start in the Army; he had met soldiers who on returning home spoke with resentment of the luxury in which the ministers lived in the capital compared with their own poor pay and the miserable existence of their families in their squalid villages. At the time, relying on what I had learned from the higher officers in Libreville, I did not give this evidence the weight it merited. There must have been much truth in it, for after the coup the President dismissed every soldier, completely disbanding the Army, and set about recruiting all new men. Doubtless the dissatisfaction among the rank and file was shared by some of the lower officers.

If M. Aubame was implicated in the coup, his motives and

purposes would be understandable, but this is a question to which we do not know the answer. The opinion of most people with whom I talked in Libreville at the time was that he had jumped on the bandwagon several hours after the coup had taken place. Evidence later available suggested that Pierre Eyéguet, Aubame's nephew and once Gabonese Ambassador in London, may have known something of the lieutenants' plot and informed his uncle before the event, but if so what role Aubame played, whether he stood aside or whether he established contact with the plotters, we do not know. All these questions were subjects of the trial, if such it can be called, later held at Lambaréné, where M. Aubame was the principal defendant. Someday someone may put together the true story.

Aubame's action in responding to the revolutionary committee's request that he take over appears in a clearer light. Léon Mba had formally abdicated the Presidency and his government in fact had ceased to exist; any qualified person, it seems to me, might without reproach have stepped in to fill the vacuum. It was on that footing that the French Ambassador had discussions with Aubame.

Ekoh, I heard from persons who spoke with him afterward, was quietly minding his business when sent for by Aubame in the middle of the afternoon to be Minister of Foreign Affairs in the Provisional Government. Ekoh had had experience in this position, having been appointed Acting Foreign Minister by Léon Mba during Aubame's incumbency whenever Aubame was away. Dr. Chambrier, who became Minister of Public Health, apparently had dropped a hint to Dr. Bonnaud of WHO a few days before the coup. Emmanuel Mbéné, who appeared as Minister of Information, Posts and Telecommunications, is related to Daniel Mbéné, one of the lieutenants, which may or may not point to his having had prior knowledge of the revolt.

Random comments such as these are all I can make; reliable information as to whether or not the individuals who joined the Provisional Government were involved in the coup is not available. However, all these men must have been troubled by Gabon's progression toward a one-party state and arbitrary government. When peaceful means to change are denied, there is a standing invitation to resort to subterfuge and force.

The Seamy Side of Grandeur

THE morning after Léon Mba had been restored, the members of the Diplomatic Corps and many others went to the Palace to welcome him. The Chinese Chargé threw his arms around the President's neck and kissed him. My greeting, more restrained, was none the less sincere.

I was glad that the President was safely back. My relations with him had been excellent and we had formed, I thought, as close a friendship as possible within the context of our respective positions. He was quick to understand a problem, gave his decisions without hesitation, and almost always agreed to my requests. He loved to talk, and would not notice the time, but about ten minutes after you had overrun the period of your appointment, his secretary would appear at the door and say "But Mr. President, so-and-so is waiting." Sometimes I would have half a dozen subjects to take up with him, so I developed a technique for getting through my agenda in the time allotted. His custom was that he and his caller sat in armchairs facing each other. When I wanted to stop him talking, I would lean forward and gently pat him on the knee. This made him pause, and in that second I would open my next point. I was really fond of that man.

What had happened to him was not right. To enter a private citizen's apartment and seize him in the dead of night is a criminal act. Whether it is the same thing when the person concerned is a head of state who had done considerable to invite this aggression is a question on which there may be different opinions. That morning, however, the President's callers were not concerning themselves with such philosophical points. We were glad to see him back, we sympathized with him because of his harrowing experience, and we looked to the future with some hope. There was a feeling of relief and relaxation in the air, and at the same time apprehension.

The evening of that first day I was in my bedroom dressing for dinner; the phone rang; the voice said, "This is Jean-Hilaire Aubame." I said, "Good evening," a bit coolly, I am afraid, for I was surprised and I could think of no title by which to address him. Then he said, "I hope that you will report to Washington the truth of what has happened here these days." Fearful that my phone was tapped, I replied only that my duty was always to report the truth to the best of my ability. Nothing more was said, but that telephone call is one of the reasons for this book. This man has been subjected to the type of treatment to which we have become accustomed in the police states which our century has spawned, most, I blush to say, in the Europe from which the ancestors of the majority of Americans came and not in the continents which we like to think of as less advanced.

It was clear to all of us in the Diplomatic Corps, and to many others, that the sensible course for Léon Mba was to adopt a conciliatory attitude toward his enemies, reduce political tension and strive to unify the country. In fact, his mood was just the opposite. He wanted punishment and retribution. The French Ambassador, undaunted by his disillusioning experi-

143

ence during the coup, saw the President daily attempting to soften his attitudes. I called on the President to support my colleague, and I tried to persuade the President to meet with the opposition, particularly M. Aubame and M. Ekoh, advice which I then believed M. Cousseran was also giving, but although Léon Mba listened to me quietly and courteously, I saw that his mind was not with me.

Nevertheless, M. Cousseran did chalk up a number of successes in rapid succession. He persuaded the President to announce that a Commission of Inquiry would be created to decide who should stand trial. He got the President to dismiss some of the more politically vindictive ministers and advisers. And, most important, he induced Léon Mba to announce that elections for the National Assembly would be held on April 12 on a pattern quite different from that previously planned. This time there would not be a single list for the whole country, but instead the voting would be by Regions for Regional lists, and any group wishing to enter a list in any Region could do so.

Then an amazing thing happened: the French Ambassador was recalled. In less than a week he boarded the Paris plane rather sheepishly and was gone. It was widely believed that Léon Mba had asked for his removal.

With Paul Cousseran's departure the trend toward more reasonable and democratic positions ended. He had arranged that the members of the Provisional Government would stay at liberty until indicted by the Commission of Inquiry, but the President was too angry to abide by this procedure. Within a few days all (except Amogho) were arrested.

In Aubame's case a car with gendarmes came to his house, ostensibly to take him to a hearing before the Commission, but delivered him instead to the airport where a plane spirited him away (without any personal articles such as pajamas, razor and the like) to an isolated place of detention far down the Coast near Setté-Cama. While he was there a friend of his who

144

claimed to have seen him came to me asking the United States to send a submarine to rescue him; if I passed the message on to Washington—which I no longer remember—it was only for form's sake as any adventure of this sort would have been utterly out of the question.

The Commission of Inquiry turned into a farce. The President's power was so great that the Commission could not stand up to his pressure. They indicted the persons the President wanted indicted, and exonerated those he considered too unimportant to bother with.

The explanation of these tawdry events is not hard to see. The French Ambassador in promoting a policy of moderation had some support from the Quai d'Orsay (the French Foreign Office), but not from the Elysée (President de Gaulle's office). During these days certain French businessmen were frequently seen at Léon Mba's elbow. De Gaulle apparently had decided that France's interests were best served by allowing Léon Mba to re-establish full authority in his own way. Although his methods were arbitrary, crude and cruel, with French troops behind him they could hardly fail to work.

Once Léon Mba was back in power, public opinion in Gabon swung sharply against France. We had observed over the past year that young Gabonese were becoming increasingly critical of their neo-colonial status and of the conduct of the French in their midst, but until France's military intervention their loyalty to and affection for France were not basically affected. The differences, the problems were still felt to be within the family, between brothers. The invasion by French troops and hail of bullets at Baraka showed France in a new light. And the very fact that the Gabonese regarded the French as brothers made their resentment, sorrow and hatred all the greater.

The initial reaction was one of shock. Then the people began to realize that a purely Gabonese revolution had been crushed, and the old order restored by the military intervention of a foreign power. As their eyes opened, they perceived also that France had done this, not for Gabon's good, but for the uranium for de Gaulle's *force de frappe* and the whole conglomeration of French businesses which had grown fat under Léon Mba.

For an American the election campaign for the members of the new National Assembly was an eye-opener. The Presidency was not at stake since Léon Mba had been elected in 1961 for a seven-year term, but in point of fact it was his policies and relationship with France that were the basic issues. A vote for any candidates put up by his party, the Bloc Démocratique Gabonais, would be a vote for him, while a vote for opposing candidates would be interpreted as a vote against him. Had the new Assembly come in with a majority against the President, it would have made no practical difference. With all power placed in his hands by the Constitution the President could simply have disregarded the deputies as in fact he had always done. But the election was a test of popular opinion.

Each of the nine Regions was to vote for its own candidates. There were forty-seven seats in all to be filled, and each Region had a number proportionate to its population. The voters, however, were not to vote for individuals but for a list. For instance, the Woleu N'Tem and the N'Gounié, the largest Regions, each had eight seats. The BDG in each put up a list of eight candidates, and the voter could chose between that list and any opposing list, of which in principle there could be any number. Under this system the man whose name appeared first on a list (the *chef de file,* or head of the line) was an important fellow, rather like the captain of the team. A vote for the government's list indicated a desire for continuance of the status quo and, in particular, approval of French intervention during the coup. A vote for an opposing list was an expression against the President and French policy. Of course, the situation throughout the country was not always this clear-cut; personalities and local problems played some role, but the overriding issues everywhere were Léon Mba and France.

While the *Daily Bulletin* carried frequent stories to the effect that it was the President's expressed wish that the elections take place in perfect honesty, he and his advisers, French and Gabonese, exhibited remarkable ingenuity in devising ploys which would help the government's men to win.

The first thing that they did was to bar anyone who had taken part in the coup or the Provisional Government from being a candidate. This excluded the obvious leader of the opposition, M. Aubame, as well as a number of other experienced politicians. The measure really was unnecessary since all these people except M. Amogho had been locked up, but the step prevented them from running while in jail. As a result the opposition was without national leadership and in each Region different people had to step forward on their own initiative to assemble lists and prepare for the contest as best they could.

The campaign was most intense in Estuaire and N'Gounié, with seven and eight seats respectively. Whichever side would carry these, given the way the other Regions were predicted to fall, would win. In both areas many people known to be anti-government were seized by the police and, without any pretense of a hearing, were locked up until after the election. In the city of Libreville the number so treated was over a thousand. Since this considerably exceeded the capacity of the jails, men were taken in airplanes and dropped off at isolated airstrips in the forests. Peter Telfair learned that the SOMIFER airstrip at Belinga was being so used and made a determined protest to a Frenchman on the President's staff, who saw nothing wrong in what was being done. Peter sent orders that food be given to the unfortunates thus dumped on his company's property. Some people were seized at night in their pajamas and taken

147

in this condition, without money or food, five hundred or so miles away, often being left among unfriendly tribes. There was little chance that they could find their way back home in time to vote. To the government's credit it must be said that, after the election, planes were sent out to recover as many of these men as could be found.

One of the casualties in these mass arrests was the president of our football team, Bekalé Grégoire. He was imprisoned on March 15 and on July 2 was tried before Judge Chango and released. The charge was simply that he had been overheard in the street advocating voting for the opposition. He only learned this, however, when he appeared in court after three and a half months in prison, which effectively deprived him of his franchise.

Other equally subtle measures were employed. Of course, all government employees received orders—not how they should vote themselves, for that was obvious, but to get out the vote and see to it that it was right. Prefects, Subprefects and village chiefs were told that if they wished to keep their jobs their districts had better turn in a good majority for the government's candidates. A most effective device was employed in the N'Gounié. There for a good three weeks before the election no one was allowed to buy gas except for government vehicles. This not only immobilized the opposition; it also immobilized the Peace Corps, who were then working in that Region. The American missionaries, who normally kept a drum or two at their different mission stations, were begged to sell a few liters, but refused knowing that this would be construed as a political act unfriendly to the government.

Although he was not a candidate, and despite his statement that he would stand above the campaign, Léon Mba went on two or three barnstorming trips. Almost everywhere he had a dreadful reception. His technique was to throw banknotes, usually in small denominations, from the platform where he was

148

President John F. Kennedy chats with Ambassador Darlington shortly before he left for Libreville.

M. Jean-Hilaire Aubame, Minister of Foreign Affairs, and Ambassador Darlington signing the AID agreement for the Peace Corps schools.

New Year's party at Palace. From right Mrs. Darlington, M. Aubame, President Léon Mba, Monsignor N'Dong, Mme. Aubame, Mr. Darlington.

Mr. and Mrs. Darlington, Christopher and Leticia, by the Ogooué River near N'Djolé where the road crosses the Equator.

In the Woleu N'Tem: stopping at a village where the people are celebrating the end of a period of mourning.

Mr. and Mrs. Darlington visiting the Catholic Mission at Oyem with Pierre Fanguinovény, Prefect of the Woleu N'Tem (in light suit).

Mr. Darlington discussing petition given him by people at Médouneu. Seated, left, Deputy Jacques Biyogho, right, Subprefect Etoughe Joseph.

"Our Football Team," the Association Sportive Darling Club. Bekalé Grégoire, the Club's President, is at the Ambassador's left.

Mr. Darlington dedicating Peace Corps school, Moussambou, morning of Coup. On the Ambassador's right: Fanguinovény and Yembit; on left: Bekalé and Nyonda.

French troops in Libreville to restore Léon Mba after the Coup.

Gabonese bearing placard saying "Down with Dictatorship; Long Live the Provisional Government." Many such crowds marched in the days after French troops put out this government and restored Léon Mba.

speaking, or from the window of his car if the crowd was too hostile for him to get out. He did this in Mouila, where there were some Peace Corps Volunteers. The crowd was antagonistic and walked away, leaving the President's money in the street.

Almost everyone expected that there would be trouble in the streets on election day, or that riots would break out when the results were known. Political antagonisms had aroused tribal passions and hatred; among the Fang in the Libreville area there were pro-Léon Mba and pro-Aubame factions, and it was feared that the losing side would attack the other. But, apart from a few scuffles here and there, there was no violence. The atmosphere was uneasy and tense, but French and Community troops, white and colored, stationed at various points throughout the town, and French patrol planes over the countryside, served to keep the people quiet. In addition, French gunboats appeared at Libreville and Port-Gentil several days before the election, staying at anchor during the critical week.

Seeing what was going on, few people expected the government to lose. On election day, April 12, it won thirty-one seats to the opposition's sixteen. But the lists sponsored by the government received only 50.38 percent of the popular vote, while those representing the opposition got 49.62 percent. In the populous Woleu N'Tem, the home of the Fang, the government lists (there were more than one on each side) received 7,410 votes; the opposition lists, 37,789. What the results would have been in the absence of fraud cannot be known, but most observers with whom members of our Embassy spoke thought that there would have been a considerable majority against Léon Mba and French domination.

Students of democratic procedures would be interested in some of the things that took place. After a voter had presented his registration card and had it stamped he was given a piece of paper which he was supposed to drop into the box of the

149

party he favored. At one polling place in Libreville a member of my staff saw a gendarme standing by the boxes hold out his hand as the voter approached; the voter instinctively gave the gendarme the paper, which he put into the government's box. Libreville is where most of the French live. The majority of them had been in Gabon since before independence and were entitled to vote. Almost all were for Léon Mba. To make sure that they would not be deterred from voting by predictions of disorders at the polling places, the government promised to give any Frenchman who voted a 10 percent reduction in his income tax; all he had to do was to attach the stamped registration card to his tax return. Of course, it was quite fair, for the card did not show how one voted. I cannot vouch for this story, but it was widely repeated and believed. Given these circumstances, it is easy to understand why the government's list won in Estuaire. But out of a total of 40,698 votes its majority was only 816, a considerably smaller number than that of opposition sympathizers imprisoned or spirited away.

In the N'Gounié the problem was handled more simply. It was believed by many that when the officials in that Region reported the results to Libreville they reversed the results, giving the government list 26,964 votes and the opposition 20,238. If this seems incredible, let me recount what occurred in the Regions of Haut-Ogooué and Ogooué-Lolo, where the government lists were headed by two men who had been on both sides of the political fence in the past and so did not have clear personal identifications. When they were speaking in a village where Léon Mba was popular, they claimed that they were government men; in opposition villages they represented the opposition. Naturally they cleaned up. Their poor opponents had no means of getting about, and since there were no newspapers or radio, they had no way to combat this fraud.

These goings-on were not part of a stage farce but took place during the first ostensibly free national election in Gabon since the country became independent. Léon Mba's was the power by which these things were done, but behind Léon Mba was France. French troops not only kept him in the Presidency but provided all the effective power to support his policies. French money financed him, and French advisers provided the brains that thought up and the skills that carried out much of the chicanery I have described. The reason was clear: de Gaulle would lose face if, after having restored Léon Mba to power by force, he had been defeated in an election. Grandeur was at stake.

I realized how much it was at stake when I called on the Frenchman, a senior judge in Gabon, who headed the panel which had investigated charges of election irregularities. The panel had completed its work with a simple confirmation of the results as published. I wanted to find out some of the details leading to this conclusion, which had been greeted with widespread cynicism. He told me that he and his assessors had found that the irregularities on both sides approximately offset each other. I appeared incredulous. He made some limp explanations, and I had my answer. When an honest man finds himself in a position where he has to distort the truth, you can see it in his eyes: they hurt. I liked this man, but he was part of the French power structure in Gabon; he was young and had his career to think of, so that was the way it was. Grandeur was served.

Despite their shortcomings the elections doubtless provided a safety valve. It helped dissipate the anger of many Gabonese who wanted to turn out Léon Mba and provided some hope, at least to the unsophisticated, that grievances could be expressed effectively and openly. Together with the trials which later took place at Lambaréné, the elections helped Léon Mba to get through the first eight months after his restoration. Both can be regarded as elements of moderation and were probably

151

viewed in this sense by many French and perhaps some Gabonese.

The French, officials and the business community alike, interpreted the elections as an endorsement of the President, but their man, instead of settling down and attempting to heal the divisions among the people, became increasingly erratic, arbitrary and dictatorial. The change in his character was tragic. Léon Mba had the sense of being a chief of state. If he had had to be responsible to some other power in Gabon— the National Assembly, the people—his development might have been different. When the French helped him to revise the Constitution, when they protected him from his own people with their soldiers, they created the conditions in which their chosen instrument degenerated. It was a sad thing to watch.

After the elections the President practically disappeared, even from his own staff. He is tired, it was said; then it was given out that he had pneumonia; then the rumor spread that he had fallen in a hot bath and burned himself. For a month or more, no one except his physicians saw Léon Mba. What had happened to him—even where he was—was a secret so closely guarded that we never learned the truth.

As he regained his strength and reassumed control of the government, bitterness, the desire for vengeance and the will to show the world that he would brook no opposition seemed increasingly to dominate his policy and actions. Men and women, sometimes only on the report that they had been overheard saying something critical of the President, were taken to jail and, without trial, beaten and held there for as long as Léon Mba chose. The villages, as always, slumbered in apathy, but in Libreville and the regional capitals fear was every man's bedfellow. The President was afraid, too. To protect himself from his own people, he had an immense masonry wall constructed around the Palace which many called *"le mur de la honte"* ("the wall of shame").

152

For all this sordid work France bears a large share of responsibility. France protected Léon Mba with French soldiers, not just for a few days but indefinitely, and when this book went to press in the summer of 1967 they were still in Gabon. Behind them he was safe, safe not only to govern, but also to give free rein to his passions. Frenchmen in the Ministry of Information helped him to keep the public misinformed. French officers in charge of the gendarmery helped him to carry out his wholesale political arrests and brutalities. A Frenchman at his behest reproduced ugly pictures of racial disturbances in Mississippi and drafted scurrilous tracts against the United States.

Most of the seasoned French administrators who were running Gabon at the end of the colonial period had gone and their places were taken by men of quite different caliber, out in Africa for a few years for the money, adventurers. These men, although financed by French aid, were employees of the Gabonese Government. They can claim, therefore, that they were only doing their duty in supporting the head of that government. Their jobs depended on pleasing Léon Mba.

The French with whom we spoke either claimed they did not know what was going on or were quite cynical. "This is Africa; you cannot apply the same moral standards here as in Paris or New York," said the new French Ambassador.

I disagreed. Almost every day Gabonese would come to my house, and sometimes to my office, to share their worries. Most were young, but not all; some had studied in France and could be called intellectuals, but in the main they were just ordinary people. They came, in part I suppose, because I had become known as someone approachable and sympathetic, but more importantly because I represented the United States, a country which they identified with freedom and which they were dimly aware was even stronger than France. So they came to talk with me. I would often find several sitting on the terrace

153

of the house waiting for me to return from the office at the end of the afternoon. Others would come during the evening. Sometimes I would keep one group sitting outside while I spoke with another inside. I never turned anyone away.

They spoke politely and softly, expressing themselves well. They thought about what they were saying and rarely exaggerated. In this they were a credit not only to themselves but to the cultural refinement that France gave to her African colonies. Yet they came to question and to speak bitterly about France. They burned under the knowledge that France had killed Gabonese to restore a pro-French President to power. I was impressed by their understanding of the issues and by their awareness of the moral questions involved. I could do nothing for them, of course, except listen; I could not, as the representative of the United States, take part in their criticisms either of Léon Mba, to whom I was accredited, or of our ally France.

But neither could I, as the representative of the United States, allow them to gain the impression that I thought that what we were witnessing was right. While avoiding direct criticism, I felt bound to indicate that, as an American, I could not condone what I saw. It was a very difficult situation. Perhaps I should have refused to see them, but since arriving in Gabon I had consistently received every Gabonese who called on me, and now when many felt that their country was in trouble it seemed wrong to change.

I have no doubt that my attitude got to the ears of Léon Mba and the French Embassy, harming my relations with both, but I feel satisfied that I represented my country as I should. I believe that I was able to make my many visitors feel that there was at least one person in Libreville, neither Gabonese nor French, who cared enough to listen, unhurried and sympathetically.

The French failed to realize, I think, how rapidly the Gabonese had been changing through the force of the very things that France had been giving them, education and the Christian religion. The time for cynicism on the part of Europeans toward Africans had passed. As for myself, I remained convinced that one of the most important ways in which the West can help the young countries of Africa is by teaching them respect for human rights as well as the tolerance and self-discipline needed to make self-government work.

Time will bring changes and the things of which I have written will tend to be forgotten. The ties between France and Gabon are strong, and French aid still pours in. I cannot believe, however, that France will again enjoy in Gabon the respect and affection it once had.

CHAPTER

XI

A Long Way from Lafayette

DURING the political crisis of February, 1963, my name
had been linked by gossipmongers with that of M. Aubame. We had no evidence how or where this rumor started;
all of a sudden it was in the wind, the talk in the shops and at
dinner tables. Matters were aggravated by M. Aubame himself.
After returning from his third visit to the United States the
previous December, he constantly allowed praises of our country to slip into his conversation and, worse still, made compari-
sons between us and France that were not always favorable to
the latter.

What circulated were hardly more than insinuations. They
died down as quickly as they had arisen and did no damage
then to our position with the President. When I called on him
to express my unhappiness and concern, he reassured me, saying, "Don't worry, rumors are common in Africa; if you ever
do anything which I do not like, I will call you and we will talk
about it." These whisperings, however, did create an identifica-

tion between M. Aubame and myself that was remembered the following year.

During these months the Peace Corps school builders made their strikingly favorable impression. We opened our beautiful Embassy on the shore boulevard, outshining the offices of the French Ambassador, and President Léon Mba eulogized the United States at our ceremony; Governor Williams' visit had been a smashing success; and President Kennedy's death had evoked an outpouring of warm feelings toward America and Americans. All this made for jealousy on the part of those who regarded Gabon as their own private garden.

In late January and early February, 1964, as the President was preparing for the elections to the new National Assembly and it was uncertain whether M. Aubame would be able to put an opposing slate into the field, the same innuendoes and rumors about me began again. I could hardly believe my ears, for I had seen M. Aubame only very occasionally, and he had not even had a meal in my house, during the past year. My work did not bring me into contact with him in his capacity as President of the Supreme Court as it had when he was Minister of Foreign Affairs.

Then came the February coup. There was a surge of emotion—family, tribal, national—revealing the intensity of the black man's solidarity when betrayed and hurt by the white. Everywhere people were saying, "The French have murdered our brothers; they have killed our children."

The instinctive reaction of the French, scared and wounded by this dreadful cataract of events, was to turn on the Americans. The desultory rumors linking our Embassy with M. Aubame and his supporters burst into full cry. We were the scapegoats. At the tennis club, in the bars, in the hotels and private houses stories spread like wildfire about *"les Américains."* "If it had not been for the coming of the United States Embassy and the Peace Corps to Gabon, everything would

157

have continued peaceful as always." "Wherever the Americans go, troubles for France follow; look at Indo-China." "The Americans were behind the revolution." "Aubame has been getting money from Darlington." Passions mounted to a point where some French stores would not sell to American Embassy families and the Peace Corps, and some French garages refused to service our cars. As I was America's official representative, I became the chief target.

The Gabonese meanwhile were demonstrating quite different feelings. After the coup mobs who were stoning and overturning the cars of Frenchmen in Libreville cheered when American cars passed.* During these days I ordered all Embassy vehicles to show the flag, but this upset the French Ambassador, who said that he felt that we were trying to separate ourselves from them. I thought to myself that if one of our Embassy cars were to be destroyed and the occupants possibly hurt because of mistaken identity, it would be a pretty expensive demonstration of American-French solidarity. In some countries American libraries have been wrecked or burned by angry mobs. One afternoon a crowd assembled outside our United States Information Service library, but it came cheering and chanting *Les Américains sont avec nous* ("The Americans are with us")—and these people were the radicals and the young.

Late on the evening of March 3 a hand grenade was thrown from a passing car at the Embassy. As it landed on the lawn, it did no more than split our wooden sign and break a couple of panes of glass. We asked the government to give us police protection after dark. This was promised, but the first night the man assigned quit after a few hours, and thereafter no one showed up.

Sunday night, March 8, my wife and I were awakened about

* This was reported in *Newsweek*.

158

eleven o'clock by a pounding on the door. We opened and saw my Deputy, Bill Courtney; the Public Affairs Officer, Henry Stephen; and Mr. Lloyd Garrison of the *New York Times,* who, like the excellent correspondent he is, was on the spot. "This time they've really done it," Courtney said. So I hurried into my clothes and went down to the Embassy, to find the windows in my office ripped with holes, broken glass everywhere, the Venetian blinds shredded, and a spatter of shot marks on the walls and ceiling. Courtney's office was the same. Outside, the building was pock-marked in numerous places. Someone in a passing automobile had raked the Embassy with a heavy-gauge gun, the kind having soft lead pellets which flatten to the size of a thumbnail. Then a bomb was thrown— we believe from the same car coming back—but as the explosion apparently took place in the air it did no damage.

No one doubted but that the perpetrators were French. The job was too sophisticated for Gabonese, and Gabonese do not have access to grenades. Mr. James Frazier of our staff lived on the Embassy grounds and Courtney lived only two doors away. Both their houses faced the shore boulevard. On hearing the first shots they rushed to their windows and saw a car containing white men. As it was after curfew the street was otherwise empty. There are no white men in Gabon, practically speaking, but French.

I drove at once to the French Ambassador's residence, and by beaming the high lights of the Embassy Dodge at his windows and blowing the horn I woke him up. M. Cousseran dressed and graciously came with me to inspect the damage. Although naturally he could not openly accept my assumption that Frenchmen were responsible, it was apparent that he was shocked and sincerely regretted what had happened.

While we were standing in the street a small car drove up, violating the curfew. The occupant, an enormously fat Frenchman properly drunk, seeing me, leaned out and uttered an unprintable epithet about "the filthy Americans." He had, unhappily for him, not noticed the French Ambassador, who stepped forward, saying, "Get out of here at once. I will see you tomorrow." The next day the man presented himself at M. Cousseran's office in his old Army uniform decked with medals and said, "My Ambassador, I have made a gaffe as big as my belly; I will never do such a thing again." But the Ambassador felt that an example should be made, and the man was expelled from the country. Strangely enough, this fellow was favorably known to us; he worked at the port where he had frequently gone out of his way to help us with our clearances. That he should have acted as he did is an evidence of the tension of these days in the French community in Libreville.

The next day when I called on the President to protest, he expressed his regrets, but with rather less feeling than I thought the event called for. He assured me that the authors of the outrage would be caught, but they were not. It was apparently not the moment for Léon Mba to criticize or apprehend Frenchmen.

Despite these shocks, I hoped that my relations with the President had not been basically affected, and I was shortly given evidence sustaining that hope. For some time we had had under option from the government one of the last available parcels of choice land on the shore boulevard, planning to use it eventually for a house for the Deputy Chief of Mission. One day we received a notice in the mail that the option had been forfeited because we had allegedly overlooked some formalities. On investigation I found that one of the President's former ministers, was using his influence to take the option away from us and secure the land for a French concern. He would, of course, do nicely in the deal. I laid the matter right on the line with the President, making it a personal issue as I had personally obtained his consent to our taking the option. The President overruled his friend and confirmed our rights. This was on March 19, a month after the coup.

But as time went on things changed. During the weeks after the elections in April the President allowed no callers. In June he began again to give a few audiences. Various members of the diplomatic corps were received by him, but to my dismay I found that I could not get an appointment. I telephoned his French secretary and was put off. I then wrote the President but received no reply. Remembering his previous kindness, I felt there must be some misunderstanding. I was at a loss to know what might have happened, or what the President's feelings toward me were.

I went to the Vice President, M. Yembit, with whom I had had so many friendly associations, and asked him to speak to the President and attempt to arrange an audience. When I saw the Vice President a week later, he said he had seen Léon Mba, who conveyed the impression that he had none but the kindest feelings and would see me soon. At about the same time a different light was thrown on the problem. At a reception I asked the President's administrative assistant, M. Pigot, a Frenchman with whom I enjoyed friendly relations and in whom I had confidence, what the difficulty was. He replied that the President had been deeply hurt by some articles by Russell Warren Howe appearing in the Washington *Post* and that he blamed me for them. I said that I had not even seen the articles and that the President should not take his anger out on me. Pigot replied that of course he realized this, but that the President regarded me as *"le chef de tous les Américains au Gabon"* ("the head of all the Americans in Gabon") and held me responsible.

After this the strains increased so that our once good life in Libreville became unpleasant. Little incidents constantly occurred. One day, driving home for lunch, I saw a small crowd of Gabonese, perhaps fifty or so, emerging into the Place

St. Anne. In the middle of the Place was an Army truck with black soldiers, Chadians I think. The French officer in command, Lieutenant Fredericks, had gotten out of the truck and was trying to prevent the Gabonese from coming into the square, pushing them and beating them over the shoulders and head with his truncheon. I knew Lieutenant Fredericks quite well, and earlier he had told me how fond he was of the Gabonese. So, driving into the Place, I slowed my car to a stop, thinking that it would be interesting to watch him expressing his affection. The Lieutenant kept shouting at the black soldiers in the truck to get down and help him. They were very slow in doing so, and he kept pushing and bashing away at the Gabonese by himself. After a couple of minutes I went on. I had been all the way over on the other side of the Place and did not get out of my car, but the next day the French community was buzzing, with considerable bitterness, with the story that Ambassador Darlington had interfered with a gendarme in the performance of his duties.

The Peace Corps also found itself involved despite constant effort on the part of both Volunteers and management to stay away from politics, even to the extent of never discussing political questions with either the Gabonese or the French.

One day I was in N'Dendé when the German Ambassador presented some radiology equipment for the dispensary at Lébamba. The ceremony took place in the main square of the town. There was a group of Peace Corps Volunteers in the crowd. M. Yembit, who was officiating, spied them and started praising their work. On and on he went, telling what fine fellows they were, and describing them at one point as *"les blancs qui travaillent,"* the whites who work. I could see from the faces of the French in the audience that this did not go down too well.

However, shortly afterward I was surprised to hear that M. Yembit was using the Peace Corps as a whipping boy in his campaign speeches. At Lébamba an American missionary who understood Ipounou, the language in which M. Yembit was speaking, heard him say that Gabon's political problems were being caused by the Americans, that the Peace Corps was responsible, and that in whatever country the Peace Corps went trouble followed. At this point his eye happened to fall on the missionary and he quickly changed the subject, obviously ashamed at being caught talking such nonsense. I heard, however, that he used this theme at a number of places, as did other government politicians. When I asked various Gabonese who were not government sympathizers the reason for such speeches, they invariably answered that the anti-American line was being pushed by the French. Jumping to the conclusion that the United States was trying to take Gabon away from them, they spread the story that the Peace Corps was an arm of the CIA and the agent of American subversion.

The story that the Americans were both anti-French and against the government of Léon Mba continued to grow despite our constant efforts to stop it. In one town the Peace Corps Volunteers saw that the French doctor who had been given the use of a new American Jeep had scratched off the U.S. AID emblem. In one of the schools in Libreville the French teachers threatened to walk out en masse unless a lone Peace Corps Volunteer, Muriel Plante, was removed. Léon Mba was on the point of ordering the girl expelled from the country (and in the American press was reported to have done so), but Colonel Wilkes and I succeeded in getting the Minister of Education, M. Nna Ekamkam, to persuade the President to reconsider.

Within the Palace the Peace Corps became an object of deep suspicion. One Sunday afternoon when two Volunteers stopped at the gates and inquired if they could see inside, the request was interpreted as a personal affront to the President. It took

Colonel Wilkes two weeks of calls and letters to quiet the matter down.

Out of touch with the country, where Volunteers were increasingly cheered, Léon Mba's distrust of the Peace Corps mounted. The twenty teachers who had come in the fall of 1963 had been a success; the French Inspecteur d'Académie, Marcel Vitte, took the lead in asking for more for the following fall. The Peace Corps agreed, and prepared a further twenty. But just a few weeks before they were to sail Léon Mba decided that they could not come. He openly stated that he feared the introduction of a group of teachers whose attitudes he could not control. So, to meet his minimum English-teaching needs, he got France to send him some young Army recruits. What they lacked in teaching skill they doubtless made up in discipline.

Our entire Leader Grant program for 1964 came to nought. Three Leader Grant visits to the United States were available to Gabon that year. Before the *coup d'état* Léon Mba had approved my recommendation to give them to three distinguished Gabonese, Jean Davin, François Méyé and Jacques Biyogho. After the coup the President advised me that they could still go if they wished. I urged them not to lose this marvelous opportunity, but although each had previously told me how much he would like to visit our country, all begged off.

One day late in April Mintsa Marcel,* who headed the

* Most Gabonese names in this book are written with what we would call the "given name," in this case "Marcel," placed first, but in some instances, as with Mintsa Marcel, the order is reversed. In the past the given name was often placed last, and many men were still addressed in this manner when we were in Gabon. In the case of each person we have used the order with which we were familiar. Gabonese custom was for a person to have but one name—not a family name, but a name that had been borne by some earlier member of the family, perhaps a grandfather. It was the French colonists who dubbed the Gabonese, men and women, with French given names, and it was natural at the start to tack these on *after* the Gabonese names.

164

winning list of deputies from the antigovernment Region of Woleu N'Tem, came to my office to say he hoped I would visit there again soon as I would "receive an ovation." While this was flattering, it was just what I did not need. Another morning the Subprefect of Mouila, Mézu Fabien, called. I said, "I am sorry not to invite you to lunch [as we did with many out-of-town visitors], but I am afraid that this might be dangerous for you." And I added, "How sad it is that things should have come to this pass in this country of which I am so fond." He replied, "Don't worry, you are loved throughout Gabon" ("*Vous êtes aimé partout au Gabon*"). That afternoon he was picked up by the gendarmes and locked up overnight.

Then one Sunday morning late in June, I received a cable from the Department saying that the Gabonese Ambassador in Washington, M. Aristide Issembé, had tried to give the Secretary of State a letter from Léon Mba addressed to President Johnson. In it the Gabonese President made several charges against me and asked that I be replaced by another ambassador. The Secretary, unwilling to give credence to charges against an ambassador of the United States, declined to accept the message.

Most of Léon Mba's charges, curiously enough, had nothing to do with me personally. One referred to critical articles in the American press; another concerned actions of some of my staff on the day of the revolution, actions which not only were quite proper but could hardly be laid at my door as I was out of town; another alleged incorrectly that one of the secretaries in the American Embassy in Paris had made some statement against the French intervention; another made an untrue accusation about our Air Attaché's plane. Only one of the accusations touched me directly: it was said that other members of the Embassy staff and I had been overfriendly with members of the Provisional Government prior to the *coup*

165

d'état. The irony of this was that most of these men then held high government positions.

Shut up in his Palace where he was protected by white French troops, the President had become a very isolated man. The Vice President, who in this period was carrying a large share of the responsibility for running the government, complained to me of the difficulties he was having in getting to the President. He told me that sometimes he had had to wait ten days after requesting an audience. The other ministers did not see Léon Mba at all. But he constantly had with him a few personal advisers, Gabonese and French, who fed his ego and encouraged him to blame his troubles on the United States. Some of the President's new French advisers were openly anti-American. These were men of quite a different stamp from the Frenchmen who had been at the President's side in the years immediately following independence. Moreover, the times had changed; the increasingly difficult attitude of General de Gaulle toward the United States was reflected by many colonial Frenchmen.

This little group around the President helped turn him against the United States and against me. They were not lacking in ammunition. There had been several critical news stories and articles in the American press, and I have no doubt that Léon Mba was wounded by Russell Howe's articles in the Washington *Post*. I later read these, as the President received them from the Gabonese Embassy in Washington, translated into impeccable French. The articles described some of the things that took place during the coup, the elections and the campaign, and they conformed essentially to my own knowledge and impressions. But they were hard-hitting and drew blood, as the truth can do. I immediately wrote to the President as nice a letter as I could, saying I regretted that our press had given him offense, but he was not mollified. I question whether the letter was allowed to reach him.

Also, this was a period of outrages against Negroes in Mississippi and other Southern states. Léon Mba, who earlier had shown understanding of our civil rights problems, now made them part of his anti-American campaign. Editorials and articles were printed in five consecutive numbers of Gabon's weekly paper, *L'Effort Gabonais,* painting the disturbances in the worst possible light and distorting the facts. When I tried to get the Minister of Information to stop the series, he indicated that he deplored the articles but could do nothing as the President had ordered them.

These developments go a considerable way toward explaining the President's attack on me, but they are not the whole story. The question remains, "What purpose was served by asking for the recall of the American Ambassador?" We believe that Léon Mba hoped he could overcome the adverse public opinion emerging after his restoration to power by blaming the coup on the United States, and particularly the American Ambassador. The story was already on the lips of most Frenchmen. It was made to order for his needs.

According to the propaganda, America coveted Gabon's natural resources and believed that if M. Aubame came to power he would hand the country over to the United States and turn the French out. If the United States was plotting to overthrown Léon Mba's government for its own ends, what could be more natural than that France, Gabon's good friend, should step in to defeat such sinister machinations? There is little doubt in my mind that Léon Mba shrewdly perceived that the more people he could convince of this theory, the stronger his position would be. And the best way to dramatize the issue was to force the United States to withdraw its Ambassador.

The various stories, mostly put out by the Presidency, took many forms, and some were quite amusing. One day Father Ledit, an assistant to the Bishop of Libreville, Monsignor

N'Dong, came to my office to show me a tract that had been circulated that morning. It accused the Bishop of trying to buy Deputy Amogho's vote for the opposition and said that the Bishop's money "came from the America of Darlington." Father Ledit said that the Bishop believed that the tract emanated from the Presidency and that it had been distributed by the police. Both the Bishop and I protested, and (would you believe it?) we heard that it had been written by the Frenchman to whom we had given the lift from Port-Gentil the night following the coup.

I must digress a minute to tell a story about Eugéne Amogho. When I arrived in 1961 he was a Minister. The President later dropped him from the Cabinet, but he turned up in the Provisional Government as Ministre de l'Agriculture et de l'Elévage, Eaux et Forêts, et Chasse (Agriculture, Stock Raising, Water, Forests and Hunting)—quite a portfolio! All of the members of the Provisional Government were promptly put in jail. But not Amogho. He was valued because of his strong tribal position in the Haut-Ogooué. The President needed his help. Notwithstanding the decree that anyone who had been in the Provisional Government could not run in the election, Amogho headed the Government's list of candidates in that Region. His list won, and in the new government following the elections he was made a Minister. He was an able and a forthright man. When I called on him to say good-bye, he had the courage to say that he regretted my leaving and added that, of course, the French had put the President up to it.

There were many other rumors about my antigovernment activities. The President told one of my colleagues that I had visited the homes of dissident students giving them each "new thousand-franc notes" ($4) to turn them against him. The Vice President told a group from the World Health Organization that he had "positive proof" that the United States Embassy had financed M. Aubame.

168

Similar stories burst out in Paris. Their wide circulation and persistence showed that they were not accidental. The Geneva newspaper, *La Suisse,* summed it up: "French commentators say that de Gaulle has proof of North American intervention in Gabon which quickly forced the French President to make the decision to send troops to reinstate the regime of Léon Mba." The American Ambassador in Paris, Mr. Charles E. Bohlen, on instructions, denied the allegations, but denials are back-page news; France had made its point.

Of course, much of the propaganda in Gabon against us was fabricated within the local French community. The colonial French are a special breed. Fiercely possessive, jealous, suspicious, many embittered by the defeats in Indo-China and Algeria, they are extremely sensitive about their former Black African possessions where they are still prospering. Gabon is not the first place where they have blamed their troubles on the Americans. Emotional, irrational—but human.

On a different plane are the actions of the French Government. What is done by calculation cannot be explained as the product of emotion. American ambassadors in a number of African countries found the official French representatives inclined to be suspicious, not infrequently uncooperative except in form, and watching for opportunities to be critical. Of more significance, in several African countries de Gaulle's government has been discovered, sometimes in little scheming ways and sometimes in ways not so little, to be working against the United States, to frustrate our policies and diminish our influence.

In Gabon in particular, the French resented U.S. Steel's large participation in manganese and Bethlehem Steel's 50 percent share in the iron ore. They were considerably disgruntled when Foley Brothers of Pleasantville, New York, obtained the contract from the World Bank to make the survey for Gabon's railroad, and they showed their jealousy of our Peace Corps by establishing a French equivalent and sending the first contingent to Lébamba, right in the area where our boys had been working.

That Paris had anything directly to do with my removal I doubt, but it is interesting that the French Government knew of it a good six weeks before it was anticipated in Libreville. A hint from them would have stopped it. One day the German Ambassador, Walter Bammer, who was always helpful, called personally on the French Ambassador, Paul Cousseran, to ask him to use his influence to put a halt to the wave of anti-Americanism in the French community, but nothing was done. I also noted that the next French Ambassador, François Simon de Quirielle, although professing personal friendship as did his wife for mine, did not lift a finger to scotch the anti-Darlington stories or to assist me in dealing with the problem. Ambassadors work on instructions.

After Léon Mba's first letter to President Johnson had been rejected, he sent off a second, stating the principle that any government has the right, without giving reasons, to refuse a particular foreign representative. This message caused the Department of State to summon me to Washington on consultation, and on July 26 I left Gabon. It was with a sad heart that I quit this little country of which I had grown so fond.

Among the many Gabonese and some French who expressed their regret was the Bishop of Libreville, Monsignor N'Dong. He told me that Léon Mba had also asked the Pope for his removal. The Pope replied, expressing the hope that all Christians would live together in love and charity, and ignored the request.

My wife, and our younger son Christopher who had come over for the summer, followed me in a fortnight. A few days before they left Christopher was talking to a staff member on the lawn in front of the Embassy. A Gabonese gardener was chopping dead fronds off one of the palms. All of a sudden a grenade dropped down at Christopher's feet out of the tree, where it had doubtless rested since March. It did not explode and was carried across the boulevard and put into the sea, a parting token from our friends.

Truly, we had come a long way from Lafayette!

XII

Epilogue

I WAS held in Washington on consultation for a year as Ambassador to Gabon. My Deputy Chief of Mission, Mr. William F. Courtney, acted as Chargé d'Affaires, a difficult assignment which he carried out with perceptiveness and skill. He was able to calm Léon Mba while avoiding the appearance of approving his repressive policies and at the same time maintaining some contacts with the suppressed liberal elements. During this period appeals came from President Léon Mba that my replacement be sent, but it was not until August, 1965, twelve months after our forced departure, that a new American Ambassador arrived in Libreville.

The long-awaited trial of the political prisoners took place at the end of August, 1964, at Lambaréné, an island where sympathizers of the accused could be kept out and demonstrations controlled. This was one of those exercises which police states go through for peculiar reasons of their own. On May 9 a decree was issued prohibiting any lawyer not a member of the Libreville bar from representing the accused. This forestalled any attempt by friends of M. Aubame in France to provide him with an attorney. There were no Gabonese attorneys, and the few French members of the Gabonese bar were government partisans.

Many people believed that the President wanted to have the prisoners executed, but the sentences were tempered, presumably on the insistence of the French Government. Even so, some were far from lenient. M. Aubame was given ten years of hard labor. His nephew, M. Eyéguet, who had been Gabon's Ambassador in London, was condemned to twenty years of the same. Others received light sentences, and some were acquitted. The judgments appeared to be a delicate balance of personal and political considerations. If there was any justice in the mix, it was not clearly apparent.

In the following months there was an orgy of arrests and beatings. A squad of thugs or gorillas (in French *"les gorilles"*) made up of foreigners—Fang from Spanish Guinea, Central Africans and Chadians—circulated through Libreville arresting anyone suspected of opposing the President. The victims often would be brought to the Palace where they were beaten, some even being taken into the President's office to be struck in his presence. Groups of these Gabonese would then be yolked together by the neck, and paraded through the streets to various places of business and even the foreign embassies, where they would proclaim their repentance. Women were not exempt from these indignities, and even one French citizen, Madame Boucat, was beaten and suffered such injuries that she lay for many days afterward in serious condition in the hospital. Another of the President's methods was to drive through the streets and set his "gorillas" on anyone who did not applaud.

The President was still protected by white troops provided by the French Government. By November the brutalities had reached a point where France apparently began to have reservations. A most interesting play then took place. The French Ambassador told the President that his government had decided that unless the outrages stopped, France might withdraw her troops. The President flew into a rage, shouted that the French Government was doing this because the Ambassador had made false reports, and said that he would take the next plane to Paris to lay his case directly before General de Gaulle, which he did. (There is a slightly different story of this incident, but this is the version that I believe is generally accepted.) What transpired between the two Presidents we do not know, but Léon Mba returned to Libreville and the French troops remained. Reports from Paris suggested that this was done "because the French had no one else." Doubtless this was true. Having supported Léon Mba so long, and having allowed him to do just as he pleased behind the shield of their power, France had no choice but to stick with him. François Simon de Quirielle soon was recalled and became the French representative in Hanoi.

It was only a few days after Léon Mba's return to Gabon that the "gorillas" assaulted one of the most beloved figures in the country, the ninety-four-year-old Abbé Walker, the first Gabonese to have become a priest. The Abbé, who had recently been made a Monsignor by the Pope, was knocked to the floor unconscious, and many of his books were destroyed. The French priest, Père Jacquard, respected head of the Collège Béssieux, was also attacked and beaten. In this way, Léon Mba lashed back at the Catholic Church, whose leaders in Gabon had opposed many of his practices.

Two years and more have passed and the situation has improved. The beatings and other brutalities have largely ceased, but French soldiers are still present, and Léon Mba's "gorillas," although less in evidence, still see to it that his critics keep their heads down. But the economy is booming. There is much new building in Libreville, prices have been stabilized, salaries have increased, money is circulating. Nearly all of this economic activity is related to foreign companies, and the progress is confined to the areas where they are. People from out in the country are being drawn increasingly into these sections, leaving the villages to stagnate. Still, the economic situation is good.

A number of the men who were out of favor with Léon Mba have been rehabilitated. But others still are in jail, and Aubame, now more than three years after the *coup d'état*, is held in solitary confinement on the Ile Perroquet. For a Gabonese, a people who depend so much on the society of their family and friends, solitary confinement is a terrible fate, and I understand that Aubame's suffering has caused some deterioration of his mental health. But Léon Mba can do as he pleases. In our times, which have known Babi Yar and Auschwitz, what does one individual matter? A sparrow falls on the ground.

Léon Mba governs Gabon now by telephone from Paris, where he is under medical treatment. Albert Bongo, who has been selected to succeed him as President, was the Director of Léon Mba's Cabinet, a civil servant, not a political figure. In fact, as a Bateké from the far southeast of the country, his tribal and geographic qualifications are not strong, but he represents a compromise in Libreville politics: close enough to the President, yet young enough—thirty-one—to be accepted by the younger ministers. In any event he is Léon Mba's choice and is acceptable to the French. He has shown skill in gathering support for himself and in the way he has administered the government during the President's long absences.

Poor Yembit, who had simply the appointive position of Vice President, was dumped, and it was arranged that Bongo be elected Vice President of the Republic, from which position he can succeed as President when Léon Mba resigns. The seven-year term for which Léon Mba was elected in 1961 would expire in February, 1968, but the Constitution was changed and the election advanced to March 19, 1967. The

175

BDG ticket with Léon Mba for President and Bongo for Vice President received 99.9 percent of the vote. In five of the nine Regions, including the Woleu N'Tem where the President's supporters lost so badly in 1964, the BDG got a full 100 percent, with not one dissenting vote!

The opposition within the country obviously could do nothing. Outside Gabon there is an opposition group which may well have contacts with the Communists in the Brazzaville Congo, Algeria and elsewhere. I do not know what their present importance is, but for the long run it should not be underestimated. When responsible opposition is suppressed, opportunities for more extreme elements are increased.

These matters at the start will not worry M. Bongo. French support will ensure that he is not disturbed by any internal dissent, and de Gaulle may be relied on to see to it that the dissidents outside Gabon's borders do not threaten France's supply of uranium. But Bongo will find that he cannot divorce himself from his generation and from the forces of nationalism in Africa. He will not be able to remain as responsive to French interests as Léon Mba. The gradual awakening of the Gabonese people will oblige him to loosen the bonds of foreign control. And if he is to retain power, I believe that he will have to conciliate and unite his country, as in fact he moved to do on April 18, 1967, when he announced clemency measures for a number of the political prisoners. His task will not be easy; I wish him well.

The relations of the American Embassy with the Léon Mba-Bongo Government now are good, and although periodically subject to tremors of suspicion, the French in Gabon also appear well satisfied with us. I hope that this state of affairs will continue, but without sacrificing our critical judgment or independence of thought.

We are familiar with police states in other parts of the world, particularly in Eastern Europe. American officials accept the conditions there as part of the established internal affairs of those nations. But the new countries of Africa, it seems to me, are different. In them I think that we should not accommodate ourselves to police states and antidemocratic methods—at least not quickly. And when the power to repress individuals and pervert democracy is supplied from outside, another dimension is added to the problem.

In the brief span of four years between January, 1963, and January, 1967, there have been fourteen *coups d'état.*

1. January 13, 1963: Togo. Sylvanus Olympio was murdered and the government seized by a Comité Insurrectionel (Revolutionary Committee) of which the Chief was Adjutant Chef (Chief Warrant Officer) Emmanuel Bodjolé.
2. August 15, 1963: Congo (Brazzaville). President Fulbert Youlou was deposed and the government seized by a civilian group led by Alphonse Massemba-Débat.
3. October, 1963: Dahomey. Hubert Maga was forced out and the government taken over by Colonel Christopher Soglo.
4. February 18, 1964: Gabon. President Léon Mba was deposed and the government seized by four lieutenants.
5. June 19, 1965: Algeria. President Ben Bella was spirited away and a new government took power headed by Colonel Houari Boumedienne.
6. November 25. 1965: Congo (Kinshasa). President Kasavubu was displaced by Lieutenant General Mobutu.
7. December 22, 1965: Dahomey. Colonel Soglo again took over, this time forcing out President Congacou, who on November 29 with Colonel Soglo's backing had ousted President Apithy and Prime Minister Ahomadegbe.

177

8. January 1, 1966: Central African Republic. President David Dacko was deposed and the government seized by Colonel Jean Bédel Bokassa.

9. January 3, 1966: Upper Volta. President Maurice Yaméogo was deposed and the government seized by Lieutenant Colonel Sangoulé Lamizana.

10. January 15-16, 1966: Nigeria. President Azikiwe and Prime Minister Sir Abubakar Tafara Balewa were deposed by a group of middle-rank officers, and Balewa, as well as the Premiers of two of the country's regions, was murdered. Power shortly was assumed by General Johnson T. U. Aguyi-Ironsi.

11. February 24, 1966: Ghana. President Nkrumah while out of the country was deposed by a combination of Army and police, the former headed by Lieutenant General J. Arthur Ankrah, the latter by the Commissioner of Police John Kofi Harlley, who then formed the National Liberation Council to organize a new government.

12. July 29, 1966: Nigeria. General Aguyi-Ironsi was killed and a government was formed by a military group headed by Colonel Yakuba Gowon.

13. November 28, 1966: Burundi. The 19-year-old Mwami Ntare V, who had deposed his father Mwambutsa IV on September 1, was in turn deposed while out of the country by Michel Micombero, the highest-ranking officer in the Burundi Army who was then the Prime Minister.

14. January 13, 1967: Togo. President Nicholas Grunitsky, who had been elected President by direct popular vote May, 1963, following the murder of Sylvanus Olympio (see No. 1), was turned out by Lieutenant Colonel Etienne Eyadema, Chief of Staff of the Togolese Army, who set up a National Reconciliation Committee headed by Colonel Marcel Dadjo.

This is quite a record. I have confined the list to coups where the incumbent chief of state was ousted and the government seized, but with a slightly wider definition I might have included earlier incidents in Burundi, when two Prime Ministers were murdered, and Uganda, where the Prime Minister, to forestall a coup, moved forcefully against his opposition.

The only state where an outside power intervened was Gabon. When Colonel Bokassa unseated David Dacko in the Central African Republic, I think that he may have been worried that France might reinstate Dacko, for he reportedly jumped into an open jeep and dashed past the Rock Hotel and the French Club yelling *"Vive la France!"* But de Gaulle, perhaps not having relished his experience in Gabon, let other revolts take their course.

Of the eleven countries where these coups took place, eight had been French colonies. I do not find this surprising. The root of much of the unrest has been the difficulty of securing change by democratic means. The young African states, particularly those with French backgrounds, have neither the institutions nor the traditions to enable them to limit the power or control the abuses of their leaders. When a leader becomes intolerable, the only course available has been to get rid of him by force. I admire young Africa for having citizens courageous enough to do this.

All but one of the fourteen were carried out by military men; they were the people who had the guns and who knew how to use them. They were able to give effective expression to their feelings, but they have generally found that it is easier to overturn a government than to run it, and that military training is not a complete education for a chief of state. I think, however, that it is fair to say of many of them that their profession, their military training, had developed in them a degree of dedication to their country so that when they saw conditions that were wrong they felt an obligation to set them right. A

179

growing number of Africans voiced disgust at the high personal expenditures of their government heads and ministers, anger at the widespread corruption, and dissatisfaction over the general mismanagement of public affairs, in particular the slow progress made in solving economic problems. The reactions toward the coups voiced by various Africans show that Africans want their governments to be democratic and their leaders honest. This is not naïve; it is an expression of basic rectitude and good sense.

Similar motives, at least at the outset, underlay the agonizing events in Nigeria, but there the situation was complicated by deep tribal problems: first Ibo resentment at Hausa dominance, then Hausa resentment that the better-educated Ibos held so many of the good jobs; and finally revenge.

In not a single case did influence from outside the country play a significant role. Neither Russian nor Chinese Communism had a noticeable hand in promoting any of the coups. In fact, the opposite could be observed: some of the coups were motivated in part by the fear that the existing governments were becoming too involved with the Chinese Communists. And the governments that assumed power in Dahomey in 1965, in the Central African Republic and in Ghana expelled Mao's representatives. The Chinese Communists, however, took quick advantage of the overthrow of Youlou in Brazzaville, and if they were not in such difficulties at home, they might now be able to exploit an opportunity in Burundi.

I do not want to imply that Communism has had no success and has no future in Africa. My judgment is that in African minds it is not a particularly important issue at present. More and more in Africa pragmatists are taking over, and they have their hands full seeking practical solutions to their countries' pressing problems and do not have much time or interest to devote to doctrines and ideologies. That is the reason, I think, why several governments which have flirted with the Communists have been thrown out; the Africans have recognized that these associations did little to cure their real difficulties.

Mao's Communism in Africa is presently in eclipse except perhaps in Tanzania and the Brazzaville Congo. Russian Communism is a different thing, for the Soviets have been making haste slowly, building quietly. Some eight thousand Africans are studying in the Soviet Union and Eastern Europe. While some have been repelled by the life they saw and have been turned away from Communism by their experiences, it must not be assumed that these are a large proportion. The great number of African students in France are also subject to Communist (and anti-American) indoctrination. Communism as a factor in Africa cannot be dismissed because of its relative lack of success to date.

I am not one of those who, reading about the African revolutions, holds up his hands in horror and proclaims that Africans are unable to govern themselves. On the contrary, I think the coups may suggest that Africans are determined to govern themselves. These early years of independence are not easy. Americans, from the vantage of our stable developed society, are often tempted to be critical of the new African states, but this is a mistake; the wise course is to be patient and understanding. This is the attitude of our government. When we encounter situations that for the moment seem intractable, we try to minimize the difficulties and work for a return to reason. There are serious problems in Africa, but progress is being made in many directions and, in my view, we should be thankful that African affairs are in as good shape as they are. I am optimistic about the future of these new nations.

PART TWO

by MRS. DARLINGTON

XIII

Opening a New Embassy and a New Life

W HEN I first heard that we were going to Gabon, I knew little more about the country than the Western Union operator who told me bluntly when I tried to send a cable to my husband: "There is no such place, Madam." I did know that it was on the Equator in West Africa, that it was where Dr. Albert Schweitzer lived and that one of the world's ugliest and most poisonous snakes was named the Gabon viper.

My husband left for his post late in September. I was to follow a few months later with such household effects as would give a personal touch to the Residence: books, pictures and *bibelots*. His letters so whetted my appetite for the adventure of this new life that as soon as I detected a faint cry of "help" in one of them I decided it was time for me to pack. Our children summed it up nicely: "He needs you and we don't. We love you, Ma, but we don't need you." I took a boat to France, spent a few days in Paris with old friends brushing up on my

French and meeting several people who had been in Libreville. Then I was off on a plane for Africa.

It was a brilliant night with full moon and millions of stars. In no time at all we had crossed the Mediterranean, then the Atlas mountains and were streaking across the Sahara Desert. Occasionally we flew over an oil station and the gas flares lit up the immense emptiness surrounding the few buildings. I did not once close my eyes. Between sips of champagne I tried to memorize the few words I had prepared in French in case I was asked to say something on arrival.

At 6 A.M. I changed planes in Douala in Cameroon. It was not quite daylight and as we breakfasted in the air-conditioned airport café the mists gradually rose. The sun got brighter and the dim forms of jungle trees along the landing strip took shape. The air was heavy and hot: everything steamed as did I. The final run to Libreville was made in a small plane, ventilated by an old-fashioned electric fan. Below was a velvety green carpet of treetops, laced by rivers and swamps. Occasionally we flew over a bit of open sea. There was no habitation of any kind until we approached the airport in Libreville. It was easy to see Charles, flanked by some Gabonese officials; there were no other planes and few other people in sight. (By the time we left Gabon this small field had been expanded to take Douglas jets and the simple houses replaced by a splendid modern terminal.) I was greeted politely by the officials, but not asked to say a word in either French or English. Then I was presented to the nine members of our Embassy and their wives, who came forward from the terrace to meet me. We had coffee on the terrace of the café while my luggage was assembled.

I remembered to shake hands with the chauffeur, Raphael, as I had been told that one does this with everyone and on all possible occasions in Africa. We got into the black Dodge and, with both flags flying (the United States flag on the right and the Ambassador's on the left) as this was considered an offi-

186

cial occasion, we drove slowly and solemnly into town. Charles pointed out the beaches, gray-blue water lapping lazily at the white sand, interesting specimens of trees, a picturesque African house, a group of brilliantly flowering bushes, but I confess I did not see much beauty in any of it at that time. Behind us the other staff cars were strung along, no one passing, as was correct.

At the main fork on the road from the airport, we turned left toward Kango. This is the only important route out of Libreville. It is the road leading to Lambaréné and the south, the only through road in the country. Our house was just short of Kilometer 5, the last house before the bush or open country. It was a pleasant, low-lying white building with a red tole or iron roof. Perched on a hill above the main road, it looked like a California split-level, not at all like an Embassy Residence. We bumped up the rocky driveway made of red laterite and stopped at the foot of a flight of broad gray stone steps where Blaise, the caretaker greeted us. A dozen or so workmen who were building a laundry room in the back of the house came forward to shake hands. Blaise took my bags while Charles showed me around. Certainly the location was splendid, as he had written. From the front terrace we looked out over the town to the harbor and the open sea. Other views were toward rolling country, open fields dotted with African huts, palms and huge sentinel trees. I would not have been at all surprised to see an elephant ambling across the skyline. The walls were of stone and white stucco partly covered with vines. There was a small cement apron on the front terrace where we would eventually have garden furniture. Just below the terrace lay a huge hole filled with dirty water which had been planned as a swimming pool and was being used by Blaise as his garbage dump for bottles and banana skins. Two fine old *manguiers* (mango trees) near the house and three *badamiers* (plane trees) gave the place a settled appearance.

Inside the house I was staggered by the amount of red-tiled floor space, the brilliance of the sun streaming in the many windows and double French doors, and the sparse quantity of rather unattractive furniture standing about ready to be placed. On the entrance level there was a large living-dining room area, kitchen, two bedrooms and bath. Down a flight of nine steps from a narrow balcony lined with empty bookcases, was another large room leading to an unpaved terrace overlooking the road winding south to Lambaréné. In the corner was a raised fireplace of heavy gray stones, most certainly for decorative purposes only, I thought as I mopped my tired face. The ceiling was twice as high as on the upper level. It was certainly going to be a challenge to make this house livable.

Our bedroom and bath opened off the balcony. The bathroom had a shower, but no tub and no shower curtain. The window faced the courtyard, where Blaise lived, and had no curtain either. The toilet was broken and there was but one towel rack. There were no curtains in the bedroom and but one armoire for clothes. Charles hastened to assure me that another one was being built and would soon be delivered. However, there were two beds, with clean sheets, and soon I was asleep to the comforting hum of the air conditioner. My first thought on waking was that I must do something at once about curtains: I could not dress crouching for long.

We lunched that first day with the Deputy Chief of Mission and his wife, Mr. and Mrs. Walker A. Diamanti, in their house on the shore boulevard. The food was delicious, the service by the Gabonese boy in his immaculate white uniform and shining gold buttons excellent, and the table settings impeccable. If such perfection could be achieved, then life in Libreville must be very charming indeed. From lunch we went to the Stadium to watch a soccer match. I was presented to an array of dignitaries and Gabonese ministers, one of whom was M. Avaro who paid me numerous gracious compliments in a resounding voice. Then we attended a reception by the French military at their mess nearby. More new faces and titles. I went to bed that first night in Gabon, numb.

The next morning Charles said he would fix breakfast; it was Sunday and Blaise was away—not that he could do anything in the kitchen in any case. When called, I sleepily went to the dining area and found the following menu: half an avocado, served with olive oil and hard round peppers, no salt, a heel of stale bread and two dark brown bananas. To drink, there was a bottle of Vittel water. No doubt at all but that I was needed! As I nibbled, I saw a small black figure dressed in white coming toward us across the front terrace. We asked him in to talk as we sat at table (something that was to happen often as we breakfasted, the French doors being open and people seeing us from the path below the terrace). He was looking for work as a cook, his name was Grégoire, he was a Bateké from Okondja beyond Franceville and he had worked as boy for a French Army officer. We liked his looks, hired him on the spot and he was with us the full three years of our stay. During that time he never once missed getting our breakfast, never once failed to show up for duty, never once got into any kind of serious trouble. He could cook for two or for fifty. We were lucky that he discovered us that first Sunday morning.

On my third day I saw to it that the stove was connected. We used bottled gas supplied by my husband's old firm, Mobil Oil. I also bought instant coffee, salt, sugar and a few more essentials. That evening we officiated at the opening of the new USIS building, the first American Cultural Center in Gabon. The President of the Republic and various ministers attended, along with all the leading people in town, the *"hautes personnalitées"* as the *Daily Bulletin* always described them. This meant not only government and diplomatic officials but religious leaders, and the heads of French businesses and banks. I heard Charles give a speech in French and was so moved with pride and so confused with the heat and the new faces that I almost fainted dead away. Luckily I was saved from disgrace by the Navy doctor attached to the Mobile Health Unit. He led me aside, said I must take salt pills until I got used to the climate and must, simply must, take a long siesta every afternoon if I was to keep healthy—advice I followed and was never ill from that time on. Champagne, whisky, beer and fruit juice were served by embassy wives and staff. There was a minor crisis when it was discovered that the plates of sandwiches were crawling with tiny ants, but these were quickly blown off and the party continued.

My next official duty was to call on Madame Pauline Mba, the No. 1 wife of the President. The hour was set for 4 P.M. on my fourth day. Joyce Diamanti lent me a hat, as I had brought none on the plane with me, and complete with white gloves, we presented ourselves at the Palace. Madame Pauline, as she was affectionately called, received us at the head of the stairs on the second floor of the building in a huge salon furnished with French tapestries, Louis XV chairs, marble-topped tables and Aubusson carpets. Brocade curtains hung from the high ceiling to the floor; thin window curtains billowed in the breeze from the sea. Madame Pauline was shy, but her French was clear and she asked about my trip and my family with all the poise in the world. She was dressed in a handsome silk print, high-heeled shoes and good jewelry. Madame Pigot, the wife of one of the French advisers to the President, signaled for champagne, cakes and cigarettes, which were brought by the butlers who were setting up a table in the dining section of the great room for the dinner to be held in our honor that evening.

I might just as well have saved myself the trouble I took in going to the hairdresser that morning. By the time I had finished with this official call, returned home and dressed for the formal dinner, my hair was nothing but a stringy mess. How

190

was I going to cope with an ever-wet head and damp hair, I wondered. At the dinner there were twenty-four guests. The French Ambassador and Madame Risterucci, and the Chargé d'Affaires of Nationalist China and Madame Leao filled out the complement of the Diplomatic Corps. Others were the Minister of Foreign Affairs and Madame Aubame, the Minister of National Economy and Madame Anguilé, the President of the National Assembly, M. Bigmann, as well as other officials with their wives. We went through seven courses. Everything was luxurious, from the linen, china and glass to the service, food and drink. Conversation was not easy for me as I sat between the President and M. Bigmann. I noticed that Madame Pauline, who sat across from her husband, watched everything he did with care. After the President gave a charming toast of welcome and Charles had responded, we retired to the Louis XV chairs for coffee and liqueurs, the women grouped around Madame Pauline and the men around the President. I was surprised to hear Madame Risterucci tell Madame Pauline that she thought the house looked quite well, that she approved of certain changes which had been made. Then she went on to tell an amusing story of her trouble with snakes coming up the stairs in the days she and her husband had lived there. When Gabon was still a colony this had been the Governor's residence and M. Risterucci had been the last Governor. It was no more than a large villa, but now as the residence of the President it had become the "Palace."

At 11:15 Charles gave me the signal to take my leave. At once everyone stood up and the party was over. It had begun to rain, and as we went out the door, sheets of water swirled around us. I had never seen anything like it. In the short walk from the car to our house we were soaked; the umbrellas had done no good at all.

It had been a busy four days. Now we had to fly south to Port-Gentil, the large seaport where we were to welcome the three U.S. ships that formed the project Amity III. They were already in harbor when we arrived, so we rushed to change our clothes and go on board. Captain Allendorfer was the commander of the group of two destroyers and one supply ship that had been visiting South and West Africa on goodwill missions. Charles was "piped" aboard and an honor guard stood at attention as he was greeted by the two captains and their officers. The men were in gleaming white, with gold *fourragères* on shoulders, a very handsome sight. Captain Allendorfer had broken his arm in South Africa so was inconvenienced by a cast, but not much. He managed to make official calls with us, carrying his dress sword, managed to drink his share of ceremonial champagne, and to dance a terrific Charleston at the reception we gave later that night. For four days we visited hospitals, schools, churches, convents and factories. In between times the American crews played soccer and basketball with the Gabonese. What impressed the Gabonese most was the jazz band from the S.S. *Forrest Sherman*. That they loved, and how they danced to it!

On our last evening we dined quietly in the apartment of Ondo Bonjean with his French wife and three friends. Ondo was the Subprefect of Port-Gentil under the French Prefect. Charles had told Ondo that he had heard something about the reputedly leftist Association of Gabonese Students in Paris and said he hoped that he could meet some Gabonese who had been members of it. Ondo said that he had been a member and invited Charles to dinner to meet some of his friends who had also belonged to it. We went and had a delightful evening. Madame had prepared Gabonese specialties for us. The hearts of palm and chicken with peanuts were good, but I could barely swallow the manioc and the plantain, a huge banana hard as cement even though cooked. After dinner Charles and Willie Jones drew out the men and listened to them discuss the future of Gabon. They were loyal to France and grateful for all it had done for them; French culture was theirs. But I remember so well one of them saying, "But does that mean we can have only France as our friend? Can we not have other windows to the world? If not, what good is independence? We might as well still be a colony." They did not seem any more left-wing than some tame New Dealers.

We returned to Libreville on the destroyer, and the crew had a fine time initiating us into the mysteries of King Neptune's court as we crossed the Equator. Charles was transferred from one ship to the other in a breeches buoy, full steam ahead, an exciting operation. Even as he descended to the deck of the other ship in the fragile little basket, the honor guard formed to receive him. He took the salute looking anything but ambassadorial in his spray-stained khakis and ill-fitting Mae West life jacket. We benefited from the fact that the ships were on the home run; Captain Allendorfer gave us an aluminum-foil Christmas tree six feet tall and collapsible, and allowed us to buy turkeys and cranberry sauce from the ships' stores for the Embassy staff Christmas dinner.

My first week was over. I had made an adjustment to the constant heat and humidity; I had learned something about my duties as an ambassador's wife and my French was beginning to come more easily. I began to feel some confidence that I could do what I had to do.

Back in Libreville it was time to get down to business with the house. There were boxes of government china, glass and silverware to unpack and put away. Cupboards had to be built for the kitchen. The furniture had to be arranged. I spent days trying to get the proper placement of tables, lamps and chairs. Electricity was a sometime thing as we had our own "group," or small diesel motor, giving us power for the air conditioner, lights and the water pump. The machine was located in a hut at the bottom of the drive. Whenever Blaise forgot to fill it with gas-oil the power went off. When we woke up stifling in the middle of the night, we knew "it" had happened again. Town power was slowly being brought toward us from the city. We eagerly watched the erection of the cement poles which would carry the lines and estimated that they would get to the house in about three months, which they did.

I was determined to have curtains, feeling all too exposed by the large windows and double French doors. During the day these were all open to the sun and the air; also to an occasional chicken, land crab or snake. But at night we closed up tightly and then the empty panes were unfriendly. I found some heavy plain material in town, Blaise rented a hand-operated Singer machine and between us we got the whole place curtained. As there was a shortage of curtain rings, I made my own from packing-case wire. What a joy it was to have some of the glare cut down during the day and to be able to sit, read and undress in privacy at night.

Our few trees were not close enough to the house to give any shade, so I ordered awnings, which were installed after six months, and only then because Charles threatened to complain of the delay to the Foreign Office and I to the President's wife who was coming to tea. Actually the last one was in place only a few hours before Madame Mba arrived. The awnings not only made it unnecessary to wear dark glasses in the house, but kept out most of the rain which had until then periodically inundated us. Even with every window and door tightly shut, floors would sometimes be awash, the wind driving the water through any little crack.

The outside of the house began to look quite decent. Blaise got the grass under control with his machete. We uncovered attractive flagstones and two flights of stone steps leading to the lower terrace. As the ragged growth was cleared away from the house, the bugs gradually retreated. At first it was impossible to sit outside at dusk, the worst time for mosquitoes and "*fouroux*," an invisible wretch that raises red itchy bumps. During the day I fought a constant battle against all manner of creepy-crawlies in the house: ants, cockroaches the size of mice (Grégoire used to pick them up by their whiskers), thousand-legged worms and scorpions. But as we cleaned, cut and sprayed, insect life diminished. Of course, the house lizards did their share. Periodically the boys would kill small snakes near the house, and such a to-do as they made about it. During three years we had snakes in the house only four times, but twice they were found in our bedroom. For a while, we had a huge lizard living in the attic; it flopped around at night making a horrid noise. One day it came out of the attic ventilator, down the vine-covered walls and was killed by the boys; it measured two and a half feet.

Blaise was trained not to throw garbage into the water hole in front of the house. Later we had it drained and a cement reservoir constructed to hold rain from the roof, which became the source of our water. A laundry, plus servants' shower and toilet, were built in back of the house next to the one-room hut already there. For over a month Gabonese workmen arrived daily at 7:00 A.M. and stayed on the property until 3:00 P.M. They finally finished the simple structure, and it was bliss to have the place to ourselves. To watch them work was maddening for they moved so slowly and talked incessantly, talking being the great African pastime. Every day or so the French contractor would arrive and yell at them for what they were doing wrong. I used to dread his visits, as his manner and language made me cringe; but the Gabonese accepted him quite calmly and with no change of expression set about to undo what they had just done. The construction of this simple building went like this: a cement box was made first; when this was up, spaces for doors and windows were hacked out; but as the door and window frames would not fit into the holes on the first try, more cement was hacked away; when the frames finally were placed, cement was bunged in to fill the gaps; finally the whole thing was whitewashed.

Probably never again will I enjoy such a sense of accomplishment as I had in getting that house in order. When, after endless calls and weeks of waiting, the plumber installed a new toilet seat and a towel rack in the bathroom, I was as pleased as a child over a new bicycle. Garden furniture which had been on order for six months arrived and we no longer had to lug dining room chairs outside to watch the sunset, the linesmen installed the last pole bringing electricity to our house, a proper metal flagpole replaced our bent bamboo one—these were triumphs of modern living!

Once we were settled, I found that marketing occupied nearly all of the morning. Everything we ate, with the exception of avocados, pineapples and bananas, was imported from France, Chad or Cameroon. Every two or three weeks a ship would stop at Libreville, notice of its arrival and the merchandise aboard having been posted in each store. Housewives could then leave an order for so many kilos of this and that, these orders to be filled before there was any sale to the public. Until I caught onto the system I was furious when I found the stores closed and was told that they were making up the "advance" orders. When the doors opened at last, only the bob ends of carrots, beets, cabbages and shallots were left. Canned goods were usually plentiful and hideously expensive —$1.25, for instance, for a can of string beans. Some fruits and vegetables were flown in weekly from France, beautiful lettuce and endive, at $2.00 a pound. We used to run from store to store in search of parsley or garlic! Beef came from Chad or Cameroon. It was cheap and good. Veal and chickens were from France, delicious but expensive: $3.00 for a tiny chicken; veal $1.50 a pound. There were queer shortages. At one time there were no potatoes in Libreville for six weeks; at another, no rice; once no sugar for a month; sometimes no mustard, or no salt. We periodically were short on onions.

There were only four main stores, all French owned and run. Their managers did all the importing. One met everyone in town over the market basket. We brought our own, of course, plus an empty bottle for peanut oil and an old newspaper for fish. The fish market was open only two or three times a week and then it was besieged by hundreds of Gabonese women who would wait for hours to get inside. There was never more than one Frenchwoman serving behind the counter. As fish was cheap and good in Gabon and as Charles loves it, I had to find a way to supply our house. One could be trampled underfoot by the good-natured but determined Gabonese, to say nothing of fainting with the heat at the same time. I learned to call the manager to find out when his next boat would arrive. Then Charles and I would present ourselves at the port before seven in the morning and buy as much as we could put into the freezer.

In the beginning all the clerks in these stores were Frenchwomen, and a ruder lot I never saw. They knew they could dispose of everything in the place without even trying and did not bother to attract trade by being pleasant or accommodating. Of course there were a few exceptions. By the time we left there were many more Gabonese behind the counters, but unfortunately they adopted the bad manners of their French predecessors. Altogether shopping was a most frustrating experience.

Once while I was waiting to be served two French nuns entered the store followed by a young Gabonese girl of about fourteen, a stocky little thing about my size. The nuns bought a crate of machetes—there must have been fifty of them with their heavy iron blades and large wooden handles. How to get the box out to the bus they were driving? The French salesman tried to push the crate to the door but could not budge it. While

197

he and the nuns argued heatedly, the young girl, with a brusque gesture, pushed them aside, made a kind of swivel motion with her arms and hips and in a flash the crate was on her *head*. She walked proudly out of the door, neck quivering a bit with the weight, but her face and manner triumphant.

There were a number of small shops in the outlying districts of the city run by Gabonese who obtained their merchandise from the French importing houses. Some of these stores, no more really than one front room in a wooden hut, had amusing names. One was called simply "Ambiance" or "Atmosphere," another "Au Petit Progrès" ("At the Little Progress"). One of the most popular bistros in town was the "Chasse Cafards" or "Chase the Blues"—a place that did a roaring business in just that, every night. All the buses and most of the taxis had names painted on their sides or printed in the rear window. There was "Ray of Hope," "Courage," "God Measures the Wind," "Venus My Love," "Thank God," "The Archangel Michael" and "God Alone Suffices."

The three local markets were uninteresting. It was a disgrace that Libreville did not have one clean, airy building where decent vegetables and fruits could be sold. At the small open market on the harbor one could buy shoelaces, cheap enamel cooking utensils, lengths of cotton or *"pagnes"* printed in Europe for the African trade, strips of tobacco and occasionally onions. Dahomians ran the place. In the covered market at Nombakélé, built during our first year, one could find dried fish from Mauritania, bananas, chili, peppers, manioc and the inevitable cooking utensils and *pagnes,* with cheap jewelry and odd bits of clothing. The place was dirty and stifling hot, having been built with no attention to ventilation, cleanliness or the proper arrangement of space. Mont Bouët's market was a higgledy-piggledy array of stalls, some covered with pieces of tole or odd bits of lumber. A good blow and the place tumbled down, to be rebuilt the next day when the storm was over. I used to buy bananas and chili there. It had nothing else available for our table. It was a meeting place for the people in the area as well as a market, and carried the same array of cheap cottons, utensils and local produce. One never saw piles of pineapples or avocados, both delicious in Gabon. We had these only because of the children who came to our door selling them. The staff at the Embassy living in quarters in the city rarely could get them except through us.

The skimpiness of the markets did not shock me until I visited other African countries and saw how exciting, colorful and useful they could be. Bangui's was bursting with delicious vegetables, meat and fish; Abidjan's was fascinating in every way, partly open, partly covered, with stalls for a large variety of produce from flowers to cooked eels.

Once I had mastered the details of everyday living, I began to feel a little at loose ends. In the United States I had always had a volunteer job. For years I had worked at Memorial Hospital as a nurse's aid, committee member and board member, and with the United Hospital Fund. Surely the one hospital here in Libreville could use me. I visited the wards one day when our boy Blaise was a patient, taking him food as was the custom since only private patients were given meals. There were lines of Gabonese standing outside doctors' offices, outside the pharmacy, outside the admissions office, outside clinics. There was obviously a great need for volunteer help. I tried the children's clinic, run by a young French woman doctor, sister of the Director General of the hospital. She showed me as much of her department as she could, her time being very limited as she had to do practically everything herself from examinations to record-keeping. She had only one trained assistant. When I offered to help her, she looked at me coolly, saying that she needed no one, her staff was quite sufficient. She had no idea, I am sure, how dependable American women can be in a hospital on a volunteer basis. In discussing my rebuff with a Frenchwoman who had lived many years in Gabon I was told that the hospital people must have thought that I was either trying to take away their jobs or acting as a spy. Service to others for its own sake was an idea they could not grasp.

For several weeks I worked with the Mobile Health Unit which our government had given to Gabon on its independence. With the unit came a U.S. Navy doctor, who was to stay for three months to train a staff of Gabonese to operate the heavy and technically perfect medical truck. He had not been able to secure a driver or the services of a nurse in several weeks. He went out alone but was worried that after his departure the unit would cease to be used. I went with him several times, helping to get the children ready for their brief examinations after school. When it was known that I was doing this, a nurse was quickly supplied. One day I even drove the unit through the main street to its garage in the hospital grounds, thereby causing a near riot at the Ministry of Health. When the naval doctor left, he begged me to keep an eye on the unit. I did. It stayed in the hospital without moving for almost a year. Because it came from the United States the French who ran the hospital found fault with it. After much prodding by officials of the United Nations Health Organization and our own AID staff, it was finally made operable again and put to work in the outlying parts of Libreville.

Since I had also worked in the field of education, as president of the local school board and as a member of the Metropolitan Opera Guild Board in charge of education, I next tried the Libreville schools. The French Director of Education was out of town, so I made arrangements with the Inspector of Primary Education to visit some schools one morning. I was shown all the primary schools in town. The two large ones near the center had French teachers; those in the poorer quarters, Gabonese. The Inspector was pleased at my interest and proud

200

to show me what was being accomplished. But when the Director returned, what a to-do there was! The Inspector was berated for having taken me on the tour without prior permission. Both Charles and I had to call on the Director to make peace for the Inspector and for ourselves. It was quite evident that the French system had no place in it for volunteers, least of all Americans. Any books we could donate to their libraries or to their English students as prizes would be welcome. But that was all.

The Chief of Protocol set up an evening English class for young government employees, the police and military. The teachers were Madame Voisin, the Scottish wife of the agricultural adviser; René Wadlow, a young American on a study grant; and myself. The French-English grammars the pupils were given were incredibly old-fashioned. For example, one exercise read: First boy (at dance): "Why are you not dancing with Cécile this evening?" Second boy: "Because she smokes and I am afraid that she might set fire to my celluloid collar." We took turns taking the classes, which only lasted three months. By then the English instruction at USIS was in full swing with a professional teacher and our makeshift affair came to an end. Until I left, however, certain of my pupils always greeted me warmly with their few words of English when we met in the post office or on the street.

Only at the little Protestant school in Baraka founded by American missionaries did I feel I could be useful without running into political complications. Embassy wives and later wives of American engineers working for SOMIFER and Foley Brothers contributed and made clothing for the children. Mrs. Bertram Saymon, wife of the AID Director, made about thirty mattress covers for their straw pallets as well as scrapbooks with bright illustrations cut from old magazines. We also collected used toys from the children in the Embassy. At the mission there was not one single article for the kindergarten: not a crayon, not a toy, not a block, not a ball. Each child had a chair and was to sit in it until told to do otherwise. Here was a place where we could use our volunteer zeal. But looking back I feel that we did not do enough; I did not push hard enough. I was afraid to "organize" in a country in which I was a guest and where so many relationships were so sensitive.

Performing my official duties kept me busy enough. There were calls to make, receptions and openings to attend, dedications to make. This was part of our job, and we felt it was important to be present at each occasion to which we were asked.

The President entertained frequently during our first year in Gabon. He gave a particularly beautiful reception celebrating the New Year in 1962, to which about five hundred people came, women in long evening dresses and men in black ties. The gardens around the palace were illuminated, and filled with small white-clothed tables. The guard of honor, with long red cloaks, stood swords in hand as the guests filed up the broad avenue of trees to pay their respects to the President and Madame Mba. A full menu from canapés to ices with proper wines and champagne was served by the boys from private houses. The *Daily Bulletin* had announced that any householder with a properly trained and uniformed boy should register him for duty. Our Grégoire was there, running about like mad earning his 700 francs and seeing the great world. There was dancing opened by the two ambassadors, the French Ambassador with Madame Pauline and Charles with the French Ambassador's wife. I followed with the Foreign Minister. Gabonese love to dance and do it extremely well, especially the new fast dances and their own brand of rock-and-roll.

There were dinners and luncheons at the Palace and occasionally a huge reception at La Péyrie, the city park. The Vice President entertained by giving cocktail parties in his house and garden on the main street of town. He usually had a small orchestra playing loudly. Townspeople lined the streets to watch. We used to have to push through crowds outside the gates to reach our car after any formal event. No one was ever rude to us, but the gendarmes had to put up with a great deal of pushing and shouting at the gates.

From time to time Madame Pauline announced an "At Home" in the *Daily Bulletin.* Anyone who wanted to call on her should telephone the Palace and be listed. The first time I went was on a boiling-hot afternoon, taking with me the other women in our Embassy. We all wore hats and gloves at Madame Pauline's request. There were about seventy women present in the huge salon, sitting around the marble-topped tables, Gabonese together, French together. There was hardly a sound in the room. I spied a vacant chair next to a Gabonese, sat down and tried to make conversation. Impossible. No one wanted to or would talk. Everyone was quite happy just sitting, drinking fruit juice, whisky or champagne. The only movement was that of the hand fans, and the serving boys bringing refills or cakes. We Americans do not like silences; and I kept exhausting myself to no purpose. Later I learned not to force the conversational pace.

Only one or two of the ministers entertained in their homes. When they did, the food was delicious with at least one Gabonese specialty. The French entertained constantly. There was indeed a hectic four-month "season" in Libreville from January through April when those in the social swim went to a luncheon, cocktail or dinner almost daily. These were chiefly all-French affairs, with Gabonese rarely attending. Dinners were given for us by all the leading French officials and businessmen. In spite of the difficulty of securing food, the menus were uniformly excellent but the service spotty. In only one French house in Libreville did I see anything of value or beauty; the majority of the French looked upon life in Gabon as a kind of camping out, something to be got through, pleasant though it might be, until time for the next home leave. Their furniture was mostly local carpentry work, china of the simplest variety, no fine linen or silver or crystal, no interesting *bibelots* unless they were African masks or spears, no pictures, no books. It was as though these families had left behind them in France every treasure of the heart and mind.

I had been noting with interest every detail of the entertaining done by the Gabonese and the French; now it was time for us to show what we could do. The electricity had reached the house and our wiring been converted; I no longer needed to worry that the lights would fail. Our engraved invitation cards arrived and were dispatched to a guest list of about 250. The day of the reception I was kept running all morning getting the necessary amount of ice to cool the necessary number of bottles, fetching it from the ice factory at the port in our own tubs. There were hundreds of details to attend to and, while the boys were willing and working hard, they did not know how Americans wanted things done. After lunch our water ran out, and a supply had to be trucked out from town. Rain fell briefly on the terrace furniture, which had to be mopped up; cigarettes had to be replaced. But in the end we managed to present ourselves at the top of the steps just at 6:30 when the first guests arrived.

President Mba and his wife came at seven, the sirens of his motorcycle escort announcing his party as it drove from town. The day was the President's sixtieth birthday, so we presented him with a handsome book of pictures of the United States, played the Gabonese, American and French national anthems from records over a loud-speaker, and Charles proposed a toast. Madame Pauline wanted to visit the whole house as she had never been in an American home. The French were curious to see what had been done to the place, known to many of them when Jean-Claude Brouillet, who had built it, lived there. Everyone came and wandered around the house and terrace. The popcorn, raw carrots and cauliflower with mayonnaise and the peanut butter and bacon canapés were successful American specialties.

Two hundred and fifty guests seemed a lot of people at that first party. I was exhausted from seeing that canapés and drinks were passed quickly enough, and from running back and forth across the terrace and down the steps to meet or say good-bye to distinguished guests. As time went on we got used to the system under which we had to get things done, but any party was quite a physical effort all the same. Our terrace made a fine setting. We had kerosene flares on the walls, which kept away the bugs and made the top of our hill look festive. It only rained once, very lightly, during the many receptions we held in the course of our three years, and then there was plenty of room inside the rambling house.

When we tried our first formal dinner party, things did not go very well. I wanted to display the government china, crystal, silver and linen to best advantage with our newly arrived pictures and personal table decorations. With great care I set the table and instructed Jean, a new boy, how to serve each course, pour the water and wine and bring in the separate courses with the proper plates. It was all in vain. During the afternoon he, the cook and the gardener disappeared into town, where they had several beers and only turned up just in time to get the dinner on the table. Our guests were two Gabonese ministers and their wives, the British Ambassador to Gabon, who resided in Brazzaville, and a British woman. As things went from bad to worse and Jean all but spilt the meat course, they whispered to me, "Don't worry, things like this happen to all of us in Africa," and "This is the best floor show I ever saw." Not exactly comforting words, however. The Gabonese did not notice anything amiss as far as one could see, even though I periodically had to go out on the terrace to bring Jean back to his duty at the table. Since there were no French present, the brilliant young Minister of Education, Jean-Marc Ekoh, was holding forth on his theories of education for Gabon. He was so interested in what he was saying he barely ate his food. When it was time to offer cold beer before their departure, there was none on hand: Jean had drunk every bottle. Charles took Jean home as soon as the guests had left. I stumbled toward our room and encountered a four-foot mustard-colored snake crawling up the steps from the living room. I yelled for Grégoire and Blaise, who came rushing with their machetes to kill it. This was the climax to a very disturbed evening. We fired Jean on the spot.

We did have other mishaps with guests. The first time the new French Ambassador and wife dined with us, a large portion of *boeuf bourguignon* sauce sluiced down her back as the boy tipped the platter the wrong way while serving her. But in time we worked out a system for entertaining that was fairly foolproof. Luncheons were always pleasant as the house was at its best at midday, with the lovely view over Libreville and the sparkling estuary and the strong light cut by the awnings. Evening receptions were always fine too because of the sea breeze on the terrace, and the bars and food tables were easily accessible just inside the wide doors. Formal dinners were the most difficult because then we tried to mix French, Gabonese and Americans. Conversation was usually adequate during cocktails on the terrace, the men and women talking in separate groups. At table all usually went well too, but afterward there was apt to be a sticky time until we adopted the practice of showing USIS films on the terrace. The guests liked them, as did our Gabonese neighbors.

In the spring of our first year I had an idea which turned out to be brilliant. Why not give a reception in honor of the National Assembly, which was then in session in Libreville? The President of the Assembly and President Léon Mba approved, invitations went to the sixty-seven deputies and their wives (two of the deputies were women), the Diplomatic Corps, the members of the Cabinet and other important people in town. Most of the deputies had never been to a diplomatic function of any kind as they came from all over the country.

We arranged transport from the Assembly Hall by using all the Embassy cars. Every deputy came, but that first time only a few brought their wives. The following year, however, over half came with wives. Shortly after this second occasion the President gave a luncheon for the deputies, the first time he had entertained them as a group. In the course of his remarks he turned toward my husband and complimented us for having traveled widely in the country and he urged the other ambassadors to follow our example.

An ambassador's wife must give entertaining the important place it deserves in the life of the embassy. I would have had a sad time indeed if I had not enjoyed having unexpected guests for lunch or dinner frequently and planned parties on an average of twice a week. We felt the house with its lovely location was there to be used, was there to help us interpret America to the Gabonese and French. I learned to cope with small numbers and large, with uninvited guests and with late arrivals. I got the ice and bottle-cooling business down to a science as well as menus, supplies and the hiring and training of extra boys. We loved having the members of our staff to parties of various kinds and tried to make our house a home for them. We enjoyed having the first contingent of the Peace Corps Volunteers for a buffet supper the night after they arrived in Gabon. After this we made certain to entertain the succeeding groups and had a Christmas party and dance for them all; it was just the house for such occasions.

It gave me great satisfaction to be given a difficult entertainment assignment and then to carry it off successfully. The hardest was when Governor Williams and his party of three from Washington plus the American Ambassadors from Congo

(Kinshasa), Congo (Brazzaville), Chad, the Central African Republic and Cameroon, and the Consul General from Angola spent three nights and two days in Libreville, the Governor staying with us. The physical work was nothing compared to the planning that was necessary for this group of distinguished people: Charles had their work schedule to put together; I had their food and drink to worry about. On Friday of their arrival we gave a formal dinner. On Saturday everyone attended the dedication of three Peace Corps schools at various locations outside Libreville, returning to our house with the Gabonese and diplomatic officials who had been invited for lunch. There were ninety, not counting a few embassy wives who helped me at the buffet tables. I managed to seat everyone inside the house and in the shade just outside the downstairs living room. I had borrowed extra plates, silver, glasses, napkins and tablecloths from everyone in the American community and from one of the hotels. The tricky thing about the lunch was that I had no idea how many to expect: it could have been fifty or ninety; luckily I took a chance on the larger figure, but when the meal was over there was not one piece of bread, one slice of meat, one bottle of wine left over.

The next day, Sunday, we held a reception at noon at the new Embassy, marking its opening, the visit of Governor Williams and his party and the celebration of our Independence Day, as the Fourth of July was only a couple of days away. We had decorated the building with flags, made tables out of desks by covering them with my tablecloths and sheets, and every embassy wife had prepared a set number of canapés; single girls were let off with making popcorn. We even borrowed the official red carpet from the Chief of Protocol for the occasion. There were four hundred guests, including President Léon Mba and all his Cabinet. Our receiving line with the Governor, the ambassadors and the attachés was an impressive sight. Although the President had said beforehand that he was too tired to give a speech, he stepped to the microphone at my husband's urging and gave a very gracious extemporaneous talk. Outrages against the Negroes in our South were then much in the news and were of deep concern to Africans. President Léon Mba went out of his way to say that he had confidence that the government of the great United States would find an acceptable solution to this problem. At that time it would have seemed unbelievable that a year hence he would be playing up our civil rights troubles and using them against us. However, that lay in the future, and on this day our Embassy was opened in an atmosphere of general goodwill to the tinkle of many glasses. It was a fine party.

That evening we had forty for a buffet supper at the house. The next day the guests departed. Every event had gone well.

Our recreation from official duties was the beach. There were miles of white sand stretching from the port in town out toward Cap Estérias. It took us no more than fifteen minutes to get there from our house, park the car and plunge in. There were fine palm and *badamier* trees lining the shore. These were fast disappearing due to the heavy tides and the constant taking of the sand for construction purposes. During the three years we were there we saw one fine tree after another undermined and finally destroyed by this double erosion. Charles' ire as a former Park Commissioner in New York State was aroused at this destruction of the fine beach, and he waged a gallant fight against the trucks which came at low tide to carry away the precious sand. He made some progress, too, by insisting that Gabon's attraction for tourists would be weakened if the beach was spoiled. Finally the Council of Ministers prohibited trucks in the area.

Of course there was no enforcement of this edict in the way of beach patrols, nothing but an *"Interdit"* sign. Charles, however, took it all very seriously. Whenever he saw a truck roaring down the beach full of sand making for an exit to the paved

209

road, he would rush out of the water waving his arms, and if he reached the truck in time he would ask the driver his name, his employer and so on. The Gabonese became very much aware of him, and I have seen drivers start down the beach, see Charles and turn their trucks around in a hurry. When we left we had given up the fight because one day when Charles said to a driver that he would report him to the Mayor of Libreville, the answer was, "But, Mr. Ambassador, these trucks belong to the town; they are sent here by the Mayor himself!"

The water was always very warm. I am sure that I perspired while swimming. It was clean, sometimes very blue, and safe as long as one did not swim out any distance. Sharks were often seen and caught in the middle of the estuary. There was a small marina where the French kept many small boats, mostly motor. The sailing was tricky, with sudden squalls that could be fatal.

The beach was unique in one way—its logs. These were huge trunks of *okoumé,* a soft wood that floated. They were always changing their positions as the tides rolled them about. They had been swept onto the Libreville beaches during World War II. The foresters had floated the logs from interior camps down the Como River and its tributaries to Owendo, the port in the Gabon Estuary, to be picked up there by freighters. With the fall of France, no more ships came to Gabon and the logs already waiting gradually broke free from their cables and were washed ashore all along this part of the coast. They made splendid back rests and picnic tables!

We also went to church fairly often, usually to the Baraka Mission in Glass founded by American missionaries. The church building was put up in the 1850's of boards sawed to measure in the United States. Because it stands on stone pillars about four feet off the ground, it has been preserved from termites and damp. In the graveyard, mostly hidden by brambles and underbrush, are many fine gravestones of Vermont marble, some standing five feet. The inscriptions are still easily legible, and what a story they tell of courage, loneliness and early death, for this was the "dread malarial coast." Many of the Americans did not long survive, but they kept on coming. There is one old woman living near the church who still speaks a few words of English, learned from an American missionary years and years ago.

Attending church meant shaking the hands of all the congregation, for the early American association is still much alive in their minds. Both the text and sermon were given in three languages, French, Miené and Fang. One day we sat in complete silence for forty minutes waiting for the pastor who had been conducting a service at the hospital on the other side of town. He had to walk back all the way for he had no car. I had thought that with this delay our service might be shortened a bit, but not at all. The children sat quietly through the whole thing. On Easter Sunday the church was so crowded that Charles and I were seated on the right side of the pulpit, just below the lectern facing the congregation. In the middle of the sermon a young Gabonese woman, tall and neatly dressed, walked in the open back door and took her stand in front of my chair. She remained standing throughout the rest of the service. I tried to make her sit down by touching her arm; there was just barely room next to me for one more person. She ignored my gesture and remained upright. No one else in the church seemed to be bothered by her. After the service I was told that she was a *"folle,"* a crazy one, and there was nothing to be done about her. I often saw old men or women half-naked in the streets, doing some strange thing, and Raphael would say, "Oh, that is a crazy one." The Gabonese were not cruel to these unfortunates; they just ignored them.

The singing was marvelous. Men sat on the right-hand side of the church and the women on the left. With their sense of rhythm and their strong voices the lack of any instrument was not noticeable. Hymns were sung in Miené or Fang, not in

French. We joined in as the printed dialect was fairly easy to follow and most of the tunes were familiar.

Charles never hesitated to take communion from the common cup, standing up with the men on his side of the church. I sat with the women, did not take communion, and shuddered at the possibilities he was exposing himself to. In time I learned not to worry unduly about disease; I did not ask if the ice I was served had been made from boiled water, the lettuce washed in permanganate and so on. Much had to be taken on faith. Léon Mba's son, who lived in Akebé, a section through which my husband drove to work, told us that the Gabonese there called Charles *"le bon blanc,"* or the good white man, because he daily stopped and picked up schoolchildren. Perhaps this goodness served as a protection.

XIV

Our Household Staff

W E were very lucky with our "boys" or servants. I got impatient when other Europeans complained of the stupidity, laziness and unreliability of the Gabonese. I was so happy to have hands to help me, I would have put up with almost anything just to keep them with me. But I found the Gabonese quick to learn, always good-natured, quite dependable, clean and honest.

First of all there was Raphael, the chauffeur. He was a Bapounou, a tribe living in the south around Mouila. He was quiet, nice-appearing and thin, and he moved slowly with a loping walk. I never saw him in a hurry. He was extremely sensitive and when corrected would stutter and become almost speechless. He never had an accident, although I don't know why not; perhaps it was because Charles would not let him go over twenty-five miles an hour. He never drove carelessly but sometimes just witlessly, speeding up as we came to traffic, and then poking along on an open road. But he was reliable and had a sweet way with him, and we became very fond of him.

One day he asked if he could bring his wife to stay at our house during the evening while he drove us to a late engagement. He was afraid to leave her alone in their section of town because of the *"diable,"* or devil, which was roaming round. He explained to me that a *diable* was a dog; not a mad dog, but one that only attacked its victim by the throat. I asked why he did not ask the police to take it away or have it killed, but he said that was impossible: whoever killed a *diable* would himself die a few weeks later. When I seemed skeptical, he assured me that one of the police had just recently died in the hospital after having killed a *diable* dog that had attacked him. The other boys in the house agreed that all Raphael had told me was gospel truth. And so his wife spent the evening in our kitchen, naturally.

A few months after this incident I was startled to receive a request from Raphael that he be allowed a week's leave to return to his village to be married. I told him I thought he was already married, but he explained that the woman I had met was only on trial. He had had her for a number of months, but as he had concluded that she was "no good," he was sending her back to her family in another part of town. He had not given any dowry, or price, for her, so she had no claim on him. But, he said proudly, beaming from ear to ear: *"Je l'ai enceinté. Elle est déja engrossie"* ("I have made her pregnant. She is already getting big"). When the time approached for the child to be born, he brought her back to his house alongside the new bride of fourteen and delivered the infant himself. Thus he was able to keep possession of it; otherwise, it would have belonged to the mother's family. The new legal wife from the country was educated—she could read and write, having attended a Catholic school for a few years. Raphael paid, I think, 60,000 francs (about $245) to her parents for her, a large sum, I thought, compared to his salary of 14,000 francs a month. He was worried because she did not conceive at once, but I told him to have patience. And sure enough, just before we left Gabon Josephine produced a son. The local expression, when told by the father, is *"J'ai fait un garçon* ("I made a boy") or *"Elle a poussée une fille"* ("She [the wife] pushed out a girl").

It is curious, but Gabonese women seem to have quantities of babies or else none at all. One theory of their sterility is that girls are used too young, there being no value at all put on virginity. Another is that as long as wives are paid for by the *"dot"*—or are bought, not to put too fine a face on it—the old men have all the advantage. It is they who have the money and can give the best prices to the father of the bride. This keeps the price up and the birth rate down. On the other hand, with the utmost frankness one of the minister's wives told me that Africans have many children because "our blood is so warm. That is why we conceive so easily. While we are nursing —maybe for as long as two years—we have nothing to do with our husbands. But the first time we are together after that—zzt, a baby starts. It is just in our blood to have children."

Our gardener was a Congolese. He had been acting as caretaker for the house and stayed on when we took over. He lived in a small room in back of the residence, cooked for himself over an open fire (once Charles saw him hotting up a mess of woolly caterpillars), and played at being "king of the castle" on our hill. He had a strong and likable personality, but he was a rascal all the same. He often got into trouble over women— stealing wives, he laughingly called it. He worked for me fairly well except that he spent too much time talking in a loud voice to all passers-by—and we had many who walked up our driveway and across a path toward town. I used to scold him regularly, and he was always penitent, promising to do better. He really worked hardest during his free time, when he went into the fields, cut grasses, spread them on our lawn to dry, and then sewed them into mattresses to be sold for 2,000 francs (about $8.00) to customers who came up our hill to buy them.

At last I had to let him go. He had asked for two weeks' leave, to which he was entitled, but he stayed away two months. I thought this a bit exaggerated, so I moved Grégoire into his house and hired Grégoire's brother to take his place. Such a to-do as there was when Blaise turned up again. Why, he had not resigned, nor left me! He had just been delayed in getting back, taking care of a sick brother. He begged and pleaded to be reinstated, but it was no use and in the end he went off to make his mattresses on someone else's time.

Very soon after my arrival I learned that to have Gabonese working happily together in the same house they must be of the same "race," that is, tribe or tribal group. When I was interviewing boys, the first question asked by Grégoire, who as the No. 1 boy had to be consulted, was "What race is he?" Grégoire said that certain races were tricky, or pushy, or dishonest, or lazy. He was a Bateké, a tribe that got on well with the Bapounou. Certainly he and Raphael never had a word of misunderstanding during our three years.

I learned a great deal from Grégoire. He was shorter than I am (five feet two), had very small feet and hands, and practically no neck. At times I wondered if he might not have pygmy blood. He was very dark, had a large smile and a soft voice. He called Charles "Chef" and me "Madame" and was always polite and good-natured. He could read enough to study a simple French cookbook and write enough to leave me endless little notes asking for an advance on his wages, or warning me about one of the other servants. One note said that Blaise was making a *"fétiche"* out of my hair combings—"not a bad *fétiche,* Madame, just one so that you will not send him away." Another one complained that he had too much work to do and wanted an assistant to help him with the pots and pans. He periodically introduced me to men who came to visit him as his "father." The first time I took him at his word and told the man what a fine son he had. When the second "father" came

216

around I was puzzled, but Grégoire explained that uncles or anyone close to him in his tribe was called "father."

One evening Grégoire came to the living room dressed as for the most formal occasion, in a smart gray suit, white shirt and polished black shoes. Charles, wearing pajamas and dressing gown, asked where he was going. It turned out that he had dressed up in order to speak to Charles "man to man." I withdrew, and Grégoire sat down to tell my husband what was on his mind. It was a rumor: he had heard that someone had told us that he, Grégoire, was putting poison in our food and he just wanted to assure us that it was not so.

Grégoire had a veritable passion for clothes, as do most Gabonese country boys. As soon as they get to Libreville, they spend their all on trousers, shirts, shoes. The minute I paid the boys they rushed off to town and came back with parcels under their arms and no cash in their pockets. In vain I tried to make them save a bit for the last few days before the next payday, but nothing I could do was successful. I tried saying, when I paid them, "Now. Here it is. I will not give anyone a single franc in advance, so put away enough so that this will last until the fifteenth [or the thirty-first]." It never worked, and in the end, after being strict once or twice, I gave in to the system.

Jean-Pierre, our second houseboy, came to work when Blaise went off on his long leave. He was a young *"petit-frère"* to Grégoire. This meant that they had one parent in common— I never found out which one it was. *Grand-frère* or *soeur* means the same father and mother.

Like Grégoire, Jean-Pierre was short, with tiny hands and feet, but had a magnificent body; broad shoulders, no hips at all, and muscles that rippled under his smooth black skin. It was a pleasure to watch him swing his machete, or lift heavy cartons, or carry furniture. He had been a day laborer before he came to us and had no training at all for gardening or working in the house. But he was willing to learn. Our children, when they visited us during our first summer, persuaded me that he was smarter than I thought and besides, "He is such a dear when he smiles, why don't you teach him to serve at table? He couldn't be worse than the extras you have to hire when you have a big party—besides he lives right here near the house." (I had made room for a second boy in the little cement building at the foot of our hill which had formerly housed the diesel motor for our electricity.) I took their advice. At first he was terrified even to try, but a white uniform, white shoes and extra pay persuaded him and he become quite good in the dining room.

Jean-Pierre had one drawback in or out of the house: his voice. It was a deep monotonous rumble and, unless he was far afield, I could hear him all day long. He was the unending gossip and storyteller of the neighborhood. His one other problem was a great attraction for women. There was a steady stream of them coming up the hill; young, middle-aged, pregnant and with babes in arms. The usual excuse was to ask for a drink of water, but if I was not on the lookout I think they got a great deal more from him than that. I finally laid down the law and said I would tolerate *no women* around the back court until after the boys had finished their work—until after three o'clock.

In time, both boys bought transistor radios. Grégoire kept his in his house, but Jean-Pierre took his to work with him as he cut the grass, or drank his coffee, or sharpened his tools. It was never more than three feet from him. They heard programs from Radio Gabon, and also from Brazzaville, Dakar and even the Voice of America. During the years we were there, the number of these transistors increased enormously. When we first settled into the house, we never heard or saw one. By the time we left young people were carrying them as they walked the road beside the house, playing all manner of programs. It is a wonderful invention for this country which has so little electricity and no real newspaper. The *Daily Bulletin* is a mimeographed sheet of eight to ten pages, completely controlled by the government and having a circulation of some three hundred—all government officials or town dignitaries.

While my Grégoire and Jean-Pierre spoke French, it was not good enough to give me any help with my own. Grégoire was pretty careful about his genders and tenses, but to the others I was always *"tu,"* and there was but one gender, masculine, and one tense, the present.

Quite by chance I found that there was a Gabonese woman who was looking for a job. Occasionally girls go out to work as laundresses, but rarely as *"boyesses"* as they are called. I tracked down Cécile and found that she was a *"métis,"* the child of a Gabonese mother and French father. She was a middle-aged woman who had been married to a Frenchman, had lived in France for a number of years and at his death had returned to her native land and family. Her French was excellent and she was eager to work for me as she had already spent six months looking for a job to no avail. The French would not have her as they did not think a woman would get on with "boys" in the house, and the Gabonese distrusted anyone who had been so long in France. She had been trained as a nurse, but the health authorities would not give her a job in the hospital, desperate though they were for help. I never could find out why. Her brother was a priest, one sister worked for the French Embassy, while another sister produced a child a year, each time by a different father.

Cécile had coffee-colored skin, and her face was marred by a reddish birthmark on one side. But despite this she was a nice-looking woman and very capable. It was a relief to have her to talk with, and to be able to trust the arranging of the dinner table to her. I knew that she would help get things ready in time for a party, and that she would answer the telephone, take messages and receive guests in my absence with something like a proper manner. When we entertained Gabonese, most of them knew her and some spoke to her in her dialect, Miené. If she did not know our Gabonese guests by sight, she knew of them by hearsay and what tales she told me! I dismissed half of them as pure nonsense. It was she who first told me that human flesh was still eaten in Libreville. When I asked her, appalled, if she meant that people were killed to be eaten, she said, oh no, but that once dead, they were not always buried. Coffins often went empty into the ground.

One evening when we had two prominent French business couples for dinner, I was congratulated on my cleverness in persuading Cécile to work for me. Before coming to me she had applied to one of these families, but had been turned down. The next morning I learned that during the course of the evening both of them had offered her a job. One had said to her, this being overheard by Blaise, "But do you really like working for Americans? With your background I should think you would be better off in a French family."

She made friends with the boys, and they trusted her up to a point, but they became jealous of her, I think, and in various ways tried to make me get rid of her. One day Grégoire complained that there was no other cook in town who had to wash the towels and dust cloths and his own pots and pans, and that all European houses had another boy to do this and a laundress to wash uniforms. If Cécile would not wash the uniforms, I should get another laundress, he said. "Cécile," he went on, "has made enemies with Joseph [a temporary boy], which is too bad, for he is a good boy, and if he were not brave she would have already killed him, as she is a vampire and has already killed two husbands with her fetishes."

I was very cross. I had taken him to Mass Sunday after Sunday, where I had supposed he followed the Christian service in his prayer book. Now I was disappointed to have this

220

reversion to tales of vampires. I gave him a lecture on telling the truth, and asked him on what possible basis he could accuse Cécile of being a vampire. His stubborn reply was: "But everyone in Akebé says so. Everyone knows this is true." My talk did some good, however. There was no more nonsense about that extra boy to wash pots and pans. Cécile stayed on for six months, until her phlebitis got so bad she had to give up the job. She then became housekeeper for a French priest, and I saw her until we left Gabon. I was very fond of her, and she of me. We embraced and wept in parting.

Our last member of the household was Marcel, another member of Grégoire's family. People used to compliment me on my three little Batekés, no one of whom came above my shoulder. Marcel was the smallest man I have ever seen. He moved quickly, was eager to learn, and if he could not understand my direction, Grégoire, his mentor, took over the training. The only problem I had with all three was finding them shoes. Their feet were so tiny that I had to get children's sizes, and these were hard to find. How I longed for our shoe stores filled with every possible shape and color. The best I could do was some old white sneakers of mine plentifully covered with white polish for one, white canvas beach shoes for another, and a pair of girl's white sandals for the third. In the dark of evening they all passed muster.

Once at a crowded cocktail party Marcel, balancing a tray of drinks, tried to pass between several large men. When he found no way, to my utter amazement he bent double and quick as a flash slipped between a pair of spread legs. Not a drop was spilled!

The three boys had a habit of sitting on the stone wall behind the house overlooking the main road below. Here they watched the world go by—trucks, taxis, cars and an endless stream of pedestrians going to and from the country. Indeed, they were all too often at this "post" rather than where they should have been, in the kitchen and the dining room, or getting out the ice and bottles for drinks. Charles had only to shout "Grégoire! Jean-Pierre! Marcel!" and the three would come running—so happily and willingly that we could never be cross with them.

I was very attached to them, and they are among the people in Gabon that I miss the most.

XV

Some Neighbors at the Residence

AFTER a year and a half the Embassy was moved from its
original location, a converted two-family apartment
across the street from the popular bistro "Le Petit Bidule," to
a spacious building, formerly the local branch of the Banque
Commerciale Africaine, on the ocean front. Instead of walking
up an outside staircase to reach his office, and answering one
of the two telephones in the building himself, my husband now
entered through a reception hall, passed a receptionist running
a switchboard, mounted gleaming stairs to the second floor,
crossed his secretary's office and entered his own sunny room
with a large covered terrace and a view looking across the
harbor to the sea. No longer did he have to shout "Raphael"
from the top of the steps to call the chauffeur from wherever
he might be lounging along the street. There was a decent place
for the drivers to sit, and a clerk to call them as needed. The
palms in front of the building were trimmed, flowers edged the
walks, and we could pride ourselves on having the most handsome building of any of the governments represented in Gabon.

Luckily, however, life at home remained casual. There were no gates to be opened or closed by Embassy guards and no house servants who insisted on formal introductions. The Gabonese who lived around us felt free to come and visit when they wished, as neighbors. Children waited at the foot of the steps in hope of a ride to school; they came to the door offering us avocados or bananas and sat outside quietly talking among themselves until we had finished our breakfast or whatever we were doing and could inspect their produce. Women on their way home from a long day in the bush, cutting wood or cultivating their bit of land, stopped for a drink of water. One day the President of the Collectivité Rurale dropped in to talk to us on an urgent matter just as we were sitting down to lunch; a plate was added and he told us what was on his mind. Another day it would be the deputy of our area, or the Minister of National Economy's *planton* (office attendant), or some neighbor who wanted a job in the Embassy.

We had a variety of tribes living around us. Across the main road there were Massangos; at the bottom of our drive and toward Sibang there were Fang; on the rolling slopes between our house and town there were Bapounous; and nearer at hand, practically on our doorstep, Bandjabis and Batekés. Each group had several huts. Some were neatly built of wood, with palm-thatched or corregated-iron roofs, grouped around a hard, bare earthen court. Others were a makeshift huddle of old doors, odd bits of lumber put together hastily to give a minimum of protection from the sun and rain. Shacks would spring up overnight. There was no government inspection or regulation. One morning I could look out at a softly rounded hill between the terrace and the town. A few days later that particular view became a hut, a smoking fire and a line of wash. Soon we absorbed the change and forgot it.

We were open to callers from dawn to bedtime. The Gabonese would stand silently at one or the other of the doors waiting until they were noticed. In the evening we liked to sit on the terrace watching the flight of hundreds of bats from the cemetery in town to the banana plantations. Below them swallows swooped about. It was marvelous at that hour as the sun dropped into the ocean and the first lights in the town below us flicked on. Callers would just quietly stroll across the lawn and join us to present their respects, to make some requests or just to chat. No neighbor intruded when they saw we had guests. But if we sat alone, they would come, and we liked it so. Even when we had entered the house, pulled the curtains and turned on the air conditioner in the drawing room, there would be visitors. They would tap on a door or a window and would call out "Monsieur l'Ambassadeur" until we heard and let them in.

When France gave Libreville television, it was decided that the American Government should own one receiver as an expression of our interest. The set was installed in our house, where it would be available to our whole staff. None of the Americans however, came to look since the shows were uniformly poor and the equipment invariably broke down. But each Sunday and Wednesday at 8:00 P.M., the two times in the week programs were given, I would turn the set on for our Gabonese neighbors. We would have all the doors open, and by twos and threes they would slip in, filling the chairs and then the floor. They watched with interest until the show was over or the machine stopped. Afterward they shook hands, thanked me and disappeared into the dark.

Sometimes, after dinner parties, we would show to our guests one of the American films that the United States Information Agency sent out. Henry Stephen, our Public Relations Officer, and his Gabonese helpers would set up the equipment on the terrace while the guests were at dinner. The films—usually pictures of parts of the United States, under titles such as "Wonderful Wyoming"—provided a welcome change from the usual evening. Most of all they pleased the Gabonese. Through the grapevine the word got around that a film was to be shown that evening, and sometimes we would have a hundred or more men, women and children sitting on the grass or standing in the shadows to watch the picture. They were always quiet and polite, and many would come up and thank us after the showing.

One of my favorite callers was Charmaine, the eight-year-old daughter of Pascal who lived at the foot of our drive. Her manners were perfect. She came frequently after school to bring me an egg or a pineapple. She would sit at the table with me drinking her orangeade and eating her biscuit with all the delicacy in the world, answering my questions about her studies and her friends with the inevitable "Madame" at the end of each statement. When she left, she pushed her chair into place, thanked me and shook my hand. The first afternoon I called on her family her mother was embarrassed because there was but one chair in the neat room. She tried to go next door to the little store to buy beer for us, but I stopped her and we sat on the simple stools talking and laughing. I learned that Charmaine was the daughter of another of Pascal's wives who lived in the country; she herself had no children; a great sorrow for her.

Our knowledge and understanding of the country and the people was constantly being widened by casual, friendly contacts.

On the first evening that Tia (our daughter Letitia) and Christopher were with us from America we were sitting on the terrace having drinks when up the steps came Charles Nze, a Fang to whom my husband had once given a lift and who since then had called from time to time with presents (usually a live chicken) for his "friend." Behind him came his father and mother, who had walked all the way from Coco Beach, 225 kilometers away, to visit him. Father was wearing sandals, khaki trousers, an old tuxedo jacket and a brown felt hat; Mother, a few paces behind him was barefoot, in a brightly colored skirt and blouse and a scarf around her head. Both faces were scarred with Fang tribal marks, dark streaks going from the top of the cheek to the chin. Charles Nze kissed both Tia and Chris, much to their astonishment, and we all sat down to beer and cigarettes. Mama smoked as fast as I could supply her, hanging onto each butt until it was nothing but a scrap of paper, then putting the fire out under her bare foot. Charles Nze talked away about Fang customs, and the damage done to plantations in the north by elephants. From time to time he asked his father in Fang for corroboration. The parents seemed quite content to sit with us, understanding nothing of our French. Like many Gabonese they did not know how to take their leave, or were quite prepared to talk the night through. So, as was our custom, we offered to drive them home, an invitation that was never refused.

Charles Nze came often to talk about his marital problems. He had a beautiful wife of fifteen who would not conceive. We advised him to be patient, but she had already been married to him for three or four years so his patience was running out. The poor girl, feeling herself unwanted, ran away to her father's house, but she could not stay there long unless the father returned her dowry which he was not of a mind to do. Charles Nze had originally given 35,000 francs ($140) for her, and gifts that he had since made to her parents, each one of which was carefully recorded as is the custom, had raised the figure to about 70,000 francs. Charles Nze earned only 9,000 francs ($36) a month working as a carpenter on the new Catholic church of Sainte Marie, so this money invested in his wife represented a very large sum.

Another man was in love with the girl, and Charles Nze would gladly have given her up to him, but this fellow could not find the money to make up the 70,000 francs. My husband suggested that Charles Nze take a certain amount down and the remainder monthly, but this lay quite outside his conception. In the end, after months of talk, the girl had to return to him and share his home with another girl whom he had married in the meantime. The second wife promptly became pregnant, and when my husband visited their hut after this, he found the first wife quiet and sad. As she grew older and her girlish freshness faded, she knew that no other man would pay the 70,000 francs for her, so she would have to stay and work in Charles Nze's house for life.

At times we shared critical moments in the lives of our neighbors. They knew that we had a telephone for they had seen the wires being strung out from Libreville and put up pole by pole until the last one arrived at our house, where the service stopped. Ours therefore became the neighborhood phone. Sometimes we were asked to telephone for the police; there had been a fight or a thief had been caught. Other times we were asked to call for an ambulance; someone was sick or having a baby. These requests usually came at night, and sometimes it was too late for the ambulance. One night a man appeared and asked Charles to pick up a woman on the point of giving birth and drive her to the hospital. Charles drove to the spot indicated, from where they had to walk a quarter-mile down a steep path in the pitch darkness to the woman's house. Seeing him, she got out of bed and walked up to the car, where as many relatives as could crowded in with them.

Another night a baby was born almost in the automobile. A trembling man beat on our door, said a woman on the main road just below our house was about to deliver. I rushed for some towels, and Charles and I hopped into the car. By the time we turned from our driveway onto the road we saw we were too late: in the light of two kerosene lanterns three women stood around a prostrate form, one of them grasping a newborn baby, the others holding children of their own. When we

228

stopped the automobile, all four pressed to get in. The newly delivered mother took care to sit on the towels I had given her, so as not to soil the seat, instead of wrapping them around her child as I had intended. The lanterns went into the car with them, and two men got into the front seat with Charles. The lanterns were finally extinguished and the whole kit and boodle were rushed off to the hospital while I walked back up to the house. In most instances the mother would come to show us the baby a few weeks later.

Sounds carry far in Africa. I could hear mothers scolding and children crying from houses far across the fields. One afternoon I was disturbed by particularly bitter sobbing and going outside found a little boy of about six standing alone in the middle of our field, the sun beating on his fuzzy head. He was barefoot, big-bellied and skimpily dressed in a pair of shorts and a brief shirt. In one hand he clutched a piece of manioc, with the other he pulled violently at one ear. I thought that someone had hit him on the side of the head. When he saw me he began to calm down and between sobs told me his trouble: Mama would not give him any money for food at school; instead she gave him this old piece of manioc and he did not want it. He was not going to eat it! I patted him, wiped his nose and he trotted off, but he threw the manioc into the bushes as he ran down the hill. He was a dreadful bellower and put on this little act by our house off and on for a month. His mother may well have been right. Gabonese parents punish their children only when it is necessary.

Other children had worse troubles. One day I saw a boy of about ten hopping along the road toward the country. One of his feet was badly cut, and the bandage was neat but bloody. His face was cheerful and he made pretty good time; at least he kept pace with the woman in front of him. I saw many sights such as this as I hung up the wash. The laundry was directly above the main road, and when I stood on the low stone wall rimming the property I had an intimate view of all that was happening on the highway below me. There was one man who walked back and forth to town each day on legs dreadfully swollen with elephantiasis. I wondered how much longer he could keep going. Another seemed always to be smiling, until I saw that his happy grin was fixed; there was no flesh around his teeth. He was one of the lepers who lived at the leper hospital in nearby N'Kembo but, as an arrested case, could go to work by the day.

One afternoon I sat on the terrace with some mending. There was a pleasant breeze from the sea and the sun had lost its harshness behind the *badamier* trees. I saw a young boy walking across the fields toward town with a huge white bandage on his foot. Every few steps he would sit and rest. At last he turned and came hopping toward our house, crawling up the steps to the terrace. His foot was a mess, badly infected, and all I dared to do was to put on a fresh bandage, give him food and water and talk to him until Charles came home with the car and could take him to the hospital. His name was Christian, he was twelve, and he took care of his four younger sisters and brothers while his parents worked their plantation in the bush. The other children went to school near their home, but as there was no room for him he had to walk all the way out to Sibang, which was a new school and not crowded. Christian asked if he could sit in the shade of our big mango tree at the lunch hour; he could not go to the shops with the other children and the school was lonesome with everyone away. So for several weeks he spent his lunch period under the tree. Grégoire and Jean-Pierre were none too gracious about giving him something to eat; perhaps they were afraid that he would be a permanent fixture. He looked at books and seemed content. When his foot was well he thanked us, said good-bye, and that was it. He was a brave and mature little fellow.

Often I was asked to give someone a lift into town, to the

hospital, the market. I enjoyed these brief contacts. One such request almost landed me in trouble. There had been a lot of talking and shouting at the foot of the drive as I set out to make some midafternoon calls. I asked Raphael to stop the car so that I could find out what it was all about and was told that a *"mauvais type"* had started a small fight, nothing serious. We started out on the main road to town and saw ahead of us a crowd of men and women attacking one lone man. There must have been fifteen at least. As we passed them, the loner broke away, leaving his shirt behind him, and ran after my car crying, "Madame, Madame, save me, save me. Take me with you." We were going quite slowly, and I did the instinctive thing, telling Raphael to stop. I had come to a full halt when the man threw open the front door and leaped in beside Raphael, but before we could start up again the crowd was on us. They pulled the man out and shook their fists at me through the window. Raphael roared away as fast as the car would go. I looked back to see the poor devil lying on the ground being kicked and beaten. Raphael told me it was not good to get mixed up in such things, and I reluctantly agreed.

In front of our house there was an open field which served as a parking lot when we had large receptions. On Saturdays and Sundays a group of young Gabonese boys from nearby parts of town, most from N'Kembo, turned up about four o'clock to play soccer until dark. It was pleasant to sit on the terrace watching them. Their black bodies, glistening with sweat, made a fine contrast with their blue, orange, red or white shorts. Many had magnificent physiques. We wondered how they could be so strong, brought up as they were on manioc, which only stuffed their stomachs and, according to all medical authorities, contained little nourishment. The younger boys who were not allowed to play acted as water boys, running up and down our steps to the outside faucet, filling the empty Vittel bottles which I supplied them. Occasionally one of the players would get hurt and would come to me for a bandage.

One day we received a formal typewritten letter delivered by three of the leading players. It explained that they wanted to enter one of the leagues and play in the tournaments in the Central Stadium. They felt they were now good enough to compete, but they would not be allowed to play in the Stadium until they had uniforms and proper soccer boots. Could we help them to buy these? It so happened that at the time Mrs. Mildred Stanley of New York was staying with us. The project interested her, and together we bought the uniforms. The group called itself the "Association Sportive Darling Club," or "Darling Club" for short, and named Charles its honorary president.

On New Year's Day the team came in a body to present its respects, bringing a chicken for Charles and flowers for me. We followed their progress and from time to time watched them play in the Stadium. After two years they became head of their league.

The slow pace of my unofficial life gave me time to look and listen, time to be aware of the changes in nature so different from the familiar ones at home. I never tired of the sudden violent storms. From our house we could see them building up and learned to estimate the time at which the downpour would hit us. The Gabonese did not seem to worry; they walked along the road at the same unhurried pace and when the rain came, plodded on, drenched to the skin but never taking shelter. I trained the boys to take the flag down before the worst of the storm was on us and to shut the doors and windows before the lamps were blown over and the cigarettes scattered from their boxes. We could see the wall of rain come toward us. Then it would blot out the windows and everything would be dark with heavy thunder and violent lightning. When the storm passed, the sun would shine again in full force, the ground steaming.

The first winter I looked forward to the summer dry season, when not one drop of rain would fall for three months. I thought it would be bliss to be without the heat and the humidity, but I was wrong. Africa without sun is sad and without rain is red and ugly. Within a few weeks the roadsides were covered with laterite dust, and the air filled with the smoke of burning brush as the Gabonese set fire to the fields around their houses to destroy the *fouroux* and mosquitoes and to prepare the ground for the next planting. These fires were scary for sometimes they would roar up very close to us. The crackle of the flames as they hit oily palms and the black smoke rising above the fields looked dangerous. The small cleared space around each hut did not seem to be protection enough from this noisy monster, nor did our driveway and the low stone wall. Ashes fell on us and occasionally sparks.

In this season the schools were closed and whole families returned to their tribal relatives in the country. Children no longer came to call or to be taken to school. The beaches were deserted for the water was as gray as the sky above and not inviting. The streets of Libreville were quiet, the stores almost empty of people and produce, and men and women walked the roads listlessly. As the summer advanced, illness increased. The coolness, combined with the humidity from the great forests breathing out their perpetual dampness, gave to the night air a raw chill. Children and old people caught colds and pneumonia, and many living by the roads developed lung trouble from the dust. Deaths mounted.

The shortage of water was a hard cross to bear. We were fortunate for we had a reservoir in which was stored water collected from the roof in the rainy season. But in town the water would be turned off except for an hour or so morning and evening; even in the hospitals it was unavailable. The women in all the little encampments and villages around us would have to walk far afield to find some brook or spring where they could fill their vessels. In the beginning they came to us and I had to issue a stern warning to the boys: drinking water, yes, but for washing clothes, no. We had just enough to see ourselves through the dry season.

We could sleep in this season without the air conditioner, with our windows open, and wake to the sound of bird songs and the voices of Africans walking along the road to work. But sleep was sometimes difficult, for all summer long each little group of huts would have periodic celebrations when they would drum for several nights, resting briefly throughout the day. They would drum for pleasure and for pain; for a wedding, a funeral, the raising (as they called the ending) of the mourning or just to dance. There were many nights when we could hear the beating of the drums nearby and could see the shadowy figures around the fires in the compounds of our neighbors. There was infinite variety in the beating, and many of the rhythms were haunting. Scuffles and fights would increase, and as the long month of August wore on and then September, there was an increasing tension.

In early September light mists fell a few times at night. These were called the rains of the mangoes and were little more than a heavy dew, but they prepared the hard-packed ground for the downpours which were to follow. Then with October came the violent rains and the sun, and Africa was itself again.

XVI

Women in Gabon

I saw and knew women in many parts of Gabon and at different levels of social development, but I never saw a lazy one. The woman works or the family does not eat. In the country it is the man's job to clear the land and build a house. The woman plants, cultivates and harvests the crops. She also hauls water, cuts and carries wood and does all other household chores. The man's duty is to keep the house in repair and build the new one every few years when the village moves to a new location. For the rest, he hunts for game or fish, and spends his time in the "palaver" house talking and smoking with the other men. By tribal custom he does not do "women's work," and this includes even helping to carry heavy loads. We have often passed a family on the move during our travels. The man walks ahead carrying a lantern and perhaps a gun or knife; the woman follows with all the household goods piled on her back, leading the children. In the towns, except for the highest paid such as the ministers, what a man earns is rarely enough to support his family; the woman must go regularly to the "plantation"—the tribal lands outside the town limits—to plant and cultivate manioc, peanuts, corn or bananas.

An American missionary of the Christian and Missionary Alliance who had lived for many years among the Massango tribe between M'Bigou and Mimongo told us this story which illustrates the feeling among these people as to what truly distinguishes the sexes. A group of women were returning in the evening from their plantations with heavily laden baskets on their backs. Among them was a man, also with a full basket. The missionary turned to a friend and remarked, "That is strange, to see a man doing women's work!" The friend replied, "That is not a man; she only seems to be a man to your Western eyes; in fact she is a woman." And the Massango went on to explain that this person (a man to us) had failed years earlier to go through with some of the cruel initiation rites of the Mwiri sect to which his people belonged. Because of this he was identified as a woman at heart, and henceforth had to do women's work, a judgment and sentence which he apparently accepted. What sexual role he played in these bizarre circumstances, the missionary did not say.

Daily I watched women walking down our driveway early in the morning as they took this short cut from town to the Lambaréné road. Each woman carried an empty basket, many had babies tied on their backs, most were barefoot. They wore brightly colored cotton skirts and blouses. Some had young children walking by their sides. I could follow their progress up the main road until they were out of sight around the bend; they walked quickly with a swinging grace. Late in the afternoon they would again pass our house on their return to town. The baskets now would be loaded with wood for the cooking fires, and occasionally a bunch of bananas would be stuck on top. Some of the women chatted gaily as though they had been on a happy picnic; others looked grim as they plodded along seemingly bent on nothing more than making one foot follow the other. But if I was spotted sitting on the terrace, they would wave and call out a pleasant greeting, and sometimes they would rest in the shade of a tree by our steps and have a drink of water. There was a faucet near our front door which became a general drinking fountain.

Even some of the more highly placed women, those married to civil servants or ministers, had their own plantations outside town. A few, surprisingly enough, actually worked them periodically, being driven out and back by their government chauffeurs. I often waved to them as they went by our gate. As soon as the dry season began in June and schools were closed, they all returned to their villages, to supervise the work on the land and to restore the roots of their tribal life. Even the wife of the President of the Republic went quite frequently to her village further along our road. She spoke to me proudly of her crops and gave me presents of pineapples and avocados.

I like to think that I made friends with a number of the Gabonese ministers' wives, even though it was a limited relationship. I felt a bond of sympathy and understanding with many of them, but it could never broaden into true friendship, perhaps in part because of the differences in our cultures, but more importantly because of the tensions which were inherent in their positions. We could talk about simple things, we could laugh together, we could have a basic give and take of information, but rarely could we discuss ideas.

Madame Pauline Mba, the wife of the President, was my first Gabonese friend in this sense. When I called on her just after my arrival, I was impressed with her poise, but it was a Frenchwoman, Madame Pigot, who was the actual hostess. It was she who kept the conversation going, who told the butler to bring drinks and pass the cigarettes. After a few months Madame Pauline received alone; the course of her instruction, which had lasted a year, had come to an end. Two French-women whose husbands were technical advisers to the President groomed her for the position of Presidential wife, a training which was finished off by a trip to France where she was received by General de Gaulle. They had the utmost respect for her intelligence and for her bravery in attacking such difficult social problems at her age and with her background. She came from the small village of Akok about forty miles from Libreville. When she was fourteen, Léon Mba loved her. Later he gave her father a *"dot"* or bride price for her. At this time he had other wives. When he was sent into exile in Bangui (now the capital of the Central African Republic) by the French, it was only she, of all his wives, who followed him. She walked much of the way, and stayed with him until he returned to Gabon. She never had a child.

When Léon became President, he told his Cabinet that he had picked Pauline to be his official wife and he ordered each of the ministers to follow his example lest there be confusion and misunderstanding in governmental and diplomatic circles. She was taught how to dress in the European fashion, how to sit (African women normally sit with knees wide apart, feet sole to sole), how to receive guests and how to take one's leave. It was the dinner table routine that bothered her the most. She said to Madame Pigot, "But you have always known how to use a knife and fork. You had parents to teach you when you were young. Here, at my age, I have to learn how to do this. Oh, when I see all those things before me on the table, I tremble with fear."

She was quick to pick up ideas. She came to a simple tea at our house, where our own wives and secretaries passed the sandwiches, fruit juice and iced tea. I moved the guests from place to place to mix the several groups. The very next time Madame Pauline gave an "at home," the white-coated boys served only drinks, while the daughters of the ministers and of the household handed round the cakes. And Madame Pauline herself circulated among the tables talking to the guests so that

238

many of us could follow her lead. She admired my so-called hats: bits of veiling stuck to a comb or bandeau, saying that they were much more practical for this climate than the French felt and feather creations that she had bought at great expense. Later I got her three from Bloomingdale's.

When my sister-in-law and the children visited us, I took them to call on Madame Pauline. Afterward she asked about each one of them every time we met. She invited me to watch TV with her when Gabon opened its own station, and how she liked the fifteen-year-old American western with the French sound track! One day when I called she was reluctant to let me go and said that she was very lonely; she felt completely isolated: she could not be friends with any of the ministers' wives because of political jealousy. Then she added, "I know that *you* see Madame Aubame and Madame Avaro all the time. You have showed them how to make popcorn and have given them clothes for the poor." I did not know until then that my movements about town were so well known! So this was what she had on her mind. The very next morning I was at the Palace with a box of clothes and a box of popcorn. We had a session in the kitchen with two cooks looking on. Madame Pauline was delighted with the noise, the size and whiteness of the popped kernels, and we parted with embraces and happy smiles.

It was common knowledge that the President had several wives in town. Our chauffeur showed me their houses, and the Embassy in fact rented a two-apartment building which the President had built for one of these women in her native quarter of Lalala. I never met any of them, but I did meet some of the children. Irène, reputedly the President's favorite daughter, was a young woman of about twenty-five who was occasionally with Madame Pauline when I called. She was said to have seven children, each by a different father. No one was considered good enough to marry her. One summer the President married Irène's mother in a civil ceremony in Libreville, perhaps to improve Irène's legal status in France for she was there at the time and there were rumors that she was going to be married. In any event it certainly rocked the people in Libreville. The mother was not popular, and it was feared she would at last realize her ambition and move into the Palace. Madame Pauline was very upset, but she came through the crisis with her position as official and No. 1 wife unchanged.

At my request she received the women Peace Corps teachers when they visited town during the Christmas holidays, after six months in the bush. She gave the girls a champagne tea and expressed amazement that they were willing to live in such faraway districts, many of which she had never visited even herself. The last time I talked to her was three days before the *coup d'état* when we attended the opening of a pilot rice-growing project run by the Chinese Nationalists near her native village. She asked me to sit with her before the ceremony began. After the coup, I was not received at the Palace. I am not at all sure that Madame Pauline received the notes or messages I wrote her in that period. I cannot think that the tentative steps toward friendship between us were nothing more than diplomatic politeness on her part. Certainly for me it was much more than that.

Another woman with whom I established a fragile bond of friendship which lasted until I left the country was Pauline Ondo. One evening we attended a dance for the benefit of the leper hospital in Oyem. It was held out of doors and, aside from the French doctor and his wife who were running the party, my husband and I were almost the only white guests. I could not but think of how we manage benefits in America: much publicity; a list of patrons who have promised to buy tickets and give dinner parties; and in the end a whacking great sum of money raised for the worthy charity. Nothing like that this evening! The Minister of Social Affairs, M. Ondo, greeted us warmly, took us to his table and introduced us to his wife. It was the first time we had ever seen this attractive woman. When she was not dancing she told Charles the story of her life, in great detail and with utter frankness.

She was a Fang from a village east of Oyem. Her husband had a number of other wives, but with independence he took her on a trip to France where she bought lots of clothes and was named his official wife. In parting I said I hoped to see her at our reception next week. She held my hand tightly saying, "Please ask my husband to bring me; if you tell him you expect me, he will not be able to refuse."

We saw her frequently after this. She would stop and call on me on the way back to town from her plantation, sometimes bringing me presents that she had grown. She used to discuss her son's future with me and said how sad it was that she did not have another child of her own, although she was kept busy managing the three other wives and thirteen children who were in the house in Libreville. She was proud of her husband and the fact that he had fifty suits in Libreville and more in the country! She spoke good French and dressed well. During our second year in Gabon, when she had passed her thirtieth birthday, she was replaced at official functions by a younger wife, Élaine, much to the annoyance of Madame Pauline Mba. Then, worse still, the Minister sent her back to Oyem, to his family house where he kept four or five other older wives who no longer suited his needs. This must have been a hard time for poor Pauline Ondo, but her fortunes were to recover. When her husband fell into disgrace, he again made her his No. 1 wife, doubtless feeling need for the help that her friendship with the President's wife might bring him.

The involved and personal nature of African politics is illustrated by a dreadful mishap which occurred to M. Ondo when he was Minister of Foreign Affairs, a position he told my husband that he hoped to keep until the end of his mandate as a deputy in 1967. In fact, he lasted only a few months. Léon Mba's daughter, Irène, finally became engaged to a Gabonese, who was then sent to France at the President's expense to be given the needed polish for the position of his son-in-law. While in Paris the boy fell in love with one of Ondo's daughters and refused to return to Libreville to marry Irène. The President was furious at this insult to his family. Elections were to be held for the Mayor and Council of Oyem, Ondo's home town. The President suggested to Ondo that he might like to run, which he could do and keep his ministerial position as well. The other candidate was Obiang Bernard. When the votes were counted, it was found that they totaled almost twice the number of the entire population of Oyem, children included. The President investigated, found that both parties were in the wrong, but that Ondo (who had won) had profited more from the fictitious votes, so he disqualified Ondo but not Obiang. Poor Ondo was stripped of his position as Minister, made to give up his house in Libreville, and forced to return to live in Oyem with Obiang Bernard as Mayor. My husband and I were on the best of terms with Obiang Bernard, but we nevertheless felt sorry for Ondo; he was such a good-natured fellow, one of our warmest Gabonese friends.

Another woman of whom I grew very fond was Madame Aubame. She was always a pleasure to be with. She had a delicious sense of humor and made jokes about her ten children and her size—she was almost as wide as she was tall. Both she and her husband were Fang, but he was monogamous. Not only were there no other wives, but apparently no mistresses. They had spent a number of years together in Paris and spoke of their life there with nostalgia. She was deeply interested in her husband's career and in politics in general. We always had much to talk about: bringing up children, the position of women in Gabon, the system of polygamy. She told me about life in the country before independence and about the rivalries

242

and jealousies between certain Gabonese families. She and her husband had taken care of Madame Pauline Mba when she was on her difficult journey to Bangui. At that time the Aubames were living in Brazzaville. They gave her food and shelter for weeks.

In spite of Madame Aubame's long stay in France and her fondness for the country and the people, she was convinced that the French wanted to destroy her husband and his influence. One night when we were dining with them, her husband had just returned from New York, where he had headed the Gabonese delegation to the United Nations General Assembly. He teased the French businessmen who were also guests about their unwillingness to build houses of wood, the greatest natural resource of Gabon. "Houses are built of wood in America," he said, "why not here in Gabon? Because you want to import all that cement from France!" As we took our leave, Madame Aubame whispered to me, "They will hate him for this. I wish he would not talk so much about American ways."

She loved to dance and was the life of any party. When others of her age went home from La Péyrie, the open park where official gatherings were often held, she and her husband would stay and dance until dawn. She took the children to the country during the dry season, where they all worked on the land. It was a fine family. After the *coup d'état* I could not even attempt to see her lest I make her situation harder than it already was. Her house was under guard, with a gendarme taking note of every visitor. Her goddaughter's husband was arrested for bringing her two radio batteries, and kept in jail over night. We received verbal messages from her brought by one of her trusted servants. One day a grenade was thrown from a passing car through her living room window. Her mail was censored, and anyone found writing to her was jailed. Her isolation was complete. Yet I do not think that she will ever give up hope for the release and complete exoneration of her husband, and for his ultimate political success.

What a contrast was Madame Yembit, a bouncy young girl from the south. She was uneducated and completely unprepared for her job as official wife to the Vice President, and yet she carried it off pretty well. She produced five children for him, and received guests at his frequent receptions with dignity. She dimpled with pleasure at any personal interest shown in her, as when I complimented her on a particular dress, or tray of canapés. I quaked for her when she christened a small boat, but I need not have worried: she walked up the steps, graciously cut the ribbon holding the bottle, and with all the poise in the world returned to her place in the crowd. She told me she got very lonesome for her *"copains,"* or pals, but her husband would not let her have them around the house—no wonder that she always seemed glad to have me call! Once I asked her age. She giggled and said she could not tell me in French, or "my way"—she would have to do it "her way"— which was to put up one finger for every four-month period of her life. That was bush counting. I reckoned by her flashing fingers that she was under twenty. When I showed her how to make popcorn, she invited the other wives who lived in back of the main house to join us in the kitchen, to watch. No introductions of course, just smiles all around. When she last came to dinner, she forsook her usual beer (she confided to Charles that she consumed a case a day) to drink wine and champagne.

Madame Avaro was every inch a minister's wife, a Galoa from Lambaréné, related to influential families in several tribes of the Miené. Her husband moved from one ministerial position to another. Unfortunately he got the impression that he was indispensable and, when Minister of Waters and Forests, committed a blunder. They survived, however, and after six months were back in favor and power again. M. Avaro had no other wives. Madame Avaro would never have permitted

244

that! The Galoa, her tribe, were monogamous, perhaps because of early Protestant influence. She spoke well, loved to sew and take care of her house and prided herself on her flower garden and her plantation. She would not trust others to cultivate her corn or her peanuts but did it all herself. She had but two children, so, to make up, usually kept a niece or a nephew in the house to love and to educate. Her husband had studied in France and frequently went to Europe on conferences. She had never gone with him but could have carried off her position as his wife beautifully. She had a natural sense of dignity, held her head high and was afraid of no one.

The most sophisticated of the ministerial families were the Anguilés. Both were M'Pongwé, a monogamous tribe from the area around Libreville. And they were both *métis,* that is, mixed Gabonese and white. Most of such whites were French, but some, such as the Walker family, were English. M. Anguilé told us that one of his ancestors was an American Indian, brought here as cabin boy to the captain of a slave ship. This lad escaped into the jungle and bequeathed his aquiline features and bronze tint to a large Gabonese family. Both M. and Mme. Anguilé were educated in France and had traveled widely in Europe. They were extremely good-looking, intelligent and charming.

Jeannine Anguilé had the figure and looks of a model in spite of six children, and she dressed beautifully. I gave her English lessons at my house for a long period, but we did not accomplish much. She was invariably late and when she did arrive we immediately began to gossip. She never talked politics except to complain of the frequent absences of her husband on government business in the United States, France, Germany or Switzerland, to say nothing of African conferences. She liked American things and clothes and yearned to visit our country.

Three of their children were in French boarding schools and she took a cure at Vichy each year. But for all her French culture she liked Americans and American ways. Each time the Minister returned from New York he brought her a dress. The Anguilés entertained with every European grace but served Gabonese specialties. Jeannine was a fine cook, and an expert gardener who could make flowers grow in the hardest of laterite. She busied herself with their plantation near Cap Estérias, and with her numerous relations scattered all over town. *Métis* seem often to marry *métis*. Certainly in both of their families this was true. We met no dark-black kinsmen at their residence.

It took a while to get used to, and be at ease with, mixed couples: a Gabonese man married to a Frenchwoman. Most of these women, curiously enough, were very blonde. All were pretty and of intellectual backgrounds. They were teachers for the most part. We knew well eight such couples, and there were quite a number more in town. On one occasion, on a flight to Paris, my seat companion was M. Mihindou, the Director of the Technical School in Libreville, who was on a Leader Grant to America for six weeks. He was sad at leaving his French wife and three children behind. He told me with some pride that he was the first of "his group" (young government officials studying in France) to marry a Frenchwoman and bring her back to Gabon. His African friends and family were furious with him. Why had he done it? Weren't the girls at home good enough for him? Did he just want to sleep with a white woman? He patiently tried to explain to them that he and his wife shared the same point of view about life, that they loved each other, that it had nothing to do with white and black.

I know that family or tribal life in Gabon came as a deep shock to these French girls after Paris, Bordeaux or Lille. They talked to me frankly about it. What they minded most was never being alone, always having members of the family in the house. And the power of the husband's mother and father was never questioned. The older members of the family controlled the children, not the French mother. She was never really accepted, yet was expected to behave in a typically tribal manner. She might even have to accept other wives.

The French wife of the Prefect of Libreville was an attractive little redhead with huge eyes and a sad, sad face. She had four children of her own under five and when her father-in-law, Jean-François Ondo, lost his ministership, she was obliged to take into her two-bedroom house five of his sons by wives other than the mother of her husband, and see that they went on with their schooling. This was the usual procedure. And no matter how difficult things became, these white women with their black children could hardly expect to be welcomed back into their parents' homes in France. Even in Libreville these wives were not accepted socially by the French community unless their husbands rose to positions of authority. I was told that when, after the *coup d'état,* four young Gabonese with French wives entered the Cabinet, the French colony was aghast at the social obligations which lay ahead.

Of course many of the small French businessmen and foresters had Gabonese mistresses, and a few married Gabonese women. Gabon had the reputation throughout Africa of being the "country of the *métis.*" This was because the early foresters who had come to Gabon on the "dread malarial coast" to work for several years at a stretch could not bring European women with them on account of the climate and living conditions. The French-African housekeeping arrangements that ensued created a large group of coffee-colored children, most of whom gravitated to the towns along the coast. This interbreeding continues apace. We had a lovely-looking Gabonese telephone girl in the Embassy. When she had to leave to have her child, she was asked if the father was a Gabonese and she answered nonchalantly, "Oh, no, he is a Frenchman."

In the chapters on our travels I describe the wives of government officials with whom we stayed. Just as the houses and villages varied, so did the women, except that they all worked hard and all managed on very little to offer us the most gracious hospitality. I always asked them to visit us when they came to Libreville, and several of them did. Madame Theodose, the dynamic wife of the Assistant Prefect in Lambaréné, came to lunch, looking very smart indeed, just before going off to a conference with the President. Auben Arsène, whom we had met as the Subprefect in Minvoul, and his wife called one Sunday afternoon. They walked all the way from town, although she was on the very point of having her ninth child. When I saw her in the hospital a few days later, she did not complain about her husband's transfer or the difficulty of housing in Libreville or the cost of living. She just said, "Ah, Madame, I am so tired." And a few months later I saw her again—pregnant with number ten. When Charles visited her, he said, "In America we have pills to deal with this sort of thing," and she begged him to have a bottle sent to her. We had letters from time to time from Madame Etoughe, wife of the Subprefect of Médouneu. Once she wrote us asking that we send her a box of canned milk for her expected baby, but before it could reach her we heard that she had died. She hemorrhaged after the birth and bled to death, there being no doctor nearer than seven hours' driving time. Her husband, broken-hearted, asked Charles to come and stay with him. Charles visited him for a week, after which M. Etoughe came to Libreville and spent a week in our house.

In 1962 the President launched two important programs: the improvement of the city of Libreville and the bettering of the condition of Gabonese women. For the latter he named 1962 "The Year of the Gabonese Woman."

Libreville had always been cleaner than many African cities. The vacant lots were filled with grass rather than garbage, and the streets were washed, eight months of the year at least, by the heavy rains. It was an improvement, however, to have more sidewalks and paved streets, and to have the ragged growth cut from along the roadsides. Any idle man was forced into the clean-up squads. Africans love nothing better than to cut down trees, so during this period many beauties were destroyed in the name of improvement. Modern cement and glass air-conditioned ministries were built to replace the former colonial offices which were scattered around the town. The ministers had to have new houses on the "Gold Coast," expensive land facing the sea. They were obliged to leave their own homes in different sections of town to live together in this ministerial compound where they had very little privacy. These houses were also built of cement and glass, without shade, and I did not know one wife who was content in her new home.

To me the worst feature of the government's spending on costly offices and houses was that it benefited so few people. Had only a fraction of the amount been devoted to a program for helping the women of Gabon, it would have made a tremendous difference to the country. The President began the "Year of the Gabonese Woman" by opening the Army to women recruits. About sixty young women joined. They marched well, a few were trained as parachutists, but the majority ended up as assistants in the police force, directing traffic or working in offices. As most of these girls were pretty, it was not long before quite a few of them were seen to be pregnant. One, an unusually winsome girl who already had one child, confided in Charles that she planned to have another as soon as she could make up her mind which man to choose for the father.

Another and very important step which the President took was to secure the passage of a law making the payment of the dowry or bride price illegal. But the practice continued much as before.

Just before independence a group of women in Libreville had started a group called the "Organization of Gabonese

Women." Their purpose was to improve the lot of women in small ways. But after a few meetings, the President decided that it was becoming "political" and ordered its dissolution. Now, to show his interest in the plight of women, he proclaimed that the organization be revitalized; it had been completely disbanded in Libreville, but the units in the country were still alive. He further proposed that our Embassy send, instead of a man, two Gabonese women on Leader Grants to the United States.

Unhappily these steps were little more than empty gestures toward the improvement of the position of women. The greatest problem facing them, and the country with its underpopulation, was and is sterility and infant mortality. Jean Kenyon MacKenzie, an American missionary in Gabon at the beginning of the century, wrote:

I think that in the geography of African misery this region of maternal anguish is the most populous. For good reasons many women are barren and many lose child after child at birth. To the sorrow of their hearts are added the burdens of superstition and blame, heavier than you can imagine.

Sixty years later this sad state of affairs was unchanged. Surely this was the place to start: improve the position of women by opening clinics where they could be taught the causes and cures of sterility and the proper care of infants. The strength and intelligence of Gabonese women would be turned to the benefit of the whole country if these basic burdens could be lightened. Later could come such public health measures as more frequent spraying against mosquitoes and flies, the covering of open sewers, and free milk for schoolchildren. But these ideas were deemed "political"; they ran into the domains of the ministries and into the realm of tribal custom. They were uncomfortable and even dangerous.

A Frenchwoman was appointed Director of the recreated

Organization of Gabonese Women. I offered to help her in any way I could, but she had no place for my advice or my services, saying that leadership must come from the Gabonese women themselves. It became apparent, however, that she wanted to keep the activity entirely in French hands. I was sure that the two young women would come back from their American trip with practical suggestions. After all, they had been chosen by the President for this very purpose. When they returned, they were full of enthusiasm and plans for getting things under way. But after a bit they told me it was best that they did not come to see me any more, best that I did not call them at the office. In the end they were completely by-passed and given no further responsibility, and they knew, and I knew, that this was because they had been to the United States. Their exclusion, as well as mine, was all part of French policy in Gabon. The French Director, it turned out, had little faith in the potentiality of the Gabonese women; she was determined to keep the work with them on the level of simple housekeeping hints. She was, after all, a very busy woman, skilled in fortunetelling and always at the beck and call of the President to read his future in the cards!

Madame Theodose had been right when she said, "The women here are still slaves."

XVII

The Woleu N'Tem and Río Muni

Travel is a very important part of the business of an ambassador and his family. It can also be great fun.

President Kennedy had said to my husband, "Don't stay all the time in your office; get out and meet the people through the country." In the letter which he sent on May 27, 1961, to each American ambassador abroad the President stressed this admonition, showing the importance which he attached to it.

"The practice of modern diplomacy," he wrote,

requires a close understanding not only of governments but also of people, their cultures and institutions. Therefore, I hope that you will plan your work so that you may have the time to travel extensively outside the nation's capital. Only in this way can you develop the close, personal associations that go beyond official diplomatic circles and maintain a sympathetic and accurate understanding of all segments of the country.

My husband naturally had to travel frequently in connection with AID projects, the Peace Corps and other matters.

In addition, he and I took a number of trips for the broader purposes of understanding the country and meeting the people. We also wanted to convey as widely as possible a feeling for the United States and Americans.

President Léon Mba was very interested in our desire to see the country, and he supervised the arrangements for each of our trips. As there are few hotels in Gabon, he asked the prefects and subprefects in whose areas we might be to receive and entertain us. I cannot speak highly enough of the President's kindness in this, or of the extremely gracious and friendly manner in which we were invariably taken care of in every part of the country.

One of our most interesting trips was to the Woleu N'Tem. It was important that we visit this Region (or state) as soon as possible since it is the home of the Fang tribe which dominates the political life of Gabon. Léon Mba is a Fang, as are Aubame, Ekoh, Méyé, Ondo, Adjomo, Engone, now in charge of Foreign Affairs, and other ministers with whom Charles had frequent business. Some Fang, like Léon Mba and Aubame, were born outside the Woleu N'Tem, but they shared the feeling for their tribe. All our Fang friends had repeatedly urged us not to delay our visit.

Oyem, the chief town of the Woleu N'Tem, is the core city of Fang tribal life. It is from there that the Region is administered by the Prefect. There are also four other towns of importance, the seats of Subprefectures: Mitzic, Bitam, Minvoul and Médouneu. In Gabon the place where a man has his family roots is important. It puts its stamp on him for life. Jacques Biyogho, Gabon's recent Ambassador to the United Nations, for instance, will say, "I am from Médouneu." From time to time he may live elsewhere, but he is always a man from Médouneu. Knowing men and women from all these towns, it was important that we should make our pilgrimage to each.

One can plan a very nice circular trip combining the Woleu

N'Tem with Río Muni, which together with the island of Fernando Po, formed Spanish Guinea, one of Spain's few African colonies. In 1964 Fernando Po and Río Muni were given a considerable measure of local autonomy. They are now called Equatorial Guinea, and their present Governor is a Fang with the well-known name of Ondo: Ondo Bonifacio.

Río Muni was not a reporting responsibility of our Embassy, but very little information was available in Washington on it. No senior American official had in fact visited it, and we knew that the Department would welcome a report. Spain is very much less sensitive about its African colonies than is Portugal, but nevertheless we felt it necessary to make quite certain that our visit would be agreeable to the government, which was then represented by a Spanish Governor. In particular we wanted the Governor to know that we would be traveling quite unofficially, that we would be on vacation and that we certainly were not coming to snoop into his country's affairs. All of this my husband set down in a letter, expressing the hope that our proposed visit would meet with the Governor's approval and requesting that someone in his office make hotel reservations for us.

There was no postal service then between Gabon and Río Muni, so a letter from Libreville, if mailed, would go to Paris, be forwarded to Madrid and thence back to Africa. It was suggested that a quicker way would be to send our letter to the Prefect of the Woleu N'Tem in Oyem, asking him to entrust it to some traveler. This is what we did, and weeks later, when we reached Oyem, the Prefect handed us a gorgeous envelope from Bata bearing the Governor's crest and sealed with red wax. Not only did he welcome our visit in the most gracious terms, but he invited us to be his guests in Bata. The reply had come as our letter had gone, carried by some kind traveler.

As our daughter, Tia, and younger son, Christopher, were

254

coming from the United States to spend the summer with us, we felt that something should be added to our trip to make it more attractive to them.

One of the most interesting things that one could do in Gabon was to go in a pirogue through the rapids of the Ogooué. This great river, the largest between the Niger and the Congo, had been one of the historic avenues into the heart of Equatorial Africa. Until recent times there was no other way except the arduous forest trails, where a traveler was at the mercy of savage tribes as well as elephants, gorillas and snakes.

Navigable to a few miles above N'Djolé, the river beyond that is a succession of rapids, where the water rushes through narrow passages between fearsome cliffs and boulders and cascades over fields of rocks. The men of the Okandé and Adouma tribes spent their lives on the river, making times without number the breath-taking descent and then the long grueling paddle back. The know-how and the secrets were passed on from generation to generation. But this was the old Gabon. Now there is the road as well as planes. The boys no longer learn the art of the river, and the strong and wise ones are almost gone.

My husband thought that a trip through the rapids of the Ogooué from Booué to N'Djolé was just what would please the children. Not only would it be exciting, but it would be seeing a life and an activity truly African that in a very few years will be ended. President Léon Mba, to whom the plans for all of our trips were submitted, hesitated because of the danger, but then, pleased that we wanted to see this part of Gabon and Gabonese life, not only gave his consent but ordered that the very best of the Okandés be engaged and, with great kindness, had the Gabonese Government pay their hire.

To my regret, it was thought that the trip would be too difficult for me, so Bill Mansfield of the Embassy agreed with alacrity to make up the party of four. They flew to Booué in a one-engine Dragon, stopping on the way at Kongo-Boumba, a foresters' station where the plane landed in a field. The subprefect at Booué gave them a very good dinner. Three of his wives were at the table, including a pretty young one who nursed her child as she sat next to Christopher. When they went to the beach after breakfast the next morning, they found to their surprise not just three or four *pagayeurs* (paddlers) but eighteen in each of the two pirogues. The pirogues were rather longer than eight-oared shells and slightly wider, hollowed out of single trees. The *pagayeurs* sat on boards attached to the gunwhales while they paddled, but when they used long poles to steady the boat or hold it from being swept into a dangerous place, they would stand on their seats balancing miraculously. In the bow the captain stood, scanning the river ahead and shouting constant orders to the crew.

While Charles and the children enjoyed their voyage, I made preparations for our motor trip. We had asked Henry Stephen to come with us. At that time we were not familiar enough with Gabon to undertake an extensive trip alone; Henry would support us and would be good company too. Moreover, as our post's Public Affairs Officer he was expected to travel and to keep a photographic record of matters of interest.

The President's office had sent copies of our itinerary to the Prefect of the Woleu N'Tem and to each Subprefect, which meant that we would be officially received and cared for along the route. But we would need enough food for two weeks of roadside lunches, things that would not spoil, as well as jerrycans of gas, tins of oil, bottled water and blankets since it would be cool at night in the north. For our party of five we took both jeeps, the Embassy's and that of the USIS.

We were late in getting started and when we arrived at Kango the Subprefect was waiting for us at the ferry. He had held it for us, having a copy of our schedule in his hand. After six hours of hard driving we arrived in N'Djolé just after the river party had landed. The *pagayeurs* swarmed around us and all wanted to shake hands with the "Mama." Two and a half days on the sunny river had turned my family into three toughs. Tia and I were put up in the deserted house of a former French doctor. It was a Charles Addams cartoon of a place. When I tried to close the shutters, they fell off. The water ran only a tiny trickle. A woman came bringing us a bucket full, some sheets and a mosquito netting. We walked up the hill behind the town to have drinks with the French noncommissioned officer in charge of the local detachment of gendarmes, and ended the day with a copious dinner with the Subprefect in his ramshackle old residence on the edge of the river. In the morning we bade good-bye to Bill Mansfield and swung up the road toward the north, Charles driving one jeep, Henry the other.

It took us eight hours to reach Mitzic, with only a short stop for lunch. We turned and twisted, up and down, endlessly on and on. There were some lovely views over the Ogooué, particularly at the point where we crossed the Equator, but most of the day we were in great forests in dim light under the high trees. The air was cool as we drove into Mitzic, and we found our way to the house of the Subprefect of the District, M. Toko Adrien. The appearance of the town was pleasing. On a low hill the Subprefect's office and his house, the gendarmery and some other official buildings fronted on a small grass-covered park with old trees. Around this center meandered rough streets where lived a few French traders in cement houses and the Gabonese in their huts under palms and banana trees. There were but two stores, carrying drums of gasoline, hardware, cigarettes and a few household supplies. Only the administrative centers in Gabon possess these amenities; the villages have nothing but their cluster of houses.

In the late afternoon we drove to the Catholic Mission to pay our respects to Madame Pauline Mba, who had arrived there on her way back from the leper hospital where she had presented a new church bell. She came out of the mission with the Bishop, Monsignor N'Dong, arms outstretched to greet us and said to me, *"Permettez-moi de vous embrasser, chère Madame,"* and kissed me on both cheeks. She was touched to see us in this little town showing Gabon to our children. We next met with a group of Crossroads Africa members installed in the Normal College giving a three weeks' course to Gabonese teachers, and then had dinner with our hosts and their other guests, the Deputy Obame Michel, the French doctor and his wife and the wife of the Subprefect of Médouneu, who was attending the Crossroads Africa session.

The Subprefect talked at some length about the difficulties of his position, a Galoa in Fang country, and about the Bwiti dances and witch doctors, saying that we would see nothing in the north compared to the south. He had, he said, often seen a dead man get up after the Bwiti dancing, walk to his grave and get into it, after which he was buried.

Our objective the next day was the Leprosarium at Ebeigne. We stopped to watch a group of girls in a ceremonial funeral dance in the open square of a small village. The elders smilingly shook hands with us while the dancers continued without interruption. At Ebeigne we were welcomed by the Director, a Frenchman named Captain Amyiot. During drinks in their pleasant house we heard a great deal about their life with its fears and problems. Madame said that at first she thought she would never be able to look at the patients, or have them around her, but after a few months she became used to them. We learned that the arrested cases are not dangerous; and that the only time the disease is contagious is when it is "pussy." Madame told us of a mission-trained girl, a Gabonese, who worked in the hospital. She had lived with a Frenchman who had returned to France leaving her with two children and another on the way. Her family wanted her to give the new baby to them as she already had two, but after the child was born she did not want to give it up. One day she was dead, poisoned. And no questions were asked; in the more remote parts of Gabon children are family or tribal property, and customs must be respected.

We were given a splendid French luncheon, well cooked and served—whether by lepers we did not inquire. Charles asked many questions so that we were well prepared for our visit to the wards. The difficulty was lack of medical help: there was no doctor on the staff at the time and only one nurse, an Alsatian missionary who had had three years' experience with Dr. Schweitzer. For the rest, treatments and dressings were given by Gabonese orderlies who themselves were cured or arrested lepers. Patients and their families lived in their own native quarters, coming to the hospital for treatment or entering the hospital wards for anything serious. The big contribution Captain Amyiot had made, it seemed to us, was in his emphasis on rehabilitation. The churches (one Protestant and one Catholic, in which we saw the new bell given by Madame Mba), the cinema, the surgical building (finished but empty of equipment and staff) had all been built by the lepers themselves. They were also doing carpentry and some leatherwork and ivory carving. Amyiot thinks it is not enough to cure or control the disease but that lepers must be taught to be useful members of society. He longs for a surgeon, and for the artificial hands, limbs and devices which we use so widely in our rehabilitation centers in America. It was obvious that he hoped that my husband would include the Leprosarium in his aid requests to Washington.

A dance was planned for us at three o'clock and word was

sent out on a huge tom-tom. When the hour came, the large square in front of the cinema and church was filled with Africans. There must have been a dozen family or tribal groups, each doing a different dance. In several there were young women, in another just young girls, in another men beating madly on tom-toms and on a bamboo xylophone.

Afterward we went back to Amyiot's house for a thorough wash-up and drink before setting out for Oyem. On the way we passed another village dance held to mark the raising of the six months' period of mourning for the dead.

Oyem is on a hill with wide, tree-lined streets, gardens and substantial houses. We went first to the Prefecture, where we met M. Pierre Fanguinovény. He is the liveliest, merriest Gabonese I have ever seen, with a beard around the edge of his face, glistening white teeth and deep-set twinkling eyes. He bounced out of his office and conducted us to his house. His wife is a tiny, very blonde Swiss.

The Prefect's residence, under huge trees overlooking a valley, was large and well furnished. Nearby were two guest houses. Charles and I were put in one, the children and Henry in the other. We cleaned up, rested and presented ourselves for drinks before dinner about 7:30. The Prefect's niece, Mlle. Mouencoula Agathe, a nurse, was staying in the house with her new baby. She had been assigned from Libreville for the summer as the clinic in Oyem did not have a single midwife. Agathe was an exceptionally attractive girl, tall with a lissome figure and a pretty face. But she was intelligent and choosy, and had found no man to please her as a husband so she remained unmarried.

Having children first is no bar to marriage in Gabon; in fact, it is the case more often than not. Girls are allowed, if not expected, to flirt; it is after marriage that they must be chaste.

I remember a luncheon in Makokou when the Subprefect's wife was talking to Charles about her children. "The oldest is not my husband's," she said, "a boy from Tchibanga got me pregnant when I was in school in Lambaréné." The place and the author were named, quite unconcernedly.

M. Fanguinovény is a scholar and linguist. He was sent to France to study by his father, a Gabonese who was one of the first to exploit the country's wood, practically the original forester of Gabon. The family property is around Lambaréné, and it was his father who gave the land for the hospital to Dr. Schweitzer. He talked well and amusingly. He said that he had worked for years on the study of local African customs and secret societies and that twice his papers had been stolen from his car. Then he told us in all seriousness that he had seen the dead walk to their graves and that the best way to cure cuts in the jungle was to place driver ants across the gash, cut off their bodies, and leave the heads like cleats to keep the wound closed till it healed.

Charles, the Prefect, Henry and I left after breakfast the next day to visit the village of Madame Marguérite Mba, one of the Gabonese women who had gone to the United States on a Leader Grant. We had entertained her in Libreville and promised to look up her family near Oyem. Her brother, after much handshaking scooped up a chicken, quickly tied its legs and gave it flapping to Charles. Her mother came out of a little mud-brick house on the way to her plantation, carrying a huge machete. She was a tall, straight-backed woman with Fang scars on her face, who understood no French. Fanguinovény told her who we were, and she smiled, shook our hands and moved off about her business with dignity. What a jump in one generation, from this background to good French and a tour of the United States by air!

We drove on to the Catholic mission, where some two hundred Gabonese were waiting for us outside the steps of the school, teachers who had come to attend a summer training school. The Abbé gave a welcoming speech, then the teachers sang the "Star-Spangled Banner" in French. I was never so moved; full African voices in four part harmony that they had arranged themselves. Then a young teacher made a speech to us, asking that we help them and reminding us of the history of our own fight for freedom and progress. Charles responded, not an easy thing to do as he was taken by surprise. Fanguino-vény had kept it up his sleeve. Then we went into the mission parlor to have communion wine and sweet biscuits with the head Sisters and Fathers of the school.

One of the pupils, Colette, ten years old, had become rather famous in the area. On her own she had written to President Léon Mba saying that her father was selling her like an animal to an old man for marriage. She insisted that she did not want to be married but wanted to stay on and study in school and begged the President to help her. President Mba sent the letter back to the Sisters, asking that they do what was possible with the father. For the moment they were keeping her safely in school, sending the father on his way each time he came and tried to collect his daughter, but the situation was difficult as daughters belong to their fathers, who *"dot"* them. Colette came in and shook our hands, had a biscuit and scampered away to play.

Later that day we all drove into the country to have a drink with one of the Deputies; he wanted us to meet his family, see his village and home. He was standing outside his neat mud-brick house to greet us. We were shown into a dark cool room, the walls made of split bamboo carefully fitted together. It was furnished with local Gabonese or African chairs and simple tables, all as neat and clean as could be. The Deputy's young wife came in holding the new baby and we met their daughters;

he explained that he had not yet "made" a boy. His tall, scarred father came in, shook hands, then sat in a corner to drink his beer while we talked. Over and over we heard on this trip: "We appreciate all the French do for us, our language is theirs, but why can't we have help from and contacts with other countries? We do not want to be so tied to France!" As we left they all stood in the twilight and waved us off. Many people from the village had gathered outside the Deputy's house.

Despite a reception and dinner that evening, we were up early the following morning to go to Minvoul. The Prefect and his wife accompanied us part way. We stopped at the Government Agricultural School, which had several nice buildings but only twenty students as there was no machinery to work with, all teaching having to be done from charts. The Gabonese Government had requested aid from our country for this institution. We walked about the fields, had drinks in the Director's house and then went on to the Cocoa Multiplication Station, a nursery where the quality of the cocoa tree is being improved. Farmers can come and get young shoots of good stock free of charge.

About 4:30 we saw a Land Rover stopped in the road ahead of us. It contained the Deputy Subprefect of Minvoul and the Gabonese head of the gendarmery who had come to escort us into town. Minvoul is on a hill standing in a sea of unbroken forest. The road ran straight up to the top, where the administrative buildings were laid out, as in all these French colonial posts, in graceful symmetry around a central green. In the middle was the flagpole, from which broad walks lined with trees led to the several buildings. All the personalities of the town were waiting to greet us, the old soldiers in their uniforms and medals. We shook hands with everyone, then crossed the square to the Subprefect's residence. As Minvoul then had no Subprefect, the Deputy Subprefect used the residence for official entertaining. There were marvelous views from the porch as far as both Cameroon and Congo Brazza.

Tia and I were given a large room with double bed on one side of the house, the men rooms on the other. None of us had running water and there was no electric light as the diesel motor was *"en panne,"* or out of order. The expression *"en panne"* was one we encountered frequently on our travels in Gabon. The diesel motors which the French officials in their time had doubtless kept running were now almost without exception broken. The same fate had befallen the scrapers which the subprefects were supposed to use to maintain the roads. When a piece of government machinery breaks in Gabon, it is likely to stay that way for months while the official waits for parts or even for the government in Libreville to give him the credit to enable him to order the parts.

While we were changing, Charles was presented to the deputies from the area. A crowd of people stood outside the house watching to see what was going on. Charles came back to get us as we were all to attend a reception to meet the head of the Collectivité Rurale and other notables. The room held about fifty people. We were seated at a huge oblong table, one of the Deputies, and Charles at the head, Tia, Christy, Henry and I on the sides. Everyone was dressed in his best with jacket and tie. Tia and I were the only women. A few wives stood outside as this was obviously a men's gathering. Drinks were passed and the meeting began.

The Deputy introduced Charles, who after a short talk said that he would be glad to answer questions. They came thick and fast, and there were some good ones. We heard over and over how they needed help with the price of cocoa and coffee, with machinery, medicines and many other things. Why cannot the U.S.A. help us? At one point a huge *chef de canton,* dressed in his uniform, got up and made an excited speech in

Fang, which was then interpreted into French by the Deputy. Charles replied to every question. Here as in other places the poor, simple people were unable to make a distinction between what they should do for themselves, what their own government could do, and what might be done by foreign aid. All they knew was that they needed, or wanted, help. My husband often tried to clarify this confusion.

During this hour and a half it got hotter and hotter and the drinks got larger and stronger. The men around the table took anything that was offered; glasses of straight gin or Scotch, gin mixed with Scotch, and one man I saw poured together gin and Cointreau. The Deputy Subprefect had been given a credit by the government to defray the expenses of receiving us.

Dripping with sweat, we finally got back across the square to our house. As we came into the room, we saw that two French priests and three Gabonese wives had turned up along with many children. Five of our hosts' children were asleep on a couch. The house was quite dark, and I am not sure just how many we were at any one time, but I do know that after endless more drinks some twenty of us sat down to dinner at about 9:30. We had been taken to see the kitchen first, a small room behind the house lit only by two open roaring fires. We could just see the grinning and sweaty faces of the two cooks and one girl who was either assisting them or keeping them company. On the way out we passed another completely unlighted hole where dishwashing seemed to be going on.

Dinner was served at one long table on the porch. The only light came from a Coleman lantern just over my head; further down the table the guests ate in darkness. We started out bravely with a fish course, then came a different kind of fish, then chicken, then meats. Altogether there were ten courses, not counting the salad which, bless her heart, our hostess forgot! She apologized and was all for sending back the dessert and

265

bringing out the lettuce, but luckily I was able to stop her. All this was served by her daughter of eleven and one boy.

At about course six, a beef stew, the daughter was serving her mother when she tripped over a dog and the bowl of meat and gravy splashed against the wall and covered her arm and dress. She threw up her hands and ran sobbing out of the room. Charles sought her out in a dark corner of the kitchen, consoled her, wiped off her dress and brought her back. Plates were changed between every course; we ate from one set while the other one was being washed in that unlighted room with no running water. At one point I asked Tia to tell Henry not to turn his back on his host who was sitting next to him. Henry shouted back that he couldn't move, the host was asleep against his shoulder! The effort, care and hard work that had gone into that meal were staggering—and practically all of it done by this tiny woman with eight children, another Galoa from Lambaréné. But perhaps getting ready for it, talking about it with the people in the village, broke the quiet monotony of their lives. We heard several times how grateful they were that we had visited them for *"ici à Minvoul, nous sommes abandonés"* ("here in Minvoul we are abandoned"). No airfield, only one small road which ends there, and all around the unbroken forest stretching to the horizon.

Our sleep that night was not very restful, and we staggered out of our beds to wash, pack and eat breakfast with unclear heads. Chris had finally gone to sleep on the couch after all the children had been taken away. Both the Deputy Subprefect and his wife ate breakfast with us and said rather wistfully that it made them sad to see us leave. After an hour's drive we approached a river and found a flowered arch had been put up for us to pass through. The ferry was waiting, also decorated with palm boughs and flowers, and on the bank were a group of women, dressed in the blue, green, and yellow uniform of

266

the Section Féminine Gabonaise. A young interpreter with them explained that they were doing a dance of welcome for us. We were most appreciative and taken completely by surprise. We got out and, of course, shook hands all around, and Charles made a little speech of thanks.

Across the river we found more women singing and dancing to welcome us. They stood in a line, the leader going up and down in front blowing a whistle to give the signal for changes. There were some quite old women in this group. After Charles again had made his speech, these old ones threw their arms around him and kissed him on both cheeks as he bent down to shake their hands. Then the rest of us got the same treatment, except for Henry who was madly taking pictures. These women did not speak any French and the young man was busy interpreting. The things I remember most clearly that they said were: "We want to know about women in America; we want to learn from them; we need medicines and a hospital; we need doctors; we have pains in our bellies and cannot have babies; our children get sick and die; help us, help us." It was hard to pull away, but we finally did, only to be stopped at two other villages for similar performances. In the last one the women stood in line and the head woman stepped up and gave us a pineapple while another handed me three eggs. We were amazed and delighted all the way to Bitam by this warm welcome.

Bitam is the center of the cocoa-producing area. We found our way to the main square, where a group of about fifty women were lined up to meet us. They were in the Section Féminine costume again, singing and dancing in the same way as the women we had met along the road. Fanguinovény turned up, with the Deputy Subprefect of Bitam, Ekoga Edouard, and we did a kind of review of the troops, shaking hands with all present before being taken on a drive around the town.

We were lodged in the empty house of the Subprefect, that

post at the moment being vacant. Madame Fanguinovény was on the steps to greet us, having driven from Oyem with her husband that morning to make sure that all was in order. We had comfortable beds, running water, a flush toilet, and were given an hour to rest and clean up before the reception at the Gabon Bar arranged by the Collectivité Rurale. When we got to the place, there were crowds standing around outside, waiting for us. Inside the door the first thing we saw was a whole cooked lamb, hanging upside down on a pole stretched between two chairs, neck and feet decorated with red flowers. Fanguinovény presented Charles, who spoke again, this time only briefly and a bit tiredly, or so the family thought. He was quick enough, though to pay tribute to the French, this being July 14, which pleased everyone.

Then one of the hosts asked me to begin the lamb, the *pièce de résistance* of the party. I pulled and struggled but made no headway with the whole shoulder, which he urged me to take. Finally he let me settle for a piece of skin and meat which I tore off the carcass. Tia then was fetched, and he helped her rip off the shoulder. After we had taken our pieces, the crowd fell upon the animal and within a few moments it was picked completely clean! The president of the Bitam Section Féminine stuck by me closely all during the party, whispering in my ear: I was to write to her, I was to help her, I was to do this and that. Chris had a young Gabonese who would not let him go, either—wanted to know all about America right then and there.

The next day was Sunday. We were off after Mass at 8:30, with the Deputy Subprefect and the head of the gendarmery, a Frenchman, leading the way to the border. They crossed on the ferry with us and we were in Spanish Guinea, or Río Muni. The frontier here was a shallow river and the ferry consisted simply of some planks laid over several old and leaky pirogues. A short drive brought us to Ebebiyin. In this colony most of the towns are close to the frontiers, where the Spanish located them to mark, or defend, the boundaries of their possession.

The streets of Ebebiyin were wide and there were flowers around the houses. In the center of town white buildings in seemingly good repair bordered a large tree-filled square. We drove to a stone house that would have been comfortable in any city, with a garden and a small swimming pool at the side. Here Captain José Javier Yndurain, the Governor's representative in the Region, came out to meet us wearing a white uniform, with red and gold epaulets. We entered his cool high-ceilinged house and were shown to immaculate washrooms. The carpets, highly polished tiled floors, pictures and *bibelots* seemed the utmost in luxury after the simple homes we had recently visited. The Captain spoke only a few words of French and things were a bit sticky until Tia tentatively brought forth her Spanish. We had no idea she was so proficient, and from then on she acted as our interpreter.

While waiting for Señora Yndurain to return from Mass we were shown about the town, visiting the cathedral, the large mission school, the hospital and the clinic. Everything was in order and seemed to be well run. There was even a garage filled with public transport buses, unheard of in Gabon. The Señora was not at all upset by having seven extra guests for lunch and gave us a variety of delicacies for hors d'oeuvres, explaining that they were Spanish specialties. Next came an excellent paella with green salad, cheeses and dessert. The waiters wore not only white uniforms with gold buttons but white cotton gloves.

We were sorry to leave this pleasant house and its charming and friendly occupants. The bouncy Ekoga Edouard kissed Charles good-bye, he and the French gendarme returned to Gabon and we set off toward Micomesen, where we were due to spend the night. The road was poor, but the villages were larger and neater than any we had seen in Gabon and the people along the roadsides appeared better dressed. Unlike the Gabonese, however, they were not eager to wave and showed little interest as our cars passed by.

Captain Manuel Pixarro and his wife were waiting on the wide terrace of their lovely house overlooking the town when we drove up in the late afternoon. With them was a Spanish statistician come to work on a census of the population. The Pixarros and their seven children lived in one wing, guests used the other, and the reception and dining rooms were in the center. Outside were well-kept gardens with shade trees, flowering bushes and many birds. The views down on the village and to the hills opposite were charming. A quiet but a pleasant place in which to live, surely.

The Leprosarium we visited on the following day served all of Río Muni. It was larger than that at Ebeigne in Gabon and appeared to us to be efficiently run by a tiny Spanish doctor who proudly took us over every inch of the place. There was no shortage of staff here: Catholic Sisters were in and out of all the spotless wards, giving love, comfort and above all a sense of order to the patients. We saw many dreadful sights, but the sick were clean and in neat beds. No families were permitted around this hospital. They brought and left the patients and were then allowed periodic visits, the European system as opposed to the Schweitzer or African one. We were shown the comprehensive card files kept on all known lepers in the country. There was no rehabilitation, but arrested cases worked as orderlies or on the grounds. It was an efficient establishment, but I thought it somewhat distant and cold except for the faces of the nursing sisters.

Another tour took us to the mission school, where several of the little Pixarros went. It was a lovely place right out of old Spain, with a central patio shaded by one huge tree, a well surmounted by a cross, and children in school uniforms, playing happily together. There was a dormitory for native orphans nearby, neat as a pin with a cover on each cot, and places at table set in the dining room, with each child's one piece of manioc and his own napkin rolled in a ring.

We then left for Bata, the capital. The drive was long, through one village after another over a road of dusty red laterite, but the last thirty kilometers into Bata were macadamized, the only paved road on which we had driven since leaving Libreville. When we arrived at the Palace, there on the steps, flanked by uniformed guards, stood the Governor, Victor Suances Diaz, and his wife together with our good friend Julio Travesi. We tumbled out of the car, mounted the great staircase and were conducted to the wing of the building that was to be our suite. And a marvelous suite it was, with two double bedrooms, one single, two baths, a kitchen with the icebox filled with drinks, and both inside and outside sun porches.

We were curious to learn how the Governor knew that we would arrive just when we did, so as to be waiting at the porte-cochere. He told us that he had the police telephone him when we passed through Sevilla de Niefang, a town some sixty kilometers away, giving him the time and an estimate of our speed from which he was able to calculate when we would be in Bata. We marveled at this exhibition of efficiency.

We spent three days in this comfortable place with these charming people. Bata was a quaint and sleepy town, as different from bustling Libreville as Río Muni was from Gabon. In Río Muni white settlers live on cocoa and coffee plantations, employing Africans who have cash to spend from their wages, so their villages appear more substantial than those in Gabon. But the Gabonese, if seemingly less prosperous, live on their own land and work it for themselves. This, of course, was five years ago. As part of Equatorial Guinea, Río Muni now has a considerable measure of self-government and can doubtless look forward to the day when it will be an independent country associated with Spain.

Thursday we left at 7:30 and drove hard over a mountainous road which was as bad as any we had seen in Gabon. We finally got to the Gabon border at six, where we were greeted by the Subprefect, Etoughe Joseph and the Deputy, Jacques Biyogho, who had been waiting for us there since four. We drove frantically the ten minutes into Médouneu through the twilight and arrived to find a crowd of at least three hundred people standing on the village green. We dashed into the Subprefect's house to clean up a little and then the four of us—Charles, Tia, Christopher and myself—with the Subprefect and the Deputy at our side, made the rounds greeting every person in the crowd, shaking hands and telling them over and over how kind it was of them to wait and how sorry we were to be late. Many had babies in their arms or on their backs. It was now dark, so the cars were driven up, headlights turned on and Charles made a speech to the patient crowd. Then we were taken back to the Subprefect's house for a *vin d'honneur.* All the dignitaries of the district had been invited in to meet us, about forty of them. This house had no electricity for the diesel was *"en panne,"* nor running water. But the wife, Marthe, (whom we had met at dinner at Mitzic) had freshly painted the so-called bathroom a bright green in our honor. Charles cracked his head twice on the low door lintel and had green hair for days as well as a big bump. She had bought new towels and soap for us from Libreville, everything to make her very simple place as nice as possible.

Charles, Tia and I were quartered in the house, Chris and Henry with the gendarmery. Cleaned and changed we stood on the narrow porch and met the guests. Charles was soon involved at one end with some wonderful old boys who kept shouting to him in Fang, the Deputy interpreting. One said, "You are a big man, they say you come from a big country;

if that is so, why can't you help us?" And later after Charles had made explanations about why he could not just put the economy of Médouneu right, another old man said, "Well, is there anyone back home where you come from who is more important than you? Then let me talk to him!" In the meantime Chris, Tia and I were at the other end of the porch, wedged in between wives and other men, all talking equally hard. I shall never forget hearing Tia in French repeating all Charles' explanations of United States policy. Then as I pushed further along through the crowd, I came across Chris doing the same thing. I hardly needed to open my mouth! Wonderful what the children had absorbed in such a short time. Later we learned that Médouneu is the real forgotten town in Gabon: not one store, once-weekly air service by a single-engine plane, no clinic, no doctor.

After dinner, we were driven some distance to the Deputy's village, where a Bwiti dance had been organized for us. All was dark except for a fire outside the church, or cathedral as they called it. We sat at the back and for some time watched a strange mixture of African and Catholic ritual. Most of the dancers were women, dressed in long white dresses, their faces whitened with powder. Red canna blossoms sewed to strips of palm leaves hung from the low ceiling; there was a kind of altar beside which, partially screened, sat two men beating a steady accompaniment on bamboo sticks and another pinging a sequence with variations on an *ngoma*. The music was rhythmic, haunting, eerie. A bell was rung to announce changes in the ceremony. At intervals men and women arose from their benches on the sides and circled round and round, one following the other, in a swaying dance. Sometimes, when the others were sitting, a single man would leap into the cathedral brandishing flaming palm leaves, and would do a wild solo. We were told the ceremony would go on till dawn, the participants fortified by *iboga*.

273

We spent three hours the next morning talking to people in the village square. They clustered around Charles telling him about their problems and asking him questions while groups danced, beat tom-toms and bamboo xylophones. These people grow potatoes, cabbages and other vegetables but have no possible way to sell them or even to get them out of the little town. And their coffee and cocoa could no longer be sold to Río Muni, where the prices, supported by the Spanish Government, are higher than in Gabon. We left with regret and deeply touched at the warmth of our reception. The Deputy and the Subprefect gave us presents and as a courtesy drove ahead of us for half an hour to start us on our way back to Mitzic. Not that we could have missed the road; it was the only one.

And what a road! It took us five and a half hours to go about a hundred kilometers, just a slow grinding up and down, watching every moment so that the jeeps did not get into trouble. Mitzic looked very good to us, and we thankfully had an early supper with the Subprefect and his nice wife and went to bed.

Since Madame Mba had been able to leave Mitzic at six in the morning Charles thought we could do it too, and we did. It seemed cruel to get off that early, but he was right, for the first part of that return road was the worst and it did not bother us too much when we were fresh and the day was young. Also, we had to keep to a tight schedule as we had planned to reach Lambaréné that night. We had three ferries to cross, and the last one, into Lambaréné, closed at 5:30. We made it and staggered into the Relais at Lambaréné almost numb and once again caked with red dust. For the last two hours I could think of nothing but the bliss of the deep bathhub (a rarity in Gabon) in that hotel. But when we arrived we found that the water was turned off until the evening because it was the dry season. It did seem strange that there on the banks of the great Ogooué River we had no water in our rooms!

When we reached home, the house in Libreville seemed the utmost in luxury and the little city itself a booming metropolis: street lights and sidewalks! We had made a wide swing through new country and, we hope, had brought to these Gabonese some understanding of Americans and of the United States.

XVIII

Independence Ceremonies of the Kingdom of Burundi

W E had been in Gabon about a year when Charles was honored by being named President Kennedy's representative at the independence celebrations of the Kingdom of Burundi. I was to accompany him officially. We were delighted at the prospect of visiting a different part of Africa. Colonel A. F. Holman, Air Attaché of the American Embassy in the Congo, took us by plane from Kinshasa (then Léopoldville) to Bujumbura (then Usumbura), capital of Burundi.

The last thirty minutes we flew along Lake Tanganyika. The mountains on the east of the lake form the barrier of the great Rift Valley. Waters on the far side run into Lake Victoria, the Nile and the Mediterranean; those on the west into Lake Tanganyika, the Congo and the Atlantic. The same mountains farther north join the Mountains of the Moon. Heavenly names and beautiful scenery! We flew over the little landmark near

276

Ujiji not many miles south of Bujumbura where Stanley "presumed" it was Livingston.

Bujumbura lies spread around the northern tip of the lake ringed by green fields and farmhouses set among clumps of trees. We were met by the Chargé d'Affaires, Herbert Olds, with his wife, Mary, and the senior members of his staff—an American Ambassador had not yet been named to Burundi—and were driven into the city through wide, tree-lined streets where masses of jacarandas were in bloom. Their purple blossoms against white walls and green leaves were lovely. Not only does Bujumbura have a beautiful setting in its valley girded by mountains, but it is a pleasing city with broad streets, a number of fine buildings and an atmosphere of spaciousness. Mr. and Mrs. Olds took us to their house, which they called Belgian colonial—that is, it was modern, comfortable and completely lacking in charm. Air conditioners were not needed; the air was dry, and cool at night.

At a cocktail party that evening given by a member of our Consulate it was quite a shock to hear English everywhere. Bujumbura had a consular staff larger than that of our Embassy in Libreville, and of course all were present, together with a number of Europeans who also spoke English. It was not until the Mwami, his Royal Highness himself, quietly entered the room that anyone used French. The Mwami was surprising in his informality. There was no motorcycle escort, no hooting of sirens. Suddenly he was just there having a drink and being introduced to the guests. He was dressed in a conservative business suit with no decorations. We were told this is the way he likes it when he goes to the houses of Americans and Europeans; no protocol. But in the evening there must be dancing. He loves the twist and becomes a problem at parties because he never wants to go home.

As we had a spare day before the start of the ceremonies, we planned to visit Kigali, the capital of the Republic of

Rwanda. We flew over low mountains all the way and could see clearly the numerous well-kept little farms snuggling down in the valleys and on the hillsides, each with its own round or square house enclosed in a round or square hedge of bushes to match.

Mr. David Manbey, the Chargé, met us with his second, Mr. Ralph Cadeaux, and the Rwandan Chief of Protocol. We drove slowly into the town, which, although a national capital, had then only about three thousand people. Charles fell in love with the place; the red road lined with huge mango trees and the well-tended bucolic atmosphere of the countryside. We passed many of the famous Rwanda cattle, large animals, mostly tan with white markings and long, curving horns. Charles had the car stopped so that he could get out and examine the cows' udders, but came back disgusted for they were quite slack. The cattle are not kept primarily for either milk or meat. No attempt is made to upgrade their quality. They are status symbols, wealth. The blood of the bulls occasionally is tapped from the neck and used as food, which apparently does the animal no harm.

The people we passed were neatly dressed and pleasant-looking but not eagerly friendly; no waving as in Gabon. These were the Hutus, the strong middle-sized people of Bantu stock who, although composing 85 percent of the population, had been held for centuries in a kind of serfdom by a small minority of tall Hamitic Tutsis. The Twas, a semipygmy people, the survivors of the original inhabitants and now only one percent, did the dirty work of life. They helped care for the cattle, which were used by the Hutus but owned by the Tutsis. In later times some Hutus in Rwanda had acquired the right to own cattle.

The town itself consisted of neat but simple European houses. The "palace" of the President was a two-story red-brick building at the crossroads. As soon as one left the main street there was nothing but the huts of the Hutus. Charles called on the Foreign Minister and some other officials and had a long talk with the Belgian Ambassador. As we left, Mr. Manbey told us again of the need to enlarge the airstrip so that there could be more access to Rwanda. The new little democracy could not survive without greater contact with the rest of the world. He hoped that my husband would add a recommendation to this effect in his report.

Back in Bujumbura the next day, the independence celebration began early. We had to be at the cathedral for the *Te Deum* at eight o'clock in the morning. There were thirty foreign delegations, and each had a reserved pew. There were many Africans as well as representatives from Belgium, France, England, Australia, Germany and, believe it or not, both Chinas! As the President of the Congo, Mr. Kasavubu, entered there was a general turning of heads. The central aisle was lined with Burundi soldiers carrying guns and wearing hard helmets. In front of us sat the Burundi ministers with their beautiful wives. The Tutsi women are lovely—tall, straight-backed, with high foreheads and finely boned faces, their hair swept up into a kind of peak. They wore pastel swathes of diaphanous material draped in toga fashion over simple blouses and skirts. Their husbands were not as impressive for, though also tall, most were too thin, with heads rather small for their height.

We had ample time to study them for we sat on these hard seats exactly one and a half hours before anything happened. Someone whispered to us that the Mwami had been out dancing at a local night spot until 5:30 that morning so was late in arising. At long last we heard the sirens of the military jeeps and then, in the distance, the marvelous roll of the Mwami's drums, *"les tambours de Sa Majesté."* Gradually the sound drew closer like approaching thunder until it ended in a crashing finale before the cathedral. The drums then continued in a muffled roll while the royal party walked up the aisle: first the members of the King's family, his second wife, his brother, his Chief of Protocol and finally his first wife, the mother of the murdered Prince Rwagasore. Then, to the louder and louder beating of the drums, came the Mwami himself, Mwambutsa IV, in a white military uniform with red epaulets, and a military cap set at a jaunty angle. He presented a fine figure, carrying himself with dignity and ease. The service was a short one, with all standing.

At the end of the service we filed out and got into our cars for the drive to the Prince Rwagasore Memorial, newly built on the open hillside above the lake. It had been just a year since the Prince, the Mwami's eldest son, had been assassinated. He was the leader of the UPRONA political party, had worked hard for independence and reforms and was considered by many to be the hope of the country. The paid Greek gunman was hanged, but no one knew for certain who was behind the killing. Several men were being held in jail, among them a member of the powerful Baranyanka family, a brother of the Burundi Ambassador to Belgium who was present at the ceremonies. The trial was to be reopened at any time.

At the Memorial there were two small graves in addition to the central one. These were for the Prince's two daughters who died one after the other soon after his assassination. We stood hatless in the blazing sun without one inch of shade for another hour and a half, again waiting for the Mwami. Finally he and his party appeared and the brief ceremony took place. The next stop was the Palace, where the visiting representatives were to be presented to him. This was a charming house, the former residence of the Belgian Governor General, with fine gardens and trees. It was good to be inside the cool rooms, to be able to sit down and have a refreshing drink. We spoke briefly to His Majesty, then made our way back to the Oldses for a change into less formal clothing, a bite of lunch and on to the new Rwagasore Stadium for the afternoon events.

The United States' seats were in the covered area just behind and to the left of the Mwami's. He entered the Stadium at three, standing in an open white car, and drove around the field smiling and waving at the throngs who had been sitting in the open seats all morning. The car stopped in front of us and he mounted the steps to his big red chair. He was wearing a tan uniform this time. We could watch him and his family and ministers as they came and went around his chair all afternoon. The program lasted just four hours. There were many long speeches, given in both French and the native tongue. Then came the parade, and it was worth waiting for. Every child, every young adult, every member of a political group or school filed past us.

The most impressive sight for us were the Mwami's two companies of drummers, one group dressed in blue togas, the other in yellow. The blues were perhaps the more famous, having performed at the Brussels Fair. There were twenty-eight men in each company, all tall and strong. Their drums are tremendously heavy, being hollowed out of large tree trunks, about four feet high, closed at the smaller end, with hide stretched over the top and fastened to wooden pegs. When walking, they carry the drums horizontally on their heads, beating them with the raised right arm. When standing, they place the drums upright on the ground before them. No one but His Majesty, the Mwami, can possess these drums. From time immemorial they have been the King's symbol. Wherever he goes they go with him, signaling his approach. The Mwami of Rwanda traditionally had similar drums. He ornamented his by tying to them, in a crown where the hide is fastened to the bole, the dried testicles of his vanquished enemies.

On this occasion the drummers stopped in front of the Mwami, formed a semicircle, set their drums down and stood

281

the chief drum in the center of the open space. Then one by one the drummers came forward to beat a solo on this drum, at the same time dancing around it and leaping over it while the rest of the men beat time. Each performer did something a little different, moving with athletic grace and leaping high into the air as he cleared the drum. It was as exciting as anything I ever saw.

The day finished with a formal banquet in the local hotel. There must have been 350 guests wedged into four long tables in a room designed for half that number. The next morning there was another command performance: all guests had to be in their places at the Stadium at nine. The Mwami was again there, greeting those who came to his chair, and there was constant movement and changes in those who occupied the seats around this place of power. The parades, dances and drumming were as fine as the day before, and we sat until it was over at noon, fascinated with every detail.

In the evening we went to the Palace at eight o'clock to present our gift to the Mwami. The large room was filled with many objects, rugs, silver punch bowls, autographed photographs and so forth, which had been brought in and unpacked beforehand. Each ambassador took a position near his gift. The Mwami entered and stood in the center of the room, made a few gracious comments and then turned to Charles, who had the honor of presenting President Kennedy's gift first. It was a handsome console hi-fi set with a number of dance records. The Mwami walked over to it and was obviously very pleased. We had been worried for the instrument had been sent from Washington just as we left Libreville; we feared that it would not arrive in time or that it would be out of order, if not broken, after the long trip. But it came through, and our airplane's crew quickly had it in fine working order.

On the final day we poked. Charles went to an exhibition of Burundi art, and later bought a straw basket woven so tightly that it could hold beer. I took a cruise on Lake Tanganyika in a small outboard motorboat. We went along the shore and had the luck to see three hippopotamuses. As they came up for air, their little ears popped open, they breathed heavily and swam swiftly away. We had to get back to the harbor by ten as after that the lake becomes rough and dangerous. Lake Tanganyika is the second deepest in the world and surely one of the most beautiful.

There was a final reception and buffet that evening at the hotel. The Mwami was most gracious, and we shook hands in farewell with him and the members of his cabinet and family. We regretted that we could not talk more with the women, who looked so intelligent and lovely as they sat in groups like so many butterflies. But it was not done; European men were not supposed to engage them in conversation and European women do not do so as they have so few points of contact. Mrs. Olds and other embassy wives told me how frustrating this was.

The woman with the strongest and most interesting face I thought was the Mwami's first wife, the mother of Prince Rwagasore. She was large, but not tall, had rather coarse features with little of the Tutsi finely chiseled look. But there was strength in her every gesture and expression. From her must have come the leadership and the drive of the dead Prince, who was an idol of the people. The Mwami's wife at the time of our visit was a young Tutsi who had given him one son, Prince Charles, then aged fourteen and in school abroad. I asked if the Burundis did not get cross with their Mwami when he spent so much time out of the country and so much money on personal extravagances. The answer was "Not at all"; he was their Mwami and could do no wrong; they expected him to live and act by a different standard from their own. But things have changed. In September, 1966, Prince Charles deposed his father, who was then living in Switzerland with his French mistress, Josie, and took over the throne, calling himself Ntare V, but in November he in turn was deposed and the monarchy after more than four centuries was replaced by a republic.

During the celebrations all the foreign representatives were given the most cordial welcome except one, a man named Apollinaire Nuwumuremyi, the Director of the Political Division of the Ministry of Foreign Affairs of Rwanda. The Rwandan Government had no airplanes so they had to ask Burundi to send one. The Burundis were somewhat less than accommodating, keeping poor Mr. Nuwumuremyi waiting all of Thursday, the day of the principal ceremonies. When he finally reached Bujumbura on Friday, he was put into a poor hotel room at 1:00 P.M. and told that someone would call in half an hour to take him to the Mwami, but he was left alone until nine in the evening.

Such are the tensions that have existed since independence between these two little countries, Burundi and Rwanda, so alike in geography, people and history.

Five days in this beautiful part of Africa gave us a store of exciting and interesting things to remember and made us aware of the enormous problems of two more emerging countries: problems stemming from aspirations outrunning present possibilities as is too often the case in the developing world.

XIX

Albert Schweitzer

Among our most exciting trips in Africa was our first, which we took toward the south. One of our purposes in selecting this route was to meet Dr. Schweitzer and visit the famous jungle hospital that he had built at Lambaréné. We had been in Gabon three months at this time, and it was the "little dry season," when motor travel is possible. Dr. Brenda Rimmer of the World Health Organization and Mr. Mansfield of the Embassy staff came with us, and we timed our arrival to coincide with Dr. Schweitzer's birthday, January 14. As Dr. Schweitzer enjoyed such an immense reputation in the United States and so many Americans came to Gabon to visit him, he was, at the Embassy, almost an "American interest," and my husband was periodically occupied with questions touching him. I will, therefore, let Charles tell about him and the meetings that we were privileged to have with him.

Lambaréné is a long, thin island-hill in the middle of the wide Ogooué River, about equidistant from the northern and southern banks. Although it is Gabon's third largest city, its population is under four thousand. The houses and shops of the French and those of the Africans are jumbled together in agreeable confusion. One of the three "international" hotels in Gabon was built in Lambaréné to accommodate the foreign visitors to *"le Grand Docteur,"* but it was rarely filled because there was a guest house at the hospital where almost every visitor was invited to stay. You could not spend the evening at the hospital and hear the Doctor play hymns on his creaky piano after dinner unless you stayed the night, for the trip back across the river in the little one-man dugout rowboats was dangerous after dark, and there was a long walk from the landing place to the hotel. So the devotees preferred the hospital guest house. We put up at the hotel, where, perspiring freely in the humid heat, we sat in the spacious dining room lounge watching the Ogooué boiling by below us.

Dr. Schweitzer's hospital, we were surprised to find, was not on the island—that is, not in Lambaréné itself—but lay on the northern bank of the river, slightly upstream. Many was the time afterward in my office in Libreville that I made pencil sketches of the area for visitors. The following morning we were fortunate in being given the Prefect's *pinasse,* or small launch, which carried us gently over to the hospital under the shade of its fringed awning. From out in the river one sees, nestling under trees on the sloping bank, a group of low-lying houses focusing in an archway connecting two of the main buildings some three hundred feet back from the shore. As we approached the small concrete landing platform, we saw the stooped figure of a man in white followed by two women, each wearing an old-fashioned pith helmet, emerge from the archway and walk to the landing. We stepped out of our pirogue to be greeted by the great Doctor and his long-time assistants or companions, Mathilde and Ali.*

* Mathilde Kottman and Ali (Alida) Silver.

286

It was then that I first sensed the reason for this man's worldwide reputation and appeal. There was majesty combined with saintliness in his bearing. I felt instantly that I was in the presence of a great man. The knowledge of his stature of course must have colored my vision, but there was more than that; his magnetism, the spell he cast over us, were real and profound. My companions felt it as did I. We walked slowly back to the buildings. Through the archway, we were at once in the midst of the hospital's busy life. There in the narrow court or passage between the front buildings and the block behind were swarms of Africans, some cooking over fires built between piles of stones, some lined up for inspections, some just lounging, and everywhere sheep, goats, ducks and chickens moving placidly about or sleeping. The Doctor showed us through a nearby door and we were in his medical office. The room was tiny and seemed dark after the brilliant sunshine. The Doctor sat at his desk, which was covered with correspondence, periodicals and books.

After a few minutes of general conversation, he inquired if we would like to visit the hospital, which Ali was then asked to show us. We first went next door into the operating room, compact and practical. A black ewe sleeping under the table did not move; whether she had been there during the morning's operations I do not know. Ali then led us with possessive pride through the various buildings. She was like a figure out of a picture book of old Europe: a severe yet kindly face, white shirtwaist, starched collar, ample gray skirt from under which we caught glimpses of square, mannish, black shoes—a very practical person, precise, efficient. Her accent suggested that she came from Holland. She had been at the hospital some fifteen years. Mathilde had been with the Doctor twice that long. A tall, sweet-faced woman, she took care of him. Earlier Mrs. Schweitzer had spent much of her time at the hospital, and Mlle. Emma Hausknecht, who had been with him for thirty years, is buried there. Like many great men he drew strength from women and was fortunate in the loyalty they gave him.

Ali took us to the maternity ward, where, with gentle scolding, she dislodged a husband who had pre-empted his wife's bed, making her lie on the floor. The wife was put back into the bed and the husband went grumbling off. We spent quite some time in the Leprosarium, part of which had been built by the generosity of the renowned American, Marion Preminger. We visited the mentally ill, of whom there was a surprising number. A very old woman wandering about naked came up to us uttering some incomprehensible staccato chatter. By each building women were preparing food, children were playing happily, and all about were animals.

Goats and sheep gave the landscape an Arcadian appearance, most of the females huge with young; ducks were everywhere; and there were geese, a couple of turkeys, antelopes in a wire enclosure, a tame chimpanzee on a long chain and several others in a cage by the dining room. The place seemed a menagerie, carefree and casual, every animal contented and at home. Sex was in the atmosphere. While I was asking Ali a question, an ewe beside us was mounted by a ram. At the door of the dining room a huge old gander covered a goose with a great flapping of wings. One tried out of politeness not to stare.

After the tour we washed our hands at an outdoor spigot fed from a bucket and entered the common room, which that day was almost filled with tables placed together to accommodate the hospital staff and the expected birthday guests. Despite the heat outside, the room was pleasantly fresh and cool and remained so throughout the luncheon although crowded with upwards of thirty people. Dr. Schweitzer, who had laid out all the buildings himself and taken a part in their construction, was proud of the ingenuity with which he had adapted them to the climate. He liked to talk about the way he did it: the buildings placed at precisely the right angle to avoid the path of the sun and to catch the prevailing breezes, peaked roofs, wide eaves, high ceilings. In this the Doctor far surpassed the French architects of the new buildings we had seen in Gabon: cement boxes with no overhang and large glass surfaces so that inside one would roast alive without air conditioning. There is no air conditioning in the Schweitzer hospital, and it is not missed.

We stood in the dining room drinking fruit juice while the doctors and nurses came in as their morning work was finished. One by one the other guests appeared; all were staying at the hospital except the Minister of the Civil Service, Edouard Adjomo, who had come to represent the Gabonese Government, and ourselves. My wife and I then had the pleasure of meeting Marion Preminger, who for years had been a patron saint of the hospital and who came each winter to spend several weeks and celebrate the Doctor's birthday. She entered the room like the fresh wind before a storm, accompanied by her distinguished husband, Mr. Albert Mayer. With her characteristic kindness she gave me an autographed copy of her latest book *The Sands of Tamanrasset*. The Africans call her *"Ma Mère,"* and soon I found myself doing the same, although she is much younger than I. There was also a dentist from Park Avenue, New York. Naïvely I asked him if spending a couple of months at Lambaréné each winter did not harm his practice, to which he replied, "Quite the contrary; it does my practice a great deal of good." Such is the magic of the Schweitzer name in America!

A young American and his wife, Dr. and Mrs. Mattison, who were working at the hospital, were there, along with Dr. R. Friedman, a heavy, black-mustached Central European who had been with Dr. Schweitzer for many years caring for the mental patients. It was a varied group, and we heard through the babel of conversation German, French and English, perhaps in that order of frequency. The Schweitzer hospital attracted doctors, as well as women to do nursing, from many countries. Some stayed a year or two, and some coming for a short time remained for many years. Most, I believe, gave their services or were just paid pocket money. They had their living at the hospital: a modest room and simple meals, and they knew where to find the key to the outside privy. All, staff and guests alike, even the Great Doctor, used this rude facility, and its odor was a surprise to the uninitiated. Thus the hospital had the services of a corps of, say, some fifteen or twenty men and women, coming from different lands, speaking different languages, but competent in medicine, psychiatry, surgery and nursing.

Luncheon, prepared and served by two bustling girls who looked as if they had come fresh from the Doctor's native Alsace, was simple but copious. The Doctor sat at the center of the long table, Mathilde at his left, Ali on his right, ministering to his wants. I sat opposite, flanked by my wife and Minister Adjomo, who took his food in silence. The Doctor and I talked across the table. With the hum of conversation I had to pay close attention for he did not raise his voice and his French had a slightly guttural accent. His preferred language was German, for Alsace when he was born and through his youth had been part of Germany. He could read English easily and could understand it, but did not use it in conversation. The French must have considered Dr. Schweitzer a German for during the First World War they interned him in France. When he returned to Africa, it was not through French assistance. It was the small tribe of Lambaréné, the Galoa, who got together the money for his passage, and the head of that tribe, whose sons Jean-Robert and Pierre Fanguinovény we knew well, gave him the land on which he built his hospital.

The Doctor told me about the hospital, the buildings, the changes of the seasons, and the ways of the great river. Nearby was a large lake, Lake Zilé, mystic, wonderful, dotted with craggy wooded isles whose tall trees were mirrored on the placid surface. But like so many things in Africa danger and death hid beneath its beauty, for it was the home of venomous serpents which chase and attack, and schools of electric eels. The Doctor told of a boy in a pirogue who was pursued by one of these vipers. The snake leaped over the low gunwhale into the boat; the boy in panic leaped into the water, where the eels clustered around and electrocuted him.

The Doctor asked us about our trip, and I told him that the next day we planned to motor south to Fougamou and then on to Mouila. He said that he had never been to Fougamou, which surprised me for it is the next town to the south on the only road, and he had then been living in Lambaréné for forty-eight years. Near the close of the meal I conveyed the best wishes of the American people, as well as our own, to Dr. Schweitzer on the occasion of his eighty-seventh birthday; Minister Adjomo also paid a grateful tribute on behalf of the Gabonese people.

For me the pleasure of the conversation was in watching Dr. Schweitzer, his great head, the rough-hewn face, the gray mane, the drooping mustache of a bygone era. His eyes would twinkle as he uttered some wise observation, and he followed every thought with animation and zest. When he addressed himself directly to me, I felt flooded by the full sunshine of his magnetic personality. One instinctively knew that here was a gentle, good and great man. After lunch Dr. Schweitzer circulated for a few minutes among his guests, then withdrew to take his rest. We said good-bye and found our way to the dock, where the Prefect's *pinasse* was awaiting us.

I have described this first meeting with Dr. Schweitzer at some length in order to convey the conflicting impressions which the day made upon us. The incongruous hospital, the welter of Africans, the strange assortment of staff and guests,

291

and at the center he who built the buildings, brought the people together and gave meaning to it all, this intense, remarkable man. The scene begins and ends with him.

In the succeeding years we visited Dr. Schweitzer several times. Once we were accompanied by Tia and Christopher. It was August, the river was low, and when it was time to go, the Doctor, Mathilde and Ali walked out with us on the sand banks to where our pirogues were moored. Henry Stephen, who was with us, took many pictures, for which Dr. Schweitzer posed very willingly. He was always most generous about being photographed and autographing books and pictures, doubtless because this gave so much pleasure to others. I never heard of anyone who was refused.

Back at the Embassy in Libreville, the presence of the famous man at Lambaréné intruded frequently. The international planes which brought the endless stream of visitors to the hospital unloaded them at Libreville, where most would take the local airline for the hour's flight to Lambaréné. Many, of course, passed through without seeing me, but some were on other business which brought them to the Embassy, and some came in just to find out how to get to Lambaréné. So I was frequently drawing my little maps and giving information.

Many of the pilgrims were interested in what would happen to the famed hospital after Dr. Schweitzer died, and as successive birthdays passed and rumors began to circulate that he was failing, people came to find out what his intentions were and to influence him in one course or another. But the Doctor was close-mouthed, and not one of them came away from Lambaréné the wiser.

The Gabonese Government quite naturally was interested in the same question, for not only was the hospital a significant part of Gabon's medical facilities but the great Doctor was the nation's most famous property. One day Georges Rawiri, one of the President's confidants, came to my office to sound me out on the theory that because Dr. Schweitzer's American following was so great, I might have some inside information. I quickly disabused Mr. Rawiri of this idea and suggested that he should go to Lambaréné himself, adding that he should plan to spend several days during which he might be able to win the Doctor's confidence. He went, stayed a week, had a fine time, but came back with nothing, which was as I had expected. I had known old ladies in America who would rather have their teeth pulled than tell anyone what was in their will; it is a human way, and Dr. Schweitzer was very human.

Perhaps the most prominent visitor from America whom I watched fail in this quest was the Boston heart specialist, Dr. Paul Dudley White, who had taken care of President Eisenhower. The Department had informed me of his coming, and he, wisely, spent several days in Libreville discussing the problem before going to Lambaréné. This man, then in his eighties, had the energy of a perpetual firecracker. His idea, as I remember it, was to persuade Dr. Schweitzer that there should be created alongside the hospital a Schweitzer Institute for Research into three common rain-forest diseases. Being sensitive to the ways of American public relations, Dr. White lined up scourges with three H's: hernia, hepatitis and hypersensitivity. It was a good effort, but it also came to nought—at that time.

Now that Dr. Schweitzer is dead this idea, and others, may form part of the future development at Lambaréné. The Doctor named as his executrix his daughter and only child, Madame Rhena Eckert-Schweitzer, a woman of high intelligence, vision and strength of will who will undoubtedly see that there is created at Lambaréné on the basis of her father's work something that will be at once a a fitting memorial to him and a blessing to African health.

For a period I became somewhat critical of Dr. Schweitzer, not on the ground that his hospital was behind the times, as some people said, but because I felt that he had failed to take advantage of the immense opportunity that was his. His reputation not only in the United States but throughout much of the world was enormous. There had never been a public appeal for funds for his work, yet money constantly rolled in to the Schweitzer Committees in the various countries, and friends could raise considerable sums by small private solicitations. If the Doctor would only give his consent—so my thinking ran—to the creation at Lambaréné of a modern medical center and research institute, what money could not be raised and what prominent men of different nationalities would not be willing to take places on its board of trustees! Thus there might be created in Gabon an outstanding medical institution based on private capital and privately run, as are our great medical centers in America. Lambaréné could be the seat— so I thought—of an institution that could do inestimable good not only for the Gabonese but for the sick anywhere in Africa who could be brought to it. The Doctor would only have to give his consent and his name, whereupon plans could be set in motion to bring such a project into being. Many of his visitors were playing with variations on this theme.

In time I came to realize that I was wrong. While the opportunity was there true enough, it was unrealistic and unjust to criticize Dr. Schweitzer for not allowing it to be taken. These plans were possible only in the years after Gabon became independent. And during this period Dr. Schweitzer was between eighty-five and ninety; he had lived at Lambaréné for half a century; his work was over, his life running out. It seems to me now unreasonable to expect that at that late hour he should have led the way, or even consented, to deep changes in his long-settled home and habits.

Those who, like myself for a time, thought that he should have done this perhaps were deluded by his mental alertness and by the thought that, once his consent was given, others would do the work. But that is too simple. He still would have had to choose between rival claimants and various plans. Nor could he have stood aside and let others make the decisions, for he would always have been the final arbiter, pulled this way and that. And when some plan had been launched, think of the chaos of architects, builders and experts, to say nothing of bulldozers and cement-mixers, that would have burst into the quiet of his little world.

In point of fact, Dr. Schweitzer did make one attempt to chart a new course for his hospital. At his suggestion, representatives of the several national Schweitzer Committees met in Basle in 1961 to try to reach agreement upon what should be done. The Alsace Committee held the deed to the Lambaréné land; the American Committee had the biggest bank account; and there were also committees in England, France, Germany, Holland and other countries, each holding itself to be the true church. The Rev. Emory Ross, the head of the American Committee, who was present and who told me about the meeting, said that after a week of arguing and bickering, it broke up having achieved nothing. Each nation wanted its ideas to prevail. After this Dr. Schweitzer apparently concluded that he would leave the problem to his successors.

There was no question but that Dr. Schweitzer's famed hospital was not just out of date; it bore little relation to what a modern hospital in the developed world should be. The Doctor clung tenaciously to the simpler past. A radio on the premises would have been unthinkable, but more than that, the hospital had no electricity although there was current in Lambaréné, and no telephone even though there was service in the town. To get a message to the Doctor, the best way was to write him a letter. If the subject were urgent, you could send a telegram, but it was little quicker than the mail for it had to be carried by hand from the office in Lambaréné and then rowed across the river.

In August, 1963, when the agreement was reached with the

Soviet Union suspending most types of nuclear bomb testing, I received a message from the Secretary of State asking me on behalf of the President to obtain, if possible, an expression of approval from Dr. Schweitzer. His endorsement was wanted in Washington just as soon as it could be gotten there. This was too important to trust to the precarious telegraph so I wrote a letter to the Doctor telling him quite fully about the agreement and saying that President Kennedy hoped that he would be willing to make a statement approving it. I asked our Vice Consul, Alfred Daiboch, to deliver this letter personally. Daiboch took the first plane to Lambaréné, which was the following morning, and in the evening was back in Libreville with a letter from Dr. Schweitzer expressing his great pleasure and satisfaction over the agreement. It was an excellent statement. In the meantime, I had received a further urgent cable asking in effect, "Where is that Schweitzer endorsement?" Apparently Washington thought that getting it was just a matter of picking up the telephone.

The absence of telephone and electricity were not the hospital's only deficiencies. The community was organized so as to resemble an African village, and the sanitary facilities were in keeping. I have already mentioned the privy—two holes in a board over a deep drop, one for men, one for women—but this convenience was for the Doctor and the white staff and guests. All the Africans—patients, orderlies and workers—just used the ditches between the buildings, or the bushes. I am not writing this just to be critical. Africans from the bush have no experience with toilets, and little even with privies, and it takes both persuasion and training, which the hospital obviously did not have time to give to the great numbers passing through it, to get them to use these modern devices.

When I first moved into our house in Libreville, I had a toilet put in for our gardener Blaise, but he simply hated to use it. I would catch him with a guilty expression on his face coming over the wall or out of the tall grass, and when I would ask sternly, "Blaise, what have you been doing?" he would look sheepish and say, *"Aw, Chef, je ne peux pas, je ne peux pas aller là"* ("Aw, Chief, I can't do it, I can't go there").

So Dr. Schweitzer did not eschew modernity entirely as a matter of personal preference, although in some matters this did appear to be the motive. Out of a reverential respect for life the Doctor was loath to kill flies and bugs. The hot climate, the river, and the sanitary arrangements conspired to give the hospital an insect population considerably higher than the tolerance of most Americans. The hospital had stocks of modern drugs and other medicines, some received as gifts; I frequently heard people complain that the Doctor refused to allow many of these to be used so they went to waste, but I have no direct knowledge of what truth, if any, there was in this report.

Visitors to Albert Schweitzer's hospital are familiar with these stories. The trouble with them is, they have the wrong focus. They concentrate on details, viewed against the background of the 1960's. They are irrelevant to life at it was on the Ogooué River when Dr. Schweitzer went there in 1913. There was no airport then, nor any road. The one road of today was not opened until more than a quarter of a century later, which explains why the Doctor had never visited Fougamou, the next town to the south; having got on quite well for so long without the road, to him it was meaningless and he never used it. The way in and out was by the river, and that sufficed.

There is a government hospital in the town of Lambaréné, recently built at a fine location on the island near the top of the hill. It is about the same size as the Schweitzer hospital, but few outside of Gabon have ever heard of it. What gave to Dr. Schweitzer's hospital its significance (apart from the person of its founder and his writings) is that when it was begun, and for decades thereafter, it was unique. Except for the scattered outposts of the missionaries no one cared for the health of the

297

Africans then. Certainly the French colonial administration did not: the natives were to be used, and when they died they were replaced; there were plenty more.

On the edge of the river the Africans could reach Dr. Schweitzer, coming by pirogue from upstream and downstream, and from the many villages around the vast lakes which connect with the river. But the hostility of the witch doctors did not make this easy and tribal divisions rendered it dangerous. In the area from which the hospital could draw there are Fang, Galoa, Okandé, Eshira, Bapounou, Seké, Oroungou and more. It was no light matter to leave the safety of one's village and venture through the territory of alien tribes and beyond to go to this white doctor. One had to be brave as well as pretty sick to try it. So the Doctor had to create a place to which Africans would be drawn, where they would feel at home. And this is precisely what he did by making the hospital another African village where a man could bring his wives to cook for him, and his children to be safe around him, while he got well. It was a wonderful idea, and it worked. Year in and year out, for decades, long before any Americans except a few missionaries had ever heard of Gabon, it worked, and countless must be the Africans who received care at Dr. Schweitzer's hands.

The stories about the hospital's backwardness, the criticisms that make up the so-called debunking of the legend of Albert Schweitzer, are true, but they are without meaning because they ignore the heart of the great man's work.

While in Gabon, I never mentioned to the Doctor any thoughts I might have had, or any of the ideas I heard from others, about what he should do. Nor did I ever touch on any political subject. Earlier he had made statements which were interpreted by some as playing with that childish and tiresome thought that the atomic bomb in Soviet hands was not a menace to peace whereas in ours it was, and I had heard from some of the American doctors at the hospital that his judgments

298

about the United States were not always kind. He never said anything to me, however, that would indicate prejudice against our country, and from the time of my arrival in Gabon in 1961 he never made any statements to which I could take exception. In any event, I did not discuss politics with him. There was always plenty to talk about without that.

Perhaps in part because I did not give him gratuitous advice or raise controversial topics, the Doctor, my wife and I got on well in an easy relationship. I was immensely pleased when in August, 1965, a few weeks before he died, I received a letter from him in which he wrote: *"Je regrette que vous ne soyez plus au Gabon"* ("I am sorry that you are no longer in Gabon"). As always it was handwritten in ink on an unheaded scrap of white paper, the stationary to which I had grown familiar and which I suppose was one of his little forms of economy. Although he was then ninety years and seven months, his writing did not show the slightest tremor. I was also happy when, after the Doctor's death, his daughter Mrs. Eckert-Schweitzer replying to my note of condolence wrote that "Your visits here were always a joy to my Father." They are certainly among our finest memories.

Before we left Gabon we went to the hospital to say "good-bye." The Doctor, as always in his white linen suit and full black bow tie, received us in the little room which was both his bedroom and his study. He sat at his desk which was all but obscured by piles of books, periodicals, papers and letters. Not feeling too strong of late, he had fallen behind in his correspondence, he apologized. One of the most remarkable things about this stupendous man was the enormous volume of correspondence he kept up, along with his hospital work and his writing, in several languages to people all over the world, day in and day out years without end. The room was so tiny that, with his cot-like bed and the desk, there was space for but one chair, so my wife and Mathilde sat on the bed. There in the half-light that filtered through the trees we chatted of the small things that made up the daily round of our lives.

When we rose to go, Dr. Schweitzer insisted on accompanying us down the little hill and out to the landing, a distance of several hundred yards. I was on the point of protesting, but Mathilde, sensing my thought, motioned to me not to, so slowly we walked together out to where our pirogue was fastened. As the boatman pushed off, Dr. Schweitzer and Mathilde waved to us, then stood there, he leaning on his cane, slightly bent but still leonine, majestic, she, a pace to the rear, faithful, watchful. The bark entering the current of the river drew away, and the two white figures grew smaller. Then with a final wave they turned and walked slowly back to the buildings.

A very great man! I pay tribute to his memory.

CHAPTER

XX

Our Last Trip in Gabon

B Y January, 1964, we were more than ready to get out of Libreville and again visit the country. During this month the rains would be light, if we were lucky. We wanted to visit the locations where the Peace Corps Volunteers were working (we missed only one) and also drive into the southeast of Gabon, parts of which we had already visited by plane. This time we intended to go alone, which meant that we had to think carefully about supplies as there would be no second car with extras, no Henry or Bill to help us out.

We took the new Embassy jeep, which was lower slung than the old Willys, comfortable and supposedly as good in the rough. We would see. In Kango we stopped briefly to inspect the Peace Corps school that had been finished since our previous visit. It was on a hill overlooking the Como River, a beautiful location but a tough one. There it stood, clean and strong, built with what courage and back-breaking labor! It seemed a miracle that a few young boys with the help of un-trained local Gabonese had managed to finish this large building, in this heat and on this site. The teachers were comfortably installed in the three new houses also built by the Peace Corps just below the school.

In Lambaréné we were the guests at a reception that evening of still another new Prefect. It seemed years since we had dined in this same house with the last French Prefect. M. Assoumou-Métou was a lively young man. His wife was a natural hostess and took good care of everyone. She had invited all the Peace Corps Volunteers in town: two teachers at the Protestant Mission and three young teachers in Lambaréné. Only the few Americans at the Schweitzer hospital were not there, although invited. There is an unwritten law that once on duty at the hospital, one stays there. The Gabonese and the French all told us how well liked and successful the PCVs were.

As we wanted to get an early start, we were at the ferry the next morning at eight. But it was a Sunday, the captain was nowhere in sight and the passengers were standing in the blazing heat patiently waiting for him to show up. We were not so patient; Charles went off in search of the man, enlisting the help of two gendarmes. They found him asleep in his house, told him to hurry up and get dressed, and forty-five minutes later we were crossing the Ogooué. The road had been greatly improved since our last trip and we bowled along at a good clip, arriving in Fougamou before noon.

Our first stop was at the Peace Corps encampment, a fairly decent cement house which served as dining room–kitchen and storage. The seven boys slept in tents. They were building two schools and several teachers' houses. We visited the sites and discussed the various problems with the Volunteers. Then we stopped at the house of the American missionaries, Mr. and Mrs. Silva, who had lived here for years, becoming fluent in the language of the local tribe, the Eshira.

When we returned to the main camp, we found Ekoga Edouard, whom we had seen as Subprefect at Bitam and later

302

at Coco Beach. He threw his arms around us and kissed us both. He had heard of our visit only the day before and had hurried down from Mandji to welcome us in the absence of the Subprefect in Fougamou. Ekoga had a good sense of humor. When we stayed with him at Coco Beach we had with us my husband's unmarried sister, Miss Caroline Darlington, an inveterate traveler, but then over fifty and by no means small. Ekoga cocked an eye at her, said that she looked as if she would make a good wife and offered Charles 60,000 francs ($240) for her. Charles replied that he thought very highly of his sister and would not let her go for less than 80,000 francs ($320). At this everyone roared with laughter—Caroline, who was a good sport, not the least—and the subject was a joke with Ekoga from then on.

From Fougamou it was a two-and-a-half-hour drive over a hard road to Mandji, a small and lonely place. It had been laid out with French attention to landscape. There was a broad avenue of mango trees leading up to the office and the residence, and a lovely view of mountains to the West. But nothing had been done to the buildings in years; they were in a wretched, run-down state. Ekoga said we could have his bed, a large one in an otherwise completely empty room. We had a brief wash, then met with the five Peace Corps Volunteers stationed in the place. Their living quarters were in a deserted cement house and were tidy as could be. The site for the school was a good one, on a broad field near the existing school. We discussed their problems of supplies, sand, laterite, wood and then went on with them to the home of a Belgian forester who had befriended them. He had built an attractive house using only local materials, furnished it with the usual Gabonese wooden chairs and tables, and decorated the whole with hunting trophies, elephant feet, python and leopard skins, plus some African masks.

He and Ekoga discussed the problems of Mandji and this

region where several thousand Gabonese are isolated and seemingly forgotten. We learned that cannibalism is still practiced in the hills, or at least the eating of human flesh after death. On occasions a little poison may be given to speed the process. *"Les hommes panthères,"* the panther men, take refuge in this region where they cannot be tracked down as there are no gendarmes and no roads. Panther men are members of a secret society, the young initiates of which must learn to kill, to drink human blood and to eat a human heart to prove their strength and courage. Sometimes they fall on a member of their own family as a particular proof of strength and sacrifice. They dress in panther skins with the claws over their hands and kill only those who walk alone at night. The whole Congo basin has variations of this savage fraternity.

We were sorry to leave Ekoga who was a genial host. After the *coup d'état* the government banned the sale of bullets and cartridges fearing that these might be used against it, but here in Mandji, the Volunteers later told us, this step caused hardship for it prevented men from shooting the game which provided an important part of their diet.

We stopped on the main road at Moudouma to visit a Peace Corps school site that was the toughest one yet. Seven boys were living in a deserted African hut made of mud bricks with a thatched roof. They were as snug as could be, had a local boy cooking for them and of course had put up a clean wooden toilet, which after Mandji was pure luxury. They were building in the midst of mud and jungle. We marveled that they had been able to stick at the place; the growth was dense and rank and the air filled with insects. However, local workmen were plentiful and the villages along the main road near them had all been cooperative and friendly.

We lunched at Mouila with the Prefect of the N'Gounié, M. Jean-Robert Fanguinovény. We had both been in the house

304

before when the French Prefect lived in it, and Charles had visited there frequently. Madame Fanguinovény had kept it up, the furniture and curtains were in good repair, and we were served a very nice meal by a white-uniformed boy. Like his brother Pierre who married the Swiss girl, Jean-Robert possesses both ability and charm. His responsibility for the Prefecture of the N'Gounié was enormous as it is the largest in Gabon. He had gone to the United States for six weeks on an AID grant and always liked to talk of this experience. He was a tower of strength to the Peace Corps in Mouila as well as in the many other locations in his Region.

Children were lined up around the almost completed new school. The ceremonies here, which we had not expected, delayed us and we were late in arriving in N'Dendé. For the last few kilometers we passed children coming from the direction of town, who shouted at us, *"à demain"* ("until tomorrow"); others called out, *"Bienvenue, Monsieur l'Ambassadeur"* ("Welcome, Mr. Ambassador"). Obviously we were expected. The square around the Subprefect's house was filled with people. M. Bekalé Robert was standing outside his office waiting for us. He had held the schoolchildren until five to welcome us, but when we did not turn up he postponed the ceremonies until eight the next morning. We apologized (having thought that this part of our trip did not constitute an official visit) and promised to be with him for the reception scheduled in our honor within a half-hour.

Bekalé had an orchestra tuning up in his dining room. After a half-hour, when only twenty guests had arrived, he stepped to a microphone and spoke formally to welcome us, expressing his sorrow at the death of President Kennedy and asking for a moment of silence in his memory. Charles then stood and made as formal a speech as possible, after which one glass of ceremonial champagne was passed to us. Bekalé kept looking out

305

the door and finally asked us where the Peace Corps people were. We told him that they did not think they had been invited. What a hoo-ha this provoked! He sent out assistants to round up the boys, all fourteen of whom we had seen sitting on the terrace of the one hotel as we drove by. They came as they were, unshaven and not too tidy, but the party immediately came to life.

In the morning we inspected the schools, going first to the present school in N'Dendé, where the Gabonese flag was raised and the national anthem sung. Charles was welcomed and gave his speech. We shook hands, the children filed into their classrooms, and we then made a tour of the three schools and six teachers' houses being built by our boys. The locations were splendid: two of the schools were in the shade of giant pepper trees which the Volunteers had insisted on saving. The fourth school, at Moussambou, a fine-looking building, and three houses were almost completed. The large open space in front was filled with people. Schoolchildren sang to us, and then a large group of village women surrounded us dancing a wild welcome. Most of them were pretty old, but there was one who was nursing her baby and as mama jumped and jiggled in the dance baby did not miss a suck. The sister of the Vice President, the *grande dame* of the village, walked about with us nicely dressed but barefoot. She understood only her native tongue, Ipounou, which we unfortunately could not speak.

The next stop was Lébamba. We took our time, wearing informal travel clothes, and were most surprised when driving into Lébamba we found a huge crowd gathered, flags flying and the Controller of the Post, Pierre Mebaley, waiting to greet us. Every European in the area was there, even several of our American missionaries. Children from the three schools—the Catholic, the Regional Public and the Protestant Mission—were standing in large groups. Each one had a different song to sing in our honor, and all the children had flowers in their

306

hands. Before we left the car Charles was able to slip on his jacket, but I just had to appear unconcerned about my lack of formality. When every hand had been shaken and the speeches finished, we were given a fine reception in the Controller's house.

That afternoon we drove for hours up a twisty road to Eteké, a plateau high in the mountainous gold-mining country. This area is also the home of the Mitsogo, the tribe in which the cult of the Bwiti originated and where it is practiced with more fervor and primitive ritual than anywhere else in Gabon. The Mitsogo rarely leave their mountain villages for jobs in town. They are intelligent and proud and many still quite wild. M. Durand, the Director of SOGAREM, the government company which is now operating Gabon's gold mining, met us in front of his house. The compound of the company looked for all the world like a part of Surrey: red brick houses, vines, flower borders, neat lawns. He said that the schoolchildren were waiting to welcome us. No! Not four times in a day! But so it was. This time there were only twenty children from the company school. After the singing, a young boy of about ten stepped forward, handed me a bouquet and read a resounding statement on the beauties of Eteké, the District of Mimongo, the aid of the United States, General de Gaulle and SOGAREM. It was a pleasure to speak to each of these children. At dusk they left us, singing as they marched two by two down the road to their homes.

We were lodged in a huge and comfortable guest house with a shower, hot water and electricity. M. Durand had secured an American flag to stand on his sideboard at dinner. His three other guests were Frenchmen working in the gold business. They had many tales to tell about the panther men who abound in these forests; they had seen them and feared them. We talked also of the *piste* of the Mitsogo, a circular trail through the mountains along which were many Mitsogo villages. Whites

307

now and then would walk this trail, a matter of many days, but it is not without danger.

The next morning we were shown the gold-mining operation, visiting stations forty-five kilometers from the main compound. We walked down to muddy streams to watch Gabonese panning and saw the grains of gold resting in the basin after the gravel had been washed away. The Mitsogo villages along the road were pin neat, each with two lines of huts facing each other across a hard-beaten earth court in the center of which stood the ceremonial Bwiti tree. Around the houses were the *iboga* bushes, the bark of which contains the hallucinogenic drug that is essential in the Bwiti ceremonies.

The *iboga* bark is often dried and powdered so as to be ingested more easily. It is very bitter and harsh on the stomach, causing dizziness, vomiting and retching. But it also banishes fatigue, so that men can drum and dance for hours on end. Initiates must consume large quantities over several days. First they experience great exhilaration, and then they go into a trance wherein they see supernatural things. When they come out of it, they are asked if they saw the "Bwiti," and they must describe him. If the description is satisfactory, they are admitted to the cult; otherwise they must go through the ordeal again. What the "Bwiti" looks like, no nonmember knows.

The views over the mountains from Eteké were extraordinary and the air clean and cool. Any kind of vegetable could be grown here, since there was enough rain but not too much. We left the friendly plateau and the well-run SOGAREM compound to wind down into the valley, then climb again to another clearing in the forest almost as high, where Mimongo is located and another group of Peace Corps Volunteers was stationed.

The road was narrow and in dreadful condition. We passed a Peace Corps truck that had fallen into the bush at one side of a steep curve. No one was hurt and several men were pulling it back on the road. Every stick of lumber, bag of cement and load of sand, plus supplies of food for the Volunteers, had to be trucked up and down roads that most people would call impassable.

We drove into the center of Mimongo through arches of palms and flags. Children were in line and the Subprefect, M. Bourounda, wearing an oyster-colored suit and hat, was waiting to introduce us to the assembled crowd. Charles' speech was brief and we were shown into Bourounda's house, the steps and floors of which had been strewn with bourgainvillea blossoms. The dignitaries who joined us for a drink poured out their troubles, all stemming from the condition of the road. They had no shops, no cars, no credits from the government— nothing but the Peace Corps as far as I could see. We walked around the small town, pleasantly located on a hilltop with gorgeous views. The Peace Corps boys were happy in their cement house but not pleased with the site the Subprefect had given them for the school, which was not the one that Charles, Dick McDaniel and Don La Voie had chosen a few months earlier. After much discussion the Subprefect was persuaded to agree to the change, and the Volunteers were pleased even though it meant that a few days' work had been lost.

Our quarters for the night were not very appealing. The house must have been lovely in earlier days, with its airy rooms and wide veranda, but the recent occupants had not bothered to repair anything. A cot had been tied to the single bed to make room for both of us. A washbasin had been filled with clean water, but after we emptied it there was no more. The toilet did not work and the floor around it was a lake of dirty water. The local officials are not entirely at fault in this. They have no revenues of their own, living entirely on what they are given by the national government, which starves them and spends lavishly in the capital. Thus Libreville becomes a little Paris while the hinterland dies. It is the same through all "French Africa."

At dinner we were overjoyed to see Prefect Fanguinovény. There was much talk about the trip we were to make the next day and the condition of the road. One woman had told me in the afternoon that it was impassable; people in N'Dendé had looked grave when we said we were driving it alone; and even the Minister of the Interior in Libreville, when pressed, had admitted only that *"on y passe"* ("one gets through"). Fanguinovény insisted that his Land Rover with his chauffeur and a second Gabonese follow us to the limit of his jurisdiction. After some time Charles agreed, and I heaved a sign of thankfulness.

That evening schoolchildren from faraway Massima gave a performance around a huge bonfire in the middle of town. They had been trucked in during the late afternoon. They acted several plays, the first time we had seen that kind of entertainment, and everyone loved it, especially the women in Mimongo. Our hostess held one of her children on her lap. Charles held another, but as it began to rain he drove his sleeping child and me back to the house. The rest of the crowd stayed on until the rain put out the fire. I certainly hated the sound of that rain! It only meant more damage to the road ahead of us.

It was a comfort to have the gray Land Rover behind us, and Fanguinovény's chauffeur knew his job. The rain gradually stopped, so that by the time it was full morning the windshield wipers were unnecessary. The road started out in fairly good repair, but soon we came to the famous bridges: several logs thrown across a stream. For these we stopped, the Gabonese chauffeur came forward, tested each log, then guided Charles across, indicating with his hands which logs to take and where to place the front wheels. The bridges were frequent and all in dreadful repair. The road now was washed out, filled with huge ruts and rocks. In places it was almost entirely hidden by the overgrown bushes and grasses. We drove in low-gear, four-wheel drive steadily; once in a while in second for a few yards, then back to low, always in four-wheel drive.

We wound along, going up to a crest and then down again into a valley. There were many villages along the way, and of quite good size. The people rushed to wave at us. The black car with the American flag was apparently quite a wonder; only an occasional Land Rover had ever passed this way. Suddenly we saw wide tracks ahead and, climbing a steep hill, came up against a rickety truck. The driver was a Hausa. He said the bridge ahead was not safe, at least not for him. We skirted by him, drove down a steep hill, and there was a fragile little bridge standing high and uncertain above a wide and rushing river. All four of us got out to study the situation. The men agreed that it would hold if taken in such and such a way. I crossed on foot and kept right on walking with my back turned; if the car and Charles were going through the bridge, I did not want to see it! Of course, both cars came across nicely.

It is no use trying to describe the road any further. I remember bad roads in the West forty-five years ago, but anyone younger than I has probably never seen a bad road in America. It took us four hours to go forty-seven miles. This brought us to a largish river, a sturdy cement bridge, and the limit of the N'Gounié. Here the chauffeur and his companion bade us good-bye and turned back. We crossed into the Ogooué-Lolo and were on our own.

At first the road seemed a bit better. The bridges had been repaired—we could see the handiwork of newly laid logs. But for the rest it was just as rocky, as closed in as before. Once in a while we would be on a high ridge, and we could breathe freely; then down again we would go, closed in by jungle and barely able to see a faint track ahead of us. The villages were more numerous, but still there were long stretches of empti-

311

ness: nobody and nothing but green, green growth and buzzing insects.

Just before two o'clock we stopped in a fairly open place to stretch. Charles had been driving steadily for eight hours, hanging onto the wheel with all his strength to wrest the car over and around the rocks and ruts. We felt pretty smug. Here we were, only four more hours of driving ahead of us if we kept up this speed (ten miles per hour). We planned to stop about thirty minutes out of Koulamoutou to freshen up and for Charles to change out of his khakis into a proper suit, since he knew there would be an official welcome because this was our first visit to this Prefecture.

In a flat and fairly open place ahead we saw some water in the road, not a long stretch, about twice the length of the car. We drove right along, and just as the front wheels were about to come out onto dry ground we stopped. The wheels on my side were so low that mud and water were almost at the door. We tried to move the car frontward and then backward—no go. Climbing out, we squashed into mud over our ankles, and we saw that the jeep was embedded.

We were standing in the road, sun beating down, bugs swarming around our heads, wondering what to do, when a couple of Gabonese walked by. We asked them to help us, and they went ahead a few hundred yards to their village to fetch more men. Just off the road there was a deserted shack which gave a little shade. Charles and I rested there while the men tried to put sticks under the wheels or dig the mud out. Periodically they would fetch one of us to try the car again. Several times Charles jacked up the car, hoping to drive it off the jack, but it was no use. We were dead beat. We told the men to stop and to show us to their village where we would rest and spend the night. We locked up the car, I took my bag filled with all my treasures—No-Pic, toilet paper, Wash-n-Dries, a bottle of water, aspirin, and cigarettes—and we set off down the road.

My head was so bitten by *fouroux* that it felt as though it were drawn into a peak. I had mud up to my knees, my skirt and blouse were covered with it, and some had splattered into my hair. Charles was a bad sight: his beard had begun to show, his eyes looked hollow, he was filthy with mud and sweat. The Gabonese men were also mud-covered, but uncomplaining, and walked behind us chattering to each other. Only two of them spoke French, and we discovered that one of these was the chief of the village. Charles tried his fluent French, but the chief did not seem to understand.

I then took a hand in my slow French, telling him that my husband was a great friend of the President of the Republic; this seemed to make an impression. Then I said that he was also a great friend of the chief of the Region, who even now would be out looking for us. That perked him up. I took out a pad and wrote the name of his village on it as he spelled it, Isala, and his own name, Idiata, for him to see. He was now won over and led us through the village. There were only twelve houses in all. We had been stranded in one of the poorest spots in the area among one of the smallest tribes, the Pové. His wife smiled at us, and moved into one of the other houses so that we could have hers.

The only furniture was a low cot covered with reed matting. There were no windows. The floor was dirt, swept clean and hard. There were no chairs, but a man immediately brought me his chaise longue made of animal hide, and another contributed a straight chair. Still another offered us three small dirty eggs, which we politely refused, saying we could not cook them. Charles flopped down on the bed to recover his strength, and I stretched out in the chaise longue, away from the door and the bugs. It seemed quite cool in the dusky little room. I rubbed No-Pic in my muddy hair to keep the bity bugs away, washed my hands with Wash-n-Dries, and smoked a cigarette. At once our hostess popped in the door to ask for one, and from then on I doled them out to her. She and another woman sat on a log in front of the door and stared in at our reposing figures. We decided that no one would think of starting out to look for us until well after the hour we were due to arrive in Koulamoutou. By then it would be dark and no one would venture on the road at night, so we might as well forget about help until morning.

Just before dark we walked back to the car, Charles to get some dry clothes and me to get my sheets, pillow, the Scotch, a box of rations, flashlight and the umbrella. On our return the second room in the house was unlocked and I was shown my bed—a hard, but clean, wooden affair covered with palm branches and reed mat. I laid out my sheets and my pillow. We ate a bit and watched the chickens and goats scurry outside the door. The hut seemed clean enough and I didn't think there would be any snakes, not with all the animals around. Chickens flew up on the roof and made funny noises, and the goats scratched themselves on the walls outside. Our hostess opened a minute window in my room, just less than a foot square, and wished us *"bon soir, Monsieur, Madame."* The men of the village sat across the road in their palaver house chatting for a long time. I kept hearing "Land Rover" and an occasional French word, so gathered that they were discussing the merits and demerits of that car and ours.

I dozed off, but was awakened about nine by thunder, flashes of lightning across my tiny window and then rain, rain, rain. Charles woke too, and we discussed glumly what this would do to the road ahead of us. We slept again and woke at dawn. It was still raining a little as we opened the door and peered out at the deserted muddy gaggle of houses, all still closed. We put up the huge golf umbrella and set off for the car. It looked a poor thing, now up to the floor in water. We could only just

314

open the doors and get in. The first thing we wanted was coffee. We mixed the instant coffee, sugar and Preem from the K rations with Vittel water and drank the mess eagerly. Charles said it was delicious and had three cups.

We returned to the house to watch the village come to life. I wondered what they ate; so far I had seen nothing edible but those three tired eggs, a piece or two of corn, and of course the chickens and goats. Doors were opened, women stretched and scratched, fires began to burn. There were few children. The people seemed to have nothing to do and little to wear.

The chief said he was calling all the women and men to get our car unstuck. He and Charles went off followed by the whole population of the village, while I sat in the shade of the house and wrote in my journal. At the car the women used their pans to empty the lake of water under the jeep. In a short time the dirt under the middle of the car was showing. The chief then directed other women to crawl under the car and scoop out the dirt with their machetes and hands. Charles jacked up the front and then the back, so the women would have more room to work. At times, he said, there were five or six women under the car at once, clawing out the dirt with their hands and splashing each other with muddy water. He was terrified lest the car slip off the jack and fall on them. But it worked. Gradually the car, with the dirt scratched out from under the axles, settled down until the wheels touched the bottom of the ruts. All this time the men had done nothing but stand around giving advice.

At the hut, I heard the motor start and the engine roar. Silence. After a bit it started again and stopped. I kept on writing. The third time there was a great shout, and in a minute Charles drove up in front of the house, surrounded by laughing, screaming women, covered with mud. I grabbed the bags and hopped into the car for we knew we must make a pretty quick getaway. We had the *"cadeau"* out and ready to distribute and did not want too much of a palaver. The chief

315

after numerous bills had been doled into his hand was just about to stop talking when he remembered that he had not charged us for his wife's house—another 500 francs settled this, plus another pack of cigarettes. He wanted one more *"cadeau,"* but gave up good-naturedly when he saw that we had reached our limit. We drove off with them all waving and shouting at us—some even running alongside the car for a bit. They had made more hard cash in that brief period than in months.

Charles and I then resolved to test every mud hole before going through to be sure to find the safe way. Whenever we came to a messy spot, I got out, walked through it tapping with the umbrella from side to side so that Charles could see how deep the ruts were. It was a good thing we did this, too. The most innocent-looking places would turn out to be above the middle of the umbrella! When this happened, Charles took diversionary action and went around the water; or when there was nothing to do but go straight through, he rushed it with as much speed as possible. Having made my soundings, I ran on ahead to be out of his way. I had my raincoat on to protect my arms from bites, and now this as well as my legs, sneakers, hands, and face were all newly coated with red mud.

We had been going for four hours since we left the village. We had been stuck once and another time had to change a tire. Then we came to a long muddy stretch just before a steep hill. I tapped through it, then ran up the hill, slipping several times as I hurried to get out of the way for this one would have to be taken at a good clip. As I reached the top, I saw a car—a Land Rover! And a Gabonese in a clean khaki shirt with a tie! It was the Assistant Subprefect from Koulamoutou, sent out to find us. He did not look altogether sure that we were the honored guests, and no wonder! He and his men had left Koulamoutou at six that morning, and had only covered thirty kilometers as they had had to cut through five trees that had fallen across the road during the night. His orders from the Prefect were to continue until he found Darlington, even if he had to go all the way to Mimongo!

It was late Friday afternoon when we rolled up to the Prefect's house in Koulamoutou, just twenty-four hours late. It was a good-sized house, with a wide cement terrace, on one of the many hills comprising the town. Madame Minko, the Prefect's wife, welcomed us as we staggered up the steps. We were so muddy we would not go into the house, but flopped down on the porch and kicked off our shoes while our luggage was unloaded from the Land Rover. In a few moments the Prefect came, having seen our arrival from his office. He was thankful that we were all right. It had been a great worry to him as well as a disappointment, for he had given a reception for us the night before with more than a hundred people, and no guests of honor.

After a pleasant cleaning up we joined our host for an *apéritif*. His Subprefect and others of his staff came in along with several French officials. All wanted to know of our journey and marveled that we had made it alone: "What, no chauffeur?" "No African at all?" M. Minko and his wife, a middle-aged couple, seemed to know just how to run a prefecture and a house. We liked them at once and admired the way they took hold of our problems. The jeep was sent for so that the tires could be repaired, the car washed and filled with gas.

The conversation dealt with just one subject: the need for a proper road from Mimongo to Koulamoutou. The people in this part of the country felt completely cut off from Libreville, physically and politically. The local stores were provisioned by truck from the Congo, or by air from Libreville to Lastoursville and then by truck back to Koulamoutou. Here in the Ogooué-Lolo anything grows—potatoes, tomatoes, lettuce, beans, corn—but there was no way to get produce to Libreville. We saw no store along the whole 187 kilometers of our drive from Mimongo—not one in any of the countless villages. What a difference if cars and trucks could safely come and go; this whole rich region could be opened up.

We were ready the next morning to make official calls with M. Minko, his Subprefect and the two Deputies from the area. We visited eleven places: all the government offices, the schools, the missions and the larger stores. Every place we went people spoke of the need for the road. M. Minko had us organized down to a split second and kept us right on time. We were impressed with the schools and the mission constructed of red brick, clean and seemingly well run. All the important buildings were on hills. People laughingly speak of Koulamoutou as built in the same manner as Rome.

Sunday morning Charles went to Mass with the Minkos. The large mission church was jammed with about a thousand people, and the singing was splendid. The French priest gave his sermon in Indjabi, the language of the Bandjabi, which impressed my husband. Before lunch the Subprefect and his wife came to say good-bye to us and to bring me a present of two mats. They said they would be *"triste ce soire"* after we had gone as so few people visited their Region.

M. Minko decided to accompany us to our next stop, Lastoursville, a subprefecture under his command. This was a nice courtesy to us and it gave him an opportunity to see how his Subprefect was doing. We left after lunch in our sparkling clean car. M. Minko and his wife followed in their chauffeured Land Rover. The drive was under three hours through fine country over a fairly good road.

At Lastoursville the Subprefect's house stands on a bend in the Ogooué River. From the edge of the terrace one looks directly down into the swirling water. It is a fine location and the house had once been fine too, with a large cement terrace, good-sized rooms and gardens, but now it was badly run-down.

Our host had been Subprefect in Booué when Charles, Tia

318

and Chris were there two years before. The Minkos and we were put into the guest house nearby—a poor place. Nothing had been painted or repaired in ages. Charles and I had the usual small double bed with mosquito netting, a washbasin supplied from an overhead barrel, with the water draining onto the ground just outside the window, and the worst WC yet. It was a small wooden stand designed for a six-year-old and apparently had not been cleaned since it was built years before. The Minkos were in the other section of the house. I could hear them talking, and I was sure they were not at all pleased with what they found. Madame Minko would never have tolerated such things, nor would her husband.

We changed and turned up for the reception on the terrace above the river. I shook hands with three young women, all his wives. Charles was a bit perplexed, as only one of them had been in Booué. The newest, a pert sexy number about sixteen, was a Fang from Río Muni. She could speak Fang and Spanish, but no French. The wives helped serve drinks, but that was the only bit of work I saw them do while we were there. The Subprefect is quite a playboy type. He wore a gray flannel suit with debonair grace, and made a pleasant toast to Charles. After the guests left and we had met everyone in Lastoursville, we had dinner.

There were thirteen at table, including the three wives. The one servant, Camille, answered all their orders and flew around the table. Eight courses this time: soup, two fish, two mutton, salad, custard and a heavy cake. During dinner the youngest wife turned on the radio, loud. The music came from Bata and was terrible. Charles was about to have it turned down, but I signaled to him to let it alone—I could not talk any more with the two wives near me, so was content to have the blast go on. Charles asked what had happened to one of the wives he had met in Booué. "I had too much trouble with her, so I sent her back to her family in Oyem," was the reply. There

319

seemed to be one principal wife in this menage (the little thing who had nursed her baby at the table in Booué sitting next to Chris)—at least she was the most in evidence. But all three chatted and giggled together as though they were the best of friends.

The next day we visited the hospital, run by a Haitian doctor and his wife. This was a very good place, freshly painted, clean and orderly. He had no electricity so did his operating in the brightest part of the day. Men were cutting the grass. It was a pleasant spot high above the river, well laid out and cared for, showing that these places can be kept up if one just wants to work or see that the work is done. We had drinks with the doctor and his wife. She had made mounds of sandwiches, and there were just a few of us to eat them: Charles and I, the Minkos, the Deputy's wife, Medzégué and his wives.

We were served a glass of champagne first. Before drinking it the doctor stood up and made a long and serious speech in our honor. Charles responded, also from his feet, although we were but nine in the room. That finished and the champagne gone, whisky was served. I don't know why we were never ill, with all the mixtures of food and drink. It is not allowed to be unhealthy on such a trip; one must just keep on going and eating and drinking. Our dinner was a bit smaller than the enormous meal we had been served the previous evening. Charles and I ate as little as possible and went to bed.

We had learned a great deal in the four days with the Minkos and said good-bye to them with warmth and gratitude, hoping to see them when they came to Libreville. The Subprefect and his wives lined up to bid us good-bye. They had entertained us with warmth and graciousness. We were glad to be traveling and on our own again. We gave a lift to two gendarmes walking out to arrest a robber in a remote village. They would have had to walk two days to get there, but they expected that the thief would be there when they arrived. They rode with us for five hours and were a great help as they knew the road well and could warn us of the bad spots. We passed several villages of naked pygmies who swarmed out to wave. We were in the deep forest.

About two hours before we got to Mounana we emerged into the open, climbed a hill, and there spread before us was beautiful rolling country. We could see the roofs of Mounana winking in the sun. The Compagnie des Mines d'Uranium de Franceville (CMUF) and its mine here supply nearly half of France's current uranium requirements. Houses for African workers are of cement, laid out in neat rows on the side of a hill. The streets are wide and paved. We inquired where the Director's house was, and wound our way up to it past offices and the mine. The houses for the French personnel are built at the top of the hill, with views of the distant mountains on all sides. There were paved roads, electricity, water hydrants and gardens. One could well be in an exclusive suburb in France.

The Director, M. de Ligneris, and his wife have the best house we have seen in Africa. It is not large, but built with a sense of style and appropriateness, using local woods, including ebony, and stone. M. de Ligneris greeted us in his short-sleeved shirt and white shorts, the uniform for so many Frenchmen in Africa. The couple charmed us at once, and we loved their house, garden and collection of Africana: taborets, M'Bigou stones, spears, masks, slave bracelets. They took us to the Case de Passage, where we were to stay in great luxury, with our own boy to look after us. We had a blissful bath in a large tub —the first since leaving Lambaréné—and spread out over the two bedrooms, sitting room and terrace.

They picked us up for drinks at Le Cercle about 5:30. This was the center of the French social life—a large, well-built club with four tennis courts (*en tout cas,* not cement) lighted for night use, swimming pool, bar and restaurant.

321

De Ligneris explained that he had come here seven years ago when the uranium was found, had planned and built the whole place, mine, factory and houses. He had left his house to the last as he knew that the morale of his top-flight personnel depended a great deal on living conditions for themselves and their families. His home was only three years old, and the garden surrounding had been created by his wife. We had a delicious dinner, just the four of us, with good conversation about Gabon. De Ligneris was most impressive. What is there about mining engineers that makes them so vital? Working out of doors? Taking such chances with nature? Creating order out of the wilderness? Telfair of SOMIFER, Durand of SOGAREM and de Ligneris had much in common.

The next day we had a thorough tour of the uranium mine from the pit to the finished product, which is neatly packed in wooden tubs for trucking to Pointe Noire. Each small tub is worth $5,000. During our rounds we met the local Subprefect and one of the deputies, who told us that the Chamber of Deputies had been dissolved by Léon Mba the day before. A new list of candidates must be prepared, and new elections held February 23d.

That evening we were given a party at the de Ligneris' house. There were about thirty people for cocktails, buffet supper and dancing. It was a very gay affair, and we were told that they often dance until six in the morning! For the first time I danced the *pas à double*. At one point a Dixie Land record got on the machine, by mistake I am sure, for they chiefly danced tangos or chachachas. Before you knew it, I was off—just like an old fire horse. Madame Le Fuhr, the wife of the head of the processing plant, joined me, and the two of us did a very neat shag-cum-lindy-cum-jitterbug to everyone's amusement. Champagne flowed all evening, and it was cool dancing on the terrace under the stars. Charles and I folded at midnight, but the others stayed much later. It was a most civilized evening, and it was hard to believe we were in the middle of Gabon, in the middle of Africa.

It was only an hour's drive to Moanda, the great manganese mine and installation of COMILOG (Compagnie Minière de l'Ogooué). As we had been there before (Charles had taken part in the opening), we stopped only briefly to make arrangements for the next day, and drove on to Franceville. This was beautiful country, for all the world like parts of England or France. There were lush green fields (or so they appeared) covering rolling hills, and here and there clumps of trees. But there were no animals! That was the giveaway: the fields were green but with a wiry scrub grass, for the ground is infertile. We crossed the ferry just outside of Franceville, having difficulty getting off, for when the gate was lowered it stuck a good three feet above the level of the road, but with the aid of planks we finally negotiated the gap. Then we roared into the town and up to the Prefect's house.

Madame Kamara was waiting for us, and her husband came over from his next-door office. They were a fine couple, both with some Congolese blood. There were no other wives. The house was a big one with a splendid view over the valleys and hills, and it was being repaired right and left. Our bedroom was comfortable, and Madame was delighted when I admired the curtains she had just made for it. We changed, for even during that short drive we had gotten covered with laterite dust, and went to inspect the hospital and the Catholic Mission. We were alone for lunch, talked at length about problems of administration and of the outlying districts of Gabon. Kamara had an important post, for his Prefecture, the Haut-Ogooué, contains both Mounana and Moanda—uranium and manganese. He had been the Subprefect here under the last French Prefect, M. Gassman, who had recommended that Kamara be given the top post.

After our rest we visited the regional school. We were taken one by one into the ten classrooms, introduced to the teachers and Charles spoke a few words to the children in each. I marveled at his ingenuity. He rarely said the same thing twice except for exhorting them to work hard and study hard, for the "richness of Gabon was not in its earth but in its human resources. This richness is in you." That evening the Kamaras gave a reception for us, including about forty of the personalities of the town.

There was a wicked storm that night, a tornado if ever I heard one. The next morning we were told that these are frequent at Franceville. After breakfast we sadly headed back toward Moanda. We would like to have gone on to Okondja, the most remote town in Gabon, which Walker Diamanti and Henry Stephen reached in the old jeep, but this was not the season for more road travel and, moreover, the clouds on the Gabonese political horizon made it necessary for us to return to Libreville.

The Prefect followed us in his car as far as the ferry, as did the Secretary of the National Assembly, Bongo Philibert. He also sent his chauffeur to follow us all the way to Moanda in case there were bad places on the road after the storm. We arrived covered with dust again, but luckily could wash and change in one of the company guest rooms before having a drink and a good lunch with M. Mailier, the acting head of COMILOG. He made arrangements for repairing and storing the jeep. It was planned that we would return to Libreville by plane and that Bill Courtney and another member of the Embassy staff would later make the return journey, a trip that never took place for the poor jeep, it was found, had given up the ghost. Months later it was bought, at a very good price, by some local person willing to take the chance of getting it running again.

At Libreville Bill Courtney, Willie Jones and Henry Stephen met us, immaculate by contrast to our travel-soiled selves.

While we were waiting for our bags a party of twenty American tourists was presented to us. They were retired couples and single women, each of whom announced his name, town and state while shaking hands. I thought they seemed a bit piqued that we had not been in Libreville to receive them. Doubtless they thought that we had just been off enjoying ourselves. And so we had.

XXI

Violence: The Congolese Riots, September 18–20, 1962

AFTER what has happened in other parts of the world in our century we may question whether cruelty does not lie somewhere within all races, but when it first showed itself among the seemingly gentle Africans around us I was shocked.

1. *Tuesday*

Tuesday morning when Cécile arrived for work she said that during the night there had been a lot of fighting going on in Louis, her section of town, because of a football game between Gabon and the Congo that had taken place in Brazzaville. I did not pay much attention but went on about my business, which was to meet Colonel Wilkes of the Peace Corps at the airport and arrange for him to come for lunch. After leaving him at the Embassy, I did my shopping and on the way home saw groups of people arguing hotly along the streets. Just below the market at Mont Bouët there was a woman, surrounded by a crowd, blood streaming down her face. A gendarme was urging her to get into a taxi. I thought that perhaps there was something in Cécile's tale after all.

I spent the afternoon as usual, resting, reading and writing, and was surprised to see Charles drive up at five to take me to the office. He said he had called, gotten no answer (I was out on the terrace) and had become worried for mobs were roaming the streets beating, maiming and killing the Congolese. As we drove to the office he explained that the Gabonese team had lost the game in Brazza, that the Congolese had treated them discourteously, playing the band only following Congolese goals, and after the game had roughed up some of the Gabonese players as well as menacing the Minister (M. Amogho) who had accompanied them. When the team got off the plane at Libreville and told of these things, the Gabonese went wild.

Up and down the streets in the main part of town gangs roamed about, armed with sharpened stakes, iron pipes and rocks, yelling and shouting as they chased the Congolese. When they cornered some exhausted victim, they would knock him down, beat him about the head and jab their stakes and pipes into the soft parts of his body. Many, we learned afterward, had teeth bashed in or eyes poked out, some had their testicles smashed and several were eviscerated.

We had two Congolese working in the Embassy: Bernard, a chauffeur, and Léon, a messenger. Willie Jones told them to stay inside the building and to sit in an inner room where they would not be seen through windows. Homes where Congolese were known to work had already been attacked. Charles and Willie did not expect that to happen at the Embassy, but the temporary building we then were in had a very flimsy door so they could not be sure. Willie telephoned to the gendarmery and was told to bring Bernard and Léon there where they would be safe. Charles and Willie felt it would be dangerous to do this in daylight and waited for the cover of darkness. Willie then took Bernard in the jeep, but Bernard wanted to go to his home first and pick up some clothes; when they reached the entrance of the Congolese section, Bernard leaped out of the car and disappeared into the darkness. An angry mob surged around Willie, who barely was able to make his getaway, feeling sure that Bernard would be killed. Later we found that he had gotten some clothes and reached the gendarmery in an Army vehicle sent to evacuate the Congolese village.

My husband, for his part, got Léon into the Dodge without being seen and made him crouch on the floor in the back. Charles then drove the two miles to the gendarmery, passing a number of roaming gangs who, had they spotted Léon, would have tried to drag him out and kill him. When they arrived at the gendarmery Charles found the officers and men all sitting around doing nothing. He asked why they were not out on the streets trying to quell the mobs and was told: "We have had no orders." The Gabonese Government, in other words, was not attempting to stop the rioting and the murder. The officers in charge of the gendarmery were French. They could have taken out their men and ended the bloodshed, but they did not do so.

2. *Wednesday*

Wednesday morning Cécile came in in a dreadful state. She said the fighting in her area had been terrible, and she was scared to death as she had been born in the Congo, although of French and Gabonese parents. We told her not to worry, she was with us. I went to the airport to meet Bill Mansfield back from a trip, and to give him news of what was happening in our peaceful little Gabon.

On returning I stopped at the Embassy, but Charles was

not there; he had had a call from Cécile that a mob was on the road below our house calling up to Grégoire and Jean-Pierre to ask if there were any Congolese working with us. The boys said "no," but the mob did not believe them. Indeed, Blaise, our gardener, had been a very militant Congolese, but he had long since left us. While they were shouting back and forth— the mob, luckily, did not come up onto the Residence grounds —Cécile telephoned to Charles. He and Jones shot out to the house, but by the time they arrived the crowd had left. Charles telephoned to both the Presidency and the Foreign Office condemning the violence and explaining that the Residence was United States property and that our employees, whoever they might be, must not be molested. He was told that nothing could be done at the moment; things were out of control.

That afternoon was terrifying. We saw truckloads of Congolese being driven out to the gendarmerie. Gangs, unhindered by the police or the gendarmes, continued to run in the streets setting upon any lone Congolese. Rumors flew like mad. It was announced over the radio that all the Congolese in Gabon would be expelled and deported to the Congo. One of the regular weekly ships from France, expected in a couple of days, would take those rounded up in Libreville and dump them off at Pointe Noire. Until then these unfortunate people had to wait in the bare enclosure of the gendarmerie. Many of them were wounded. No food was provided, nor any shelter, nor anything but the bare ground to lie on. Members of their families who were left behind—wives or husbands who were Gabonese—brought them their necessities. When the ship arrived, this hapless band was marched the mile and a half to the port with very little protection, and along the way they were reviled by Gabonese who threw stones and struck them with sticks. This exercise was carried out by the gendarmery commanded by French officers.

Anyone who was Congolese had to leave. Even M. Lassy,

the excellent Mayor of Libreville, and his wife were not exempt. She and all seven of their children had to go on this ship while he flew to Paris a couple of days later, not to return for many months. My butcher was in despair: he had lost seven men, all trained, and had one killed before his eyes in front of his shop.

We learned from M. Risterucci, the French Ambassador, that a mob had come right into the Embassy grounds and had grabbed his *maître d'hôtel* who was in the garden. This man, although a Congolese, had been living in Gabon for nineteen years, had a son in the Gabonese Army, had been decorated by President Léon Mba and often served at the Presidency. The Ambassador saved him by calling the President, who sent his own motorcycle escort to retrieve the man from the mob and take him to the gendarmery, where he also would be held until deported. We were surprised that Risterucci would allow this to be done to a man who had worked for him for so many years. When Charles queried the Ambassador about this, he replied that it was France's policy, since she had given these African states their independence, to allow them to conduct their affairs, including making their mistakes, without interfering.

3. *Thursday*

Thursday we had guests for lunch. They were due at 12:30. At about eleven, when the table was being set, Cécile suddenly called me to look toward Akebé—fires! Sure enough, we watched as one house after another caught and went up in flames. I telephoned the Embassy and learned that the Gabonese were burning the entire section of Libreville where the Congolese had lived. It was a nasty thing to see.

At 12:30, just as our guests were arriving, the President went on the air and told the people to stop fighting. He said

330

all Congolese were leaving Gabon, there must be no more bloodshed or rioting. Everyone was to go back to his proper job and get off the streets. And that is just what happened. As soon as he told them to stop they did. It was obvious to us that the forty-eight hours of rioting had been allowed by the government, which had made little effective attempt to interfere with the mobs, to call out the police or military, or to protect the lives and rights of the Congolese minority.

4. *Afterward*

Friday, after everything was over, two Gabonese soldiers arrived at our house, complete with submachine guns, provided by the Gabonese Government, to stand guard over the Residence. The two nice young men spent the day sitting in chairs on the terrace. I made the mistake of giving them lunch at the same time we had ours, only to witness them eating their own loaf of bread and tin of sardines after they had finished our handout. The two times during the day when they seemed most alert were before luncheon and at the end of the afternoon, when they stood at the top of the steps at attention, guns at the ready, waiting for the Ambassador to return from the office. The next morning we called the Adjutant and told him not to bother to send his men again.

Altogether I think there were seven deaths and some sixty to seventy serious injuries. The hospital was filled to overflowing and every doctor worked frantically stitching, mending, giving transfusions, setting broken bones, bandaging broken heads. The tearing apart of families and the loss by these poor people of all they had was heart-rending. Congolese were good workmen. They were quicker and perhaps more easily trained than many of their Gabonese fellows and so had risen to jobs of responsibility. They were electricians, butchers, waiters, cooks, chauffeurs. A young man, Pascal, who changed all the wiring in our house when we switched from a generator to town electricity, was a Congolese, the French electrician's best workman. He was driven out, leaving, besides his wife and child, a new motorcycle and all his household effects which were promptly stolen by his envious Gabonese neighbors.

In the Congo the reaction was violent. When the ships arrived in Pointe Noire and landed the hundreds and hundreds of Congolese, many hurt and all destitute, mobs turned on the Gabonese living there. As there were few of them, the mob's rage was visited on other Africans, principally the unfortunate Dahomians. Men had their limbs hacked off, or were eviscerated with sharp sticks. Pregnant women were attacked, their bellies slashed open and the unborn children wrenched out and smashed on the ground.

What a sad period! Even though the Congolese had lived peaceably in Gabon for years, normal relations between human beings went by the boards. Perhaps this is in the makeup of the Black African, a legacy of centuries of tribal warfare; perhaps it will change with education. The Gabonese had only two weeks earlier given a very fine account of themselves. The half-yearly Conference of the Chiefs of State of the African and Malagasy Union had just been held in Libreville. The whole city had been made as beautiful as possible: sidewalks were laid, streets swept, junk removed from empty lots. There was a general atmosphere of goodwill and progress. Then this!

We tried to find an explanation for the sudden madness. The Abbé Fulbert Youlou, President of the Congo (Brazzaville), had for a long time been sending arms and money into Gabonese districts on the Congolese frontier, both to the rich uranium and manganese area about Franceville and to the iron-ore district around Makokou, hoping to detach them from Gabon and make them part of the Congo. Then in Libreville during the Conference of the Chiefs of State, Abbé Youlou had gone out into the city talking with Congolese workers, and had counseled them to press for higher wages. When the Conference closed, Léon Mba was furious at Youlou, and Youlou was smarting because of the rebuff which he had received from his colleagues in his desire to support Tshombé and an independent Katanga. The two Presidents were in many ways to blame for the explosion. As the French Ambassador said, *"C'était un coup de folie"*—an attack of madness.

In this miserable story the Gabonese Government bears a heavy responsibility. What took place at the football game in Brazzaville was hardly more than a bit of unpleasantness. The rioting and the killing started in Gabon. And the fact that the Gabonese fell on the Congolese in all parts of the country—in Port-Gentil, in the N'Gounié and the Nyanga, and at Moanda —at about the same time suggested some foreknowledge and planning.

Any self-respecting state has a responsibility to maintain law and order and to protect minorities. Our dear Gabon and its government did not do this. They allowed the bloodbath to run its course unchecked for two days and two nights. It made us heartsick.

XXII

More Violence: The Coup d'État and Its Aftermath

O N a Saturday in February, 1964, we attended the opening of an agricultural demonstration project near Akok, set up by Chinese from the Republic of China to teach the Gabonese how to grow rice. With incredible energy and very little mechanical equipment—the bulldozer promised by the Government of Gabon never materialized, so they went ahead by hand—a dozen or so wiry little Chinese cleared acres of forest, got rid of stumps, and in the rich jungle soil laid out neat rows of rice. They built a simple pump and wheel which brought the muddy water from a nearby stream into the irrigation ditches. Around the rice they planted runner beans, melons, cucumbers and lettuce. Members of the Gabonese Government, various officials and all the Diplomatic Corps with the exception of the French Ambassador, whose country had just recognized Communist China, were present for the ceremony. Charles and Bill Courtney talked with the crowd, but there was no discussion of the forthcoming elections to the National Assembly. I sat with Madame Mba for a time, chatting in a most friendly manner. On the way home after the ceremonies we gave her old father, head of the village of Akok, a lift along the dusty road.

The next day we met Mr. Randolph A. Kidder (now Ambassador) and Mr. Robert A. Hancock, the two Foreign Service inspectors who had come from Washington to conduct the Embassy's biennial inspection. After lunch we installed them in the quarters where they would live and work for the duration of their two weeks' stay. On Monday Charles flew to Mouila.

Tuesday at 4:00 A.M. I was awakened by a telephone call from Willie Jones, our Administrative Officer. He said in a hushed voice, "The Presidency has been surrounded by soldiers. Our landlord [M. Anguilé, the Minister of National Economy] and his family are here in our house. Don't show any lights and if you hear shooting, call me." I prowled around in the dark listening to the unearthly quiet. I was glad when dawn came and even more relieved when I heard Grégoire in the kitchen making coffee.

At seven, members of the Embassy telephoned to give me further details. While I was at breakfast a military sound truck went by, soldiers sitting on top with guns in hand, announcing, "The Government of Léon Mba has fallen. Foreigners will be safe as long as they do not interfere. Schools are closed; businesses are closed. Léon Mba and all his men are under arrest."

Raphael arrived, having walked across the fields from his house in Akebé. He was very nervous, but he had not been stopped. All businesses may be closed, I thought, but there is one that will be open no matter what: Pélisson, the baker. Raphael and I got into the car, and stopped in Akebé to see that the two inspectors were all right. They were standing in front of their house with Willie Jones, watching the military

335

trucks go by, and were quite unperturbed. For them revolutions were no great novelty. Willie told Raphael to fly the flag on the car, and we drove along the deserted streets to the center of town.

At Pélisson's there were crowds, all in the best of humor, getting bread as usual. M. Davin, the Secretary General of the Ministry of Foreign Affairs, came to the car to talk with me, along with M. Mihindou, the Director of Technical Education. They were all in good spirits and did not seem worried. They said it was rumored that an Army plane had been sent to arrest M. Yembit and M. Nyonda in N'Dendé. I thought what a surprise that would be to Charles, standing there with both of these men dedicating a school! I was also told that all other ministers had been arrested and were being held at the Army barracks in Baraka and that a provisional government would soon be announced.

On the way home I stopped at the Embassy to pass on my news. Bill Courtney was worried that I was in town and urged me to go to the house and stay there. I did. Raphael and Marcel left and I settled down with Grégoire and Jean-Pierre, who sat on the terrace wall with instructions to report any unusual occurrence on the road. No cars moved, nobody walked; everyone in our neighborhood was inside, listening to their radios if they had them. I looked at the trays I had stacked in the hall to lend to Madame Cousseran for the reception she was to give that very afternoon in the French Embassy for French and Gabonese Army officers. Surely these men could not have known of the plotting going on in their midst.

At about noon it was announced on the radio that the Government of Léon Mba was ended and that there would be elections the next Sunday, until which time the Army would be in control. Then Léon Mba read his resignation in a broken voice. Later came a message to the prefects and the subprefects urging them to keep the people in their districts under

336

control and telling them that Libreville was calm. During the afternoon rumors and action quickened. Planes flew in from the south. I wondered if Charles could be on one of them, but the Embassy said they were the French military. I waited and listened.

At five o'clock the Embassy had a flash from the control tower at Port-Gentil that Charles and Henry were on a red Cessna headed toward Libreville. But could they land and get home? The French had taken control of the airport and were not allowing any planes to come in, and the Gabonese had set up roadblocks between the airport and town. At six Peter Telfair, whose house was near the airport, called to tell me he had seen a red Cessna land, stop briefly far out on the runway and take off again; Charles and Henry must have been on it. They were, and not long afterward Willie Jones, who had gone out to meet them, drove Charles to the house.

That night at eleven the Belgian Chargé called to tell us he had been summoned to the Presidency to confer with the Revolutionary Committee. He was preparing Charles for a similar call. Not knowing that my husband had returned, the Presidency telephoned Courtney, who, after the security of the Americans in Libreville had been raised, agreed to go to the meeting and report the results to the Ambassador.

At daybreak we were awakened by the roar of planes circling over the house. As it grew lighter the shooting began, all aimed at the military barracks. From our terrace we could see the planes circling to swoop down on Baraka and hear the barking of the machine guns. Charles talked with the Embassy, reporting on how it looked from where we were, they on how it sounded in the Embassy. The Counselor of the French Embassy telephoned, and later the Ambassador, to tell us that this exercise was just to maintain order—nothing to be alarmed about.

Jules Mbah, former Gabonese Ambassador to the United

States, came to our door, having walked across the back fields from his house in N'Kembo so as not to be seen. He asked, "What is happening? Is it true that the French are killing our Gabonese? Can this be possible?" We told him the little we knew and he disappeared. After three hours the planes stopped circling and the firing died down. The radio announced that the barracks were in the hands of French troops and that the only legal government was that of Léon Mba. All arms should be laid down. The French Embassy telephoned to say that the Ambassador had gone to speak with the Revolutionary Committee in the Palace, which was now surrounded by French troops.

After a quick trip to our Embassy, Charles returned for me. I was needed to run the switchboard as none of the local employees could leave their houses. I acted as doorkeeper, too, locking and unlocking it as members of the Diplomatic Corps and Embassy staff came and went. At one time I had Washington on the telephone and was terrified lest I pull the wrong cord. A curfew was announced for seven o'clock, so we spent the night next door at the Courtneys'. There was no news about Léon Mba; the French troops could not find him. The following morning we heard his voice on the radio announcing that he was back in power. He declared he would pursue the instigators of the rebellion and punish them as they deserved, chasing them and their families from wherever they might try to hide. It was a frighteningly vindictive speech.

On our way home we drove past several houses belonging to French businessmen. In front of each there were large groups of people of all ages. Later I learned that French families were spending the nights together for protection, until the women and children could be sent back to France. We had not ordered similar precautions for the American personnel, but a week or so later there was a street fight between anti-Léon Mba Gabonese and gendarmes in the section of town called Lalala where two of our Peace Corps families were living. Street fights were ugly. All the Gabonese had were clubs, machetes and stones while the gendarmes had guns. After this incident we moved these families with their six children into other staff houses nearer the center of town.

A message then reached our Embassy from the French Embassy to the effect that the Americans were spreading panic by their evacuations. In truth, the only Americans who had left Gabon were the Peace Corps Director, evacuated because he was very ill, and the USIS Director's family going on long-scheduled home leave. The only moves in living quarters that had been made were of the two Peace Corps families with small children. But numerous French families had been doubling up for protection from the very beginning, and French women and children, as well as husbands, were piling on the planes to France as fast as they could get space.

Daily we heard of more French families leaving; each flight was jammed. "It's finished, it's destroyed" (*C'est fini; c'est fichu"*), they said, referring to the protected and comfortable life they had enjoyed. They knew that after French troops had shot down Gabonese, the country would not be the same for them again. At the port there were hundreds of Dahomians, the small businessmen of Libreville, waiting for the next ship. This was a bad sign. Their countrymen had been persecuted so often they could sense danger before others did.

The exodus of Gabonese from town to country along the main road in front of our house was a sad thing to watch. Women with all their household goods on their heads and backs trudged toward the bush followed by their children. Others waited by the roadside until picked up by bus or truck. I asked one man why the women were leaving. He replied that bad times were coming, tribe against tribe; better to have the women and children in their villages. Charmaine's mother sat on our steps and told me of her worries: it would be Fang against Fang—the "Léon Fangs" against the "Jean Fangs." She was a Léon Fang, but across the road they were all for Jean-Hilaire Aubame. She did not think the Gabonese would ever turn against the whites, but only against each other.

Then came a terrific storm which knocked out our telephone for six weeks. The Embassy tried to set up a walkie-talkie for me, but it did not work. French troops and blacks from other French African states under the command of white French officers patrolled our road and stood at all main intersections of town. Periodically truckloads of soldiers toured the streets, their guns much in evidence. The Gabonese Army was disarmed and disbanded. Former Gabonese soldiers walking along the road, going home, would stop and talk with us, often to ask for bus fare to their villages. It was announced that the elections would be put off again. Crowds that gathered in the markets and around the Palace were dispersed by French troops using tear gas. People were picked up every day by the score and thrown into jail.

We decided that we should evacuate the two Peace Corps families with small children. Before we got them out one group spent a day and night with me, a mother with four little children and another on the way. While washing clothes for them in our laundry behind the house I looked down the road and saw two Gabonese men talking together as they walked up the hill toward town. An Army jeep came over the crest toward them; it stopped and four soldiers jumped out with their guns pointed. The two Gabonese tried to run into the bushes. They were pursued, caught, brought back to the road, beaten and thrown into the jeep, which turned around and sped back to town. All of this I saw between "rinse" and "dry."

When the Peace Corps family left, our Air Attaché from Brazzaville, Colonel Edward Hensch, flew in with his crew. I barely had time to change the sheets before they reached the house. They brought a proper two-way telephone for me so that at last I was not shut off from the Embassy. "Station 1 calling Station 2. Do you read me? Over." It added to the general atmosphere of unreality. The speaker was always ready to alert us if anything went wrong in town, and we could alert others if trouble broke out in our section.

It was a comfort having the four American airmen in the house. When another violent storm put out our electricity, ice-box, deep freeze and water pump, the crew mechanic was able to fix the whole line within a few hours. They were perfect house guests, leaving their rooms neat, taking breakfast and lunch out, but returning to us for dinner because of the curfew. Plans were perfected for the evacuation of all Americans in Gabon. With the Peace Corps the number had grown to over 130. The missionaries probably would not leave but were included in our planning. The plane would shuttle us all to Río Muni, only forty minutes away. I learned that I was slated for plane trip No. 4. I told Charles that I would not go, but he said I would obey orders. The other Foreign Service wives in the Embassy already had their bags packed.

The plane was to stay in Libreville until things had calmed down. There had been two and a half weeks of constant tension. It was reported that the people of the Woleu N'Tem, Fangs who supported Aubame, would march against Libreville and against the southern tribes, which were pro-Léon Mba. This rumor went so far that members of tribes such as the Bateké and Bapounou, living at the edge of town, were terrified. Marcel refused to go home at night; more and more families left for their villages and the bush.

March 8 was a sunny Sunday. We went to the beach and, although there were soldiers stationed at all important intersections and in front of the Lycée, there were no crowds or demonstrations. We lunched with the air crew, who were making plans to return to Brazzaville the next morning. That night our Embassy was shot up and bombed, but the plane left on schedule. We watched it out of sight from the terrace.

I saw Madame Cousseran in the street and thought she looked very bad, she who had been so gay and pretty notwithstanding all her responsibilities and her five vigorous sons. I determined to call on her at once, for we had been very friendly. She was touched that I came, saying that life recently had been insufferable. There were threatening telephone calls day and night. "But now we are leaving." When I looked as astounded as I felt, she said, "Didn't you know? We have been recalled at Léon Mba's request and go at once. I thought that was why you came to see me, to say good-bye." I had not known nor had anyone at our Embassy. In two days the Cousserans were gone.

The elections were put off, and we knew that until they were held the tension and fears would not lessen. I was told that I should be careful what I said on the telephone, which was probably bugged. Gabonese came every day to talk about the elections and the people under arrest. We never took sides or said anything against the government; we were there to listen and to answer questions about American elections, American politics and American democracy. Messages were brought by faithful employees of some of the men in prison, but we sent none back. Madame Ekoh, whose husband was awaiting trial, came to call on me one afternoon with a friend. They had taken a taxi to the corner of St. Anne, then walked the rest of the way. She wanted to tell me what was going on in her family and in her section of town, but did not ask for help; she came simply to talk. She would not let me drive them back to town, fearing that it would be dangerous for us to be seen together. She said the spy lines of Léon Mba were everywhere. And this I believed when I heard from one of the other ambassadors that American cigarettes which I had offered to callers one evening had fallen into Léon Mba's hands and were being used as evidence of our complicity in the revolution.

During the campaign I met the priest, Père LeFévre, for whom Cécile kept house. He told me she was in the hospital with a bad leg. I went at once to see her, and we had a long visit. She told me that one day the President had driven into the courtyard of the hospital and that all the staff and patients were asked to go out and greet him. He wanted a demonstration in his favor. But only a few straggled outside, and certainly there was no hint of enthusiasm. Furious, he threw a handful of franc notes out of the car and drove away. Cécile was on the balcony outside her room looking down at it all. The notes lay untouched for some time, then disappeared.

One day as my husband picked up two of the little boys he regularly took to school he asked, "Well, Emmanuel, how are things? What is the news today?" "Oh, you are going to be assassinated, Mr. Ambassador." "Is that so?" "Yes," said Jean-Paul, "you will be assassinated, Mr. Ambassador." Perfectly calmly they repeated the talk that they had heard that morning in their homes. That same day a Belgian forester whom we had met at Mandji, where he had settled after his father had been murdered during the disorders following Congolese independence, called on Charles at the Embassy to say that he had seen a notorious gunman in Libreville and told Charles to "beware." Charles thought that this was too much of a good thing, so, after informing the Department by cable, he passed on the report to the French Ambassador, who had the Gabonese Government pick up the man and deport him.

It was an unhappy time for us, but occasionally some little incident would warm our hearts. One day I drove the car myself to market; Raphael was in the hospital for a hernia operation. As I came to the crossroads at St. Anne I saw ahead of me a large gathering of angry Gabonese. A gendarme came up to my car and said, "I would not try to go any further, Ma-

343

dame," but as I could not turn around just where I was, there was nothing for it but to go ahead. The mob stopped me and swarmed around the car, but as I leaned out of the window a young man yelled, "Oh, that is Madáme Darlington, she can certainly pass," at which they slapped my rear fenders and I roared off. In the mirror I could see other cars not getting through.

Another day I drove past the main market and saw that the Dahomians (the few still in town) were putting up their shutters. The streets were deserted. I decided that I would only make one stop for bread. At Pélisson's I learned that a riot was forming. I drove home as fast as was safe, passing knots of Gabonese at nearly every corner. When I called the Embassy to report, I heard that the schools were closing on the rumor of more trouble.

Nothing could upset Libreville as much as a shortage of bread. Pélisson's main shop was the hub of town and his small bread-dispensing stations in outlying quarters always had crowds around them. For several days these stations were not supplied as there was fear that the trucks might be upset or some damage done. Everyone therefore converged onto the main shop. The gendarmery had to be called to regulate the crowds. It was an unpleasant wait, but I had a nice thing happen once: a tall Gabonese gendarme spied me all but buried in the crowd and called out, *"Bonjour, Mamam, passez, passez,"* and made the others let me go through.

When I called on Raphael in the hospital, I was greeted warmly by other patients and the Gabonese attendants. In the French shops I felt no particular animosity, but there was a guarded air about everything. French women talked together but not as freely as before I came in and, while they were polite to me, I was not included.

I met Madame Minko, the capable wife of the Prefect at Koulamoutou on the shore boulevard, and expressed pleasure

344

and surprise at finding her in Libreville. She had come with her husband when all the prefects had been summoned to the capital and as Libreville was her home had not returned to the south. She did not accept my invitation to the house so I asked if I might call on her. She seemed surprised, but we agreed on a day. I drove myself and parked the big black car in front of her simple cement house, very different indeed from the Prefect's residence in Koulamoutou. No one was about. The door was open, so I called *"Bonjour, Madame!"* several times until out came Madame, barefooted and dressed in a loud cotton *pagne*. This was an entirely different woman from the one who had entertained us so pleasantly on our trip. She was being aggressively native, it seemed to me, or perhaps just unconsciously relaxed. Certainly she acted surprised that I had actually come to call.

We talked briefly, and she offered no refreshments until her sister-in-law came in and offered me beer. I could sense that they were uneasy about me: Why was I here? What was I trying to find out? And on my side, I was determined to show them that the rumors about us were stupid and that I was being natural and decently polite because of the hospitality they had shown to us. We chatted about that trip and the hazards of the road—not a word about the elections, of course. Shortly two other family members came into the small room, nephews or sons, obviously civil servants of some sort. They were coolly polite but thawed considerably when they heard us talking about traveling the roads of Gabon. I made them laugh as I described my difficulties in parking the big car. After a proper interval I stood up, shook hands and took my leave. By now a crowd had gathered around the house, a quiet and apparently friendly one, and I waved good-bye as I drove off. I was sure the news of my visit had already reached the President, and I hoped that my act of politeness and gratitude had not hurt the Minkos.

When the elections were finally over and the new deputies arrived in Libreville for the spring meeting of the National Assembly, we gave our third annual reception for them. Not only did nearly all of them come with their wives, but almost the whole Cabinet as well and most of the invited French officials. Léon Mba and his wife, however, did not appear, and a few of his closest associates also stayed away. We later learned that the President thought we should not have entertained the deputies this year, as they included a number who were opposed to him.

We wondered what the turnout would be for our Fourth of July reception. I took special pains to deliver all the invitations myself, with the help, of course, of Raphael. He could not read, but he knew the ever-changing locations of all the government bureaus. I sat in the back of the car sorting the envelopes, handing the appropriate ones to him as we stopped. We had worked out a convenient route during the years. In spite of my care a number of invitations went astray, and this time I was sure it was not accidental: certain French advisers were either not given them or they said they had not received them, and so were spared the embarrassment of showing up at the American Ambassador's and possibly risking President Léon Mba's displeasure. But in spite of these small annoyances it was our best reception: there were over six hundred guests. It was as though the Gabonese and many French alike were showing their belief in the United States and in us. Even the Vice President and his wife attended, while ten days later, at the July 14 reception at the French Embassy, he was resting at his village of Moussambou.

Two weeks afterward our younger son, Christopher, arrived to visit us and to work for the rest of the summer in the Embassy. He had taken a French boat down the coast from Bordeaux. Three days later Charles received word that he must leave at once for Washington on consultation; Christopher and

I were to stay on, making no change in our mode of living until our scheduled return in September.

One evening he and I were waiting on the terrace of La Paillotte, a small restaurant on the shore. Out of the darkness walked the Gabonese Ambassador to Washington, Aristide Issembé and his brother. The Ambassador looked dumfounded at seeing me, but recovered quickly and came forward to kiss my hand, his usual greeting. I introduced him to Christopher and then he asked where the Ambassador was, although he knew perfectly well. I replied, "Oh, he is in Washington, while you are here in Libreville." We laughed and he went on into the restaurant. By the time our hosts had arrived, a circle of at least eighteen French contractors and small businessmen had grouped around Issembé. Christopher helped me count them. They had drinks and after a period left singly or in twos and threes. They seemed to have come by foot. I think Issembé must have advised Léon Mba that the rest of the Darlington family should leave the country for it was shortly after this that my orders came.

Bill Courtney was summoned to see the Minister of Foreign Affairs, Pierre Avaro. The purpose was to ask about my plans: specifically, when was I going to leave Gabon. He said that although he was devoted to Madame, for whom both he and his wife had the highest regard, it was not good enough that I leave in early September. The President did not want to have me in the country over the Gabonese Independence Day, August 17, lest there be some manifestation on our behalf. As the State Department did not wish to expose our government or me to the possibility of a diplomatic rebuff, Christopher and I packed and left Gabon within a week.

Everyone in town knew what had happened when they saw the lift van suddenly appear outside the house and came upon me packing china, books and pictures. A few French friends came to the Residence to express their regret at the sudden change in our plans, as did the whole Diplomatic Corps. I spoke to no Gabonese in any position of authority but did receive good-bye calls from a number of the families who lived around us.

There were several French couples, far removed from the circle of Presidential advisers, who showed us continued friendship and support. They were appalled by the rumors circulating against us. After Charles was recalled to Washington they were particularly kind to me and to Christopher. And when he and I had to leave on such short notice, two of them, having then returned to France, came to meet our plane and greet us on arrival in Paris—a most warmhearted and understanding gesture.

At the airport in Libreville Christopher and I bade good-bye to all the Americans and the Diplomatic Corps. The French Ambassador and his wife, who had entertained us a few days before at a beach party, were there to see us off and were particularly friendly. She had in tow her Consul General, who had been rude enough to say to me at that party, "I don't like Americans, Madame Darlington, but I find your son very sympathetic." He was there, I thought, to make some kind of amends for this remark for he alone from the French Embassy staff was present.

The only Gabonese to see us off were our servants. No one else dared take the chance, nor would we have had them do so.

Index

Adam, Archbishop Jérome, 136
Adjomo, Edouard, 289
 tribal affiliation of, 253
Adouma tribe, 255
Adrien, Toko, 257
Africa:
 ambassadors' role in, 53–59
 coups d'état (1963–1967),
  177–179
 U.S. policy on, 72–73
Africa Institute (Switzerland), 55
African Development Bank, 96
Afrique sans Frontières, L'
 (Anguilé and David), 67
Afro-Malagasy Common Organi-
 zation, 96
Agathe, Mouencoula, 260
Agence France Presse, 127
Agency for International De-
 velopment (AID), 74–100,
 252
 aid to Gabon, 85–92
 cooperation with Peace Corps,
  103
 policies of, 78–79, 80
 self-help requirement, 93–95

Aguyi-Ironsi, Johnson T. U., 178
Ahlert, Mary Jo, 4
Ahomadegbe, Justin, 177
Algeria, 177
Allendorfer, Captain, 192–193
Ambassadors (United States),
 49–60
 entertainment allowance, 52
 role in Africa, 53–59
American Board of Commission-
 ers of Foreign Missions,
 69–70
Amogho, Eugène, 12, 147, 327
 appointed Minister of Public
  Works, 48
 tribal position of, 168
Amyiot, Captain, 258–260
Anguilé, André-Gustave, 12, 67,
 80, 131, 191, 245–246, 335
 appointed Minister of National
  Economy, 48
Anguilé, Madame André-Gustave,
 191, 245
Ankrah, J. Arthur, 178
Apithy, Sourou Migan, 177
Arsène, Auben, 248

Association of Gabonese Students, 192

Association Sportive Darling Club, 232

Assoumou-Métou, 302

Aubame, Jean-Hilaire, 36, 45–46, 94, 120, 143, 144, 156, 191, 340
  appointed Minister of Foreign Affairs, 48
  background of, 13
  excluded from 1964 election, 147
  February Coup and, 132–140
  jailed, 16
  resigns, 119
  sentenced, 173
  tribal affiliation of, 253

Aubame, Madame Jean-Hilaire, 191, 239, 242–244

Augur, Newell, 127

Avaro, Pierre, 12, 120, 188–189, 347

Avaro, Madame Pierre, 239, 244–245

Azikiwe, President, 178

Balewa, Sir Abubakar Tafara, 178

Bammer, Walter, 170

Bandjabi tribe, 26, 30, 224, 318

Bank of America, 66

Banque Commerciale Africaine, 223

Bapounou tribe, 12, 26, 30, 213, 216, 224, 298
  language of, 29

Baraka Mission, 210–212

Baranyanka family, 280

Barron, Monsignor, 71

Bateké tribe, 175, 216, 224

Baum, Norman, 4, 109

Bekalé, Robert, 305–306

Bell, David, 84

Ben Bella, 177

Benga tribe, 29

Bergus, Donald C., 75

Bernard, Obiang, 242

Bernard (chauffeur), 327–328

Béssieux, Msgr. Jean-Rémi, 71

Bethlehem Steel Corporation, 63–64, 169

Bigmann, Louis-Emile, 6, 69, 131, 191

Biyogho, Jacques, 164, 253, 272

Blaise (servant), 187, 188, 193, 216, 220, 296–297

Blancke, W. Wendell, 49

Bloc Démocratique Gabonais (BDG), 45, 118, 146
  election of 1964, 146–152
  election of 1967, 175–176

Bodjolé, Emmanuel, 177

Bohlen, Charles E., 169

Bokassa, Jean Bédel, 178, 179

Bongo, Albert, 131, 175–176

Bonifacio, Ondo, 254

Bonjean, Ondo, 192

Bonnaud, Marcel, 96–97, 140

Botswana, Republic of, 35

Bouanga, Athanase, 108

Boucat, Madame, 173

Boumedienne, Houari, 177

Bourounda, 309

Brandstetter, 129

Brazza, Pierre de, 37

Brazza, Savorgnan de, 71

Brouillet, Jean-Claude, 204

Bruhns, Fred C., 84

Burundi, Kingdom of, 276–284
  coup d'état (1966), 178

350

independence ceremonies, 276–284

relations with Rwanda, 284

women in, 279

Bushnell, 70–71

Bushnell, Rev. Albert, 70

Bwiti ceremonies, 258, 273, 307, 308

Cabrol, Claude, 16

Cadeaux, Ralph, 278

Cameroon, Republic of, 25, 66, 113

Cannibalism, 25, 304

Catholic Mission, 323

Cécile (servant), 219–220, 221, 326, 328, 329, 343

Central African Republic, 10, 66, 238

  coup d'état (1966), 178, 179

  expells Chinese Communists, 180

Chad, Republic of, 10, 66

Chaillu, Paul B. du, 71

Chambrier, Dr., 132, 140

Chango, Judge, 148

Charles, Prince, 283–284

Charmaine, 226

Chatenay, Paul, 40

China, Republic of, 36

Christian (student), 230

Christian and Missionary Alliance, 30, 68, 113, 236

Churchill, Sir Winston, 14

Cocoa Multiplication Station, 263

Collectivité Rurale, 224, 264

Collège Béssieux, 71, 174

Comité Insurrectionel (Togo), 177

Commission of Inquiry (Gabon), 144–145

Communism, 176, 180–181

Compagnie des Mines d'Uranium de Franceville (CMUF), 39, 321

Compagnie Minière de l'Ogooué (COMILOG), 62, 64–65, 68, 323, 324

Congacou, President, 177

Congo, Republic of (Brazzaville), 10, 35, 66, 181

  coup d'état (1963), 177

  reaction to Gabonese riots, 332

Congo, Republic of (Kinshasa), 117, 276

Coup d'état of 1964 (Gabon), 126–141, 177, 179, 334–348

  casualties, 133–134

  French intervention in, 132–139

  reasons for, 139

  tribal reaction to, 341

Courtney, William F., 137, 159, 172, 324, 334, 347

Cousseran, Paul, 120, 135–136, 144, 159–160, 170

  recalled, 144, 342

Cousseran, Madame Paul, 336, 342

Cox, Joe, 4, 126

Crossroads Africa, 258

Dacko, David, 178, 179

Dadjo, Marcel, 178

Dahomey, Republic of, 10, 131, 177

  expels Chinese Communists, 180

351

Daiboch, Alfred, 296
Daily Bulletin, 147, 189, 202, 203, 219
Darlington, Caroline, 303
Darlington, Charles F.:
  appointed ambassador to Gabon, 5
  background of, 5–6
  recalled, 170–171, 348
Darlington, Christopher, 170–171, 226, 254–256, 264, 266, 292, 346–348
Darlington, Letitia, 26, 254–255, 264, 268, 269, 292
David, Jacques, 67
Davin, Jean, 13, 164, 336
De Gaulle, Charles, 15, 118, 133, 145, 238
  conference with Mba, 174
De Ligneris, 321–322
Delano, Frank E., 24
Denis, King, 37
Diamanti, Walker A., 4, 9, 49, 76, 77, 102, 188, 324
Diamanti, Mrs. Walker A., 188, 190
Diaz, Victor Suances, 271
Diseases, 23–24, 230
Dowry system, 24, 249
Durand, 307, 322

East African Common Services Organization, 96
Eckert-Schweitzer, Rhena, 293, 299
Economic Commission for Africa, 96
Edou, Ndo, 130, 134
Edouard, Ekoga, 267, 269, 302–304

Effort Gabonais, L', 167
Eisenhower, Dwight D., 35, 293
Ekamkam, Nna, 163
Ekoh, Jean-Marc, 6, 40, 68, 102, 109, 140, 144, 206
  appointed Minister of National Education, 48
  in 1964 coup, 132–133
  tribal affiliation of, 253
Ekoh, Madame Jean-Marc, 342
Elephantiasis, 230
Ellert-Beck, Rodolphe, 84
Engone, 253
Equatorial Customs Union, 67
Erdman, Marshall, 104, 105, 107
Eshira tribe, 12, 30, 298
  language of, 29
Essone, Valère, 130–131
Etoughe, Madame, 248
European Development Fund, 85, 89
European Economic Community, 67, 114
Evangelical Church of Paris, 70
Explorations and Adventures in Equatorial Africa (Chaillu), 71
Export-Import Bank, 80, 81
Eyadema, Etienne, 178
Eyéguet, Pierre, 140, 173

Fabien, Mézu, 165
Fang tribe, 7, 13, 149, 224, 253, 298
  early migrations of, 25
  language, 211
  location, 25–26
  population, 26
  tribal marks of, 227

352

Fanguinovény, Jean-Robert, 127, 267, 290, 304–305, 310
  background of, 261
Fanguinovény, Mrs. Jean-Robert, 127, 129, 268, 305
Fanguinovény, Pierre, 260–262, 290
Fernando Po, Island of, 254
Fiemeyer, Michel, 85
Filaria, 23–24
First National City Bank of New York, 66
Flesch, Wayne, 128
Foreign Assistance Act (United States), 97
Forrest Sherman (ship), 192
Frazier, James, 159
Fredericks, Lieutenant, 162
Fredericks, Wayne, 61
Friedman, R., 289

Gabon, Republic of:
  aid from Agency for International Development, 85–92
  ambassadors accredited to, 36
  association with France, 37–43
  beaches, 209–210
  climate, 20, 21, 23, 233–234
  Congolese riots in (1962), 326–333; Brazzaville reaction to, 332; causes of, 327; Mba and, 330–331
  coup d'état (1964), 126–141, 177, 179, 334–348; casualties, 133–134; French intervention in, 132–139; reasons for, 139; tribal reaction to, 341
  early missionary work in, 68–71

  economy, 17, 174–175; French control of, 112–117
  education, 40–43, 200–201, 263
  election of 1964, 123–125, 142–155
  election of 1967, 175–176
  exports, 66, 67, 112
  government of, 3–18, 45–48; centralization of, 11; election districts, 123; regional districts, 11–12
  imports, 66–67
  independence, 10, 46
  interior regions, 11–12, 301–325
  language, 38, 211
  national flag, 33
  population, 24
  resources, 62–64, 74
  roads, 187, 310–311
  U.S. interests in, 61–73
  villages, 31–32, 33
  women in, 24, 215, 235–251; Bwiti dances and, 273
Gabon: Nation-Building on the Ogooué (Weinstein), 44
Gabon viper (snake), 185
Gabonese Exchange Control, 113
Galoa tribe, 244, 245, 290, 298
  language of, 29
Gambia, 35
Garrison, Lloyd, 159
Geiger, Paul, 68
Ghana, Republic of, 178, 180
Giblin, Milly, 4, 49, 64
Gondjout, Edouard, 46
Gondjout, Paul, 45–47, 120
  imprisoned, 46–47
  in 1964 coup, 132–133

Government Agricultural School (Gabon), 263
Gowon, Yakuba, 178
Greer, Virginia, 4, 49
Grégoire (cook), 27, 148, 189, 202, 216–217, 219, 220–221, 230, 329
Gregory XVI, Pope, 71
Grunitsky, Nicholas, 178
Guinea, Republic of, 25
  U.S. interests in, 61–62

Hancock, Robert A., 335
Harlley, John Kofi, 178
Hausa tribe, 25, 180
Hausknecht, Emma, 287–288
Henderson, Loy, 49–50
Hensch, Edward, 340
Holman, A. F., 276
Howe, Russell Warren, 161, 166
Hull, Cordell, 5, 100
Hutchinson, Edmond C., 78, 83, 92
Hutus tribe, 278, 279
Hyland, 129

Ibo tribe, 25, 180
Indjabi language, 30, 318
International Bank for Reconstruction and Development, 64
Ipounou language, 163, 306
Issembé, Aristide, 165, 347
Ivory Coast, Republic of, 10, 113

Jacquard, Père, 174
Jean-Pierre (servant), 27, 217–218, 219, 230, 329

Johnson, Lyndon B., 35, 51, 72, 117
  foreign aid requests, 99
  Mba's letter to, 165, 170
Jones, Willie, 4, 49–50, 114–115, 117, 192–193, 324, 327, 335–336
Joseph, Etoughe, 42, 272

Kamara, Madame, 323–324
Kasavubu, President, 279
Kennedy, John F., 3, 35, 51, 56, 61, 72, 99, 252
  appoints ambassador to Gabon, 5
  death of, 59–60, 157
Kergaravat, General, 63, 131, 133, 135
Kiavué, Roger, 4, 6, 9–10
Kidder, Randolph A., 335
Korry, Edward M., 95
Kottman, Mathilde, 286, 290, 292

La Voie, Don, 33, 309
Lambaréné, Gabon, 274, 285
  population, 32, 286
Lamizana, Sangoulé, 178
Lassy, Major, 329–330
Le Fuhr, Madame, 322
Leader Grant program, 164, 250
Leao-Tchoung-Kin, 36, 191
Ledit, Father, 167–168
LeFévre, Père, 343
Lepers, 230, 258–259
Leprosarium (Ebeigne), 258–259
Leprosarium (Lambaréné), 288
Leprosarium (Río Muni), 270

Lesotho, 35
Libreville, Gabon, 19–21, 25, 248–249
 beaches, 50
 construction boom in, 114
 food markets in, 196–199
 population, 31
Libreville Mission (French aid program), 85
Livingston, David, 277
Louis, King, 37
Lukens, Alan W., 50

McCaw, Sandy, 104, 107
McDaniel, Dick, 3, 107, 309
McGlauflin, Arthur W., 79, 80
MacKenzie, Jean Kenyon, 250
Maga, Hubert, 139, 177
Mahogany industry, 22
Mailier, 324
Malagasy Republic, 113
Malaria, 23
Manbey, David, 278, 279
Manganese industry, 62–65, 169
Mansfield, William, 4, 21, 49, 77, 255–256, 257, 285, 328
Marcel, Mintsa, 164, 221
Massango tribe, 30, 224, 236
Massemba-Débat, Alphonse, 177
Mattison, Dr., 289
Mattison, Mrs., 289
Mauritania, Islamic Republic of, 6
Maury, Philippe, 132
Mayer, Albert, 289
Mba, Irene, 239–240, 242
Mba, Léon, 3, 6–10, 15–17, 36, 45–49, 63, 68, 75–76, 117, 142–143, 202, 204, 208

anti-American campaign of, 167
 arrested, 335
 background of, 7–8
 conference with de Gaulle, 174
 Congolese riots and, 330–331
 elected president, 47
 executive powers, 10–11, 118–125
 in exile, 238
 imprisoned, 128–129
 letter to Johnson, 165, 170
 1964 coup and, 126–141
 terrorism of, 173–174
 tribal affiliation, 253
 U.S. automobile gift to, 83
Mba, Madame Léon, 190, 194, 202, 203, 204, 237–240, 258, 335
 background of, 238
Mba, Madame Marguérite, 261
Mbah, Jules, 337–338
Mbéné, Daniel, 130, 140
Mbéné, Emmanuel, 140
Mebaley, Pierre, 306
Méyé, François, 48, 164
 tribal affiliation of, 253
Michel, Obame, 258
Micombero, Michel, 178
Miené language, 29, 69, 211, 220
Mihindou, 246, 336
Minko, 317–320
Minko, Madame, 317–320, 344–345
Mission of Aid and Cooperation (France), 85
Missionaries, 30, 113, 148, 238, 259, 306
 early settlements, 68–71
Mitsogo tribe, 26, 307, 308

Mobil Oil Corporation, 5, 65, 68
Mobile Health Unit (Gabon), 200
Mobutu, Joseph, 177
Mombo, Jacques, 130
Morgan Guaranty Trust Company, 66
M'Pongwé tribe, 26, 245
  language of, 29
Murphy, John, 127, 129
Mwambutsa IV, King, 178, 280, 281–283
  deposed, 283–284
  drum symbols of, 281–282
Mwiri sect, 236
My Ogowe (Nassau), 70

Nassau, Robert Hamill, 70
National Assembly (Gabon), 10, 15–16, 47
  dissolved, 123
  election of 1964, 146–152; results of, 149
  U.S. diplomatic reception for, 206–207
National Liberation Council (Ghana), 178
National Reconciliation Committee (Togo), 178
N'Dong, Bishop, 167–168, 170, 258
N'Dong, Philippe, 132
Neo-colonialism, 112–113
New York Times, The, 159
Newsweek, 158
N'Goua, Joseph, 119, 131
Niger, Republic of, 10
Nigeria, Federation of, 25, 80
  coup d'état (1966), 178

Nkrumah, Kwame, 178
Normal College, 258
Ntare V, King, 178
Nuwumuremyi, Apollinaire, 284
Nyonda, Vincent de Paul, 12, 103, 128, 336
Nze, Charles, 226, 227–228

Ogooué River, 25, 255
Ogooué-Lolo tribe, 12
Okandé tribe, 255, 298
Olds, Herbert, 277
Olds, Mrs. Herbert, 277, 283
Olympio, Sylvanus, 139, 177, 178
Ondo, Bonjean, 91
Ondo, Elaine, 241
Ondo, Jean-François, 90, 119, 240–242, 247
  tribal affiliation of, 253
Ondo, Madame Jean-François, 119, 240–241
Organization of African Unity, 96
Organization of Gabonese Women, 249–250, 251
Oroungou tribe, 298
  language of, 29

Pahouins tribe, 25
Panther men, 304, 307
Parliman, John A., 113
Parti de l'Unité Nationale Gabonaise (PUNGA), 46, 119
Peace Corps, 24, 55, 70, 79, 83, 162–163, 252, 308–309
  AID cooperation with, 103
  number of volunteers (Gabon), 106–107, 110
  Rural School Construction Project, 101–110

Pélisson (baker), 335, 336, 344
Péyrefitte, Alain, 138
Philibert, Bongo, 324
Pigot, 161
Pigot, Madame, 190, 237, 238
Pixarro, Manuel, 270
Plante, Muriel, 163
Polygamy, 13–14, 24, 242
Population:
    Fang tribe, 26
    Gabon, 24
    Lambaréné, 32, 286
    Libreville, 31
    Oyem, 32
    Port-Gentil, 31
Pové tribe, 26, 313
Preminger, Marion, 68, 288, 289
Project Amity III, 192
Protestant Mission, 306
Pygmies, 25, 321–322

Quirielle, François Simon de, 170, 174

Radio Gabon, 7, 218
Raphael (chauffeur), 186, 214, 216, 231, 312, 344
Raux, Etienne, 13
Rawiri, Georges, 292–293
Réalités Gabonaises, 132
Rimmer, Brenda, 285
Río Muni, 252–275
    government, 254, 271–272
    leprosarium, 270
Risterucci, Jean, 36–37, 47, 102 135, 191, 330
Risterucci, Madame Jean, 191
Roosevelt, Franklin D., 100
Roosevelt, Mrs. Franklin D., 68

Ross, Rev. Emory, 295
Rural School Construction Project, 101–110
Rusk, Dean, 117
Rwagasore, Prince, 280
Rwanda, Republic of, 277–278
    relations with Burundi, 284

Sandoungout, Marcel, 12
Sands of Tamanrasset, The (Preminger), 289
Saymon, Bertram B., 79–80, 83, 84, 96
Saymon, Mrs. Bertram, 201
Schweitzer, Dr. Albert, 61, 185, 262, 285–300
    death of, 299
    in World War I, 290
Schweitzer Committees, 295
Schweitzer Hospital:
    construction of, 288–289
    location, 286
    significance of, 297–298
Seké tribe, 29, 298
Senegal, Republic of, 10, 35
Shriver, Sargent, 103
Sibang tribe, 224
Silva, 302
Silva, Mrs., 302
Silver, Ali, 286, 287, 292
    background of, 287
Sizaire, General, 62–63
Société des Mines de Fer de Mékambo (SOMIFER), 63, 201, 322
Soglo, Christopher, 131, 177
Sousatte, René, 46, 119
Stanley, Sir Henry Morton, 271
Stanley, Mildred, 232

Stephen, Henry, 126–127, 129, 159, 225, 292, 324
Stevenson, Adlai, 61
Sudan, Republic of the, 25
Suisse, La, 168

Tanzania, United Republic of, 181
Tasca, Henry, 61
Technical School (Libreville), 246
Telfair, Peter, 63–64, 68, 147, 322, 337
Telfair, Mrs. Peter, 63–64
Texaco Company, 65
Theeten, Paul, 81
Theodose, Madame, 248, 251
Togo, Republic of, 177, 178
Trade Agreements Act (United States), 100
Travesi, Julio, 271
Tribes, 224
   differences in, 25
   political organization, 25–29
   reaction to Gabon *coup d'état,* 341
   social organization, 25–29
   See also names of tribes
Tsetse fly, 22, 24
Tshombé, Moise, 333
Tuberculosis, 23
Tunisia, Republic of, 80
Tutsi tribe, 278, 283
Twas tribe, 278

Union Démocratique et Sociale Gabonaise (UDSG), 45, 47, 118–119
United Nations Technical Assistance Programs, 85

United States Information Service (USIS), 55, 189, 225
   English instruction, 201
   library, 158
United States Steel Corporation, 62, 64–65, 169
Upper Volta, Republic of, 10, 178
UPRONA Party, 280
Uranium, 146, 321–322

Vitte, Marcel, 103, 164
Voice of America, 218
Voisin, Madame, 201

Wadlow, René, 201
Wadlow, Mrs. René, 55
Walker, Abbé, 174
Walker-Deemin, 113–114
Washington Post, 161, 166
Wattel, Gérard, 102
Weinstein, Brian, 44
Welker, Colette, 4, 49
White, Paul Dudley, 293
Wilkes, William, 107, 163–164, 326
Willaumez, Bouët, 37
Williams, G. Mennen, 61, 157, 207–209
Witch doctors, 258, 298
Woleu N'Tem (region), 252–275
   government administration of, 253
Women:
   Burundi, 279
   Gabonese, 24, 215, 235–251; Bwiti dances and, 273
"Wonderful Wyoming" (film), 225

358

World Health Organization (WHO), 88, 168, 285
   1963 Gabon study, 96

Yaméogo, Maurice, 178
Yaoundé Convention, 67
"Year of the Gabonese Woman, The" (program), 248–249
Yembit, Paul-Marie, 12, 59, 118–119, 126, 161, 162–163, 175, 336
   campaign of, 127–128
   requests French intervention, 138
Yembit, Madame Paul-Marie, 244
Yndurain, José Javier, 269
Yndurain, Mrs. José Javier, 269
Yoruba tribe, 25
Youlou, Abbé Fulbert, 122, 131–132, 139, 332–333
   deposed, 177

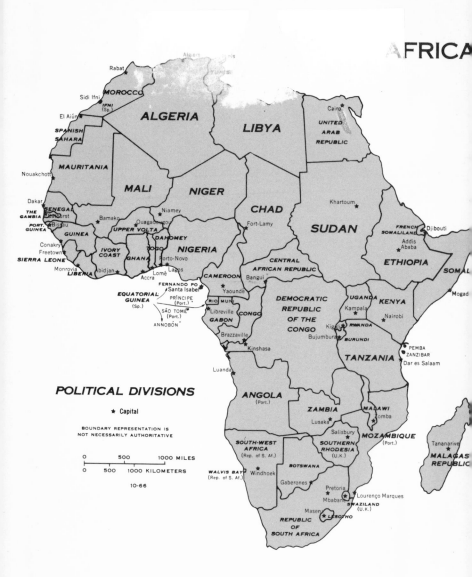

AFRICA

Rabat ★

MOROCCO

Sidi Ifni
IFNI
(Sp.)

El Aiún ★

SPANISH
SAHARA

ALGERIA

Algiers   Tunis

LIBYA

Cairo ★

UNITED
ARAB
REPUBLIC

Nouakchott ★

MAURITANIA

MALI

NIGER

CHAD

Khartoum ★

SUDAN

FRENCH
SOMALILAND
Djibouti ★

Dakar ★

SENEGAL
THE   Bathurst
GAMBIA

PORT.   Bissau
GUINEA

Conakry ★
Freetown ★
SIERRA LEONE

Monrovia ★
LIBERIA

GUINEA

Niamey ★

Bamako ★

Ouagadougou ★

UPPER VOLTA

IVORY
COAST

GHANA

Abidjan ★

DAHOMEY

TOGO

NIGERIA

Porto-Novo ★

Lomé
Accra ★   Lagos

CAMEROON

Fort-Lamy ★

CENTRAL
AFRICAN REPUBLIC

Bangui ★

Addis
Ababa ★

ETHIOPIA

SOMAL

Mogad

FERNANDO PO
Santa Isabel ★

EQUATORIAL
GUINEA
(Sp.)

PRÍNCIPE
(Port.)

SÃO TOMÉ
(Port.)

ANNOBÓN

RIO MUNI

Libreville ★

GABON

CONGO

Brazzaville ★

Yaoundé ★

DEMOCRATIC
REPUBLIC
OF THE
CONGO

Kinshasa ★

Kigali ★
RWANDA

Bujumbura ★
BURUNDI

UGANDA

Kampala ★

KENYA

Nairobi ★

PEMBA
ZANZIBAR
Dar es Salaam ★

TANZANIA

Luanda ★

POLITICAL DIVISIONS

★ Capital

BOUNDARY REPRESENTATION IS
NOT NECESSARILY AUTHORITATIVE

| 0 | 500 | 1000 MILES |
| 0 | 500 | 1000 KILOMETERS |

10-66

ANGOLA
(Port.)

ZAMBIA

Lusaka ★

MALAWI
Zomba ★

Salisbury ★

SOUTHERN
RHODESIA
(U.K.)

MOZAMBIQUE
(Port.)

Tananarive ★

MALAGAS
REPUBLIC

SOUTH-WEST
AFRICA
(Rep. of S. Af.)

WALVIS BAY
(Rep. of S. Af.)

Windhoek ★

BOTSWANA

Gaberones ★

Pretoria ★

Mbabane ★
Maseru ★
LESOTHO

Lourenço Marques ★

SWAZILAND
(U.K.)

REPUBLIC
OF
SOUTH AFRICA